Thomas Monro

**Olla Podrida**

Thomas Monro

**Olla Podrida**

ISBN/EAN: 9783337267131

Printed in Europe, USA, Canada, Australia, Japan

Cover: Foto ©ninafisch / pixelio.de

More available books at **www.hansebooks.com**

B

# PREFACE.

A PREFACE to a Work, if read at all, is generally read the firſt; though as generally, I believe, written the laſt. Few authors know the limits of their undertaking till their work is finiſhed; but moſt Readers begin a book with the peruſal of page the firſt.

This cuſtom of writing a Preface when the work is complete is attended with peculiar advantages.— An Author having diligently purſued the thread of his labours, through a

ſpace

fpace of five hundred pages, may then certainly fit down and inform his readers, with great deliberation, what he intends to do.

It may not be impertinent to fuppofe him modeftly beginning in fome fuch manner as this:

" It is my intention, in as fhort a compafs as the nature of the fubject will admit, to offer, with becoming humility, fome important truths to the confideration of my Readers, which will, I truft, convince them that the narrative of Captain Lemuel Gulliver abounds with grofs and palpable mifreprefentations, geographical miftakes, and botanical errors; and will moreover imprefs conviction on their minds that the whole of that too popular hiftory is a catchpenny account, which deferves no credit. I am clearly able

able to prove, that fuch a commander as Captain Lemuel Gulliver never ferved in our navies—I fhall alfo in the courfe of my work add a few obfervations on the nature of truth and falfhood, and conclude with a lift of Britifh Commanders from the time of Admiral Drake inclufive—The whole will form an ufeful repofitory of fcience, be dedicated to the people of Great Britain, and is ferioufly recommended to the ufe of fchools."

Thus are we preface-writing authors juftified in fpeaking of ourfelves and our performances. Nor is it often that we reft fatisfied with a protracted enumeration of our particular accomplifhments; we are frequently defirous to enhance their value by afferting boldly, that all who have preceded us in fimilar attempts have poffeffed no one requifite for the proper execution of their tafk.

Upon

Upon the whole, however, nothing can be fo proper as for an author to recommend his own work. Is not he who writes a book the moft likely perfon in the world to know its excellencies? The feeming indelicacy of becoming the herald of our own accomplifhments, ought not to refift the good of the community. Befides, I would ask, who fcruples to commend to a purchafer his dog, his horfe, or his daughter? " They are well-bred, Sir, and well-managed—This from the Godolphin-Arabian — that from Pompey of Northumberland—the other by my firft wife, with a well-ftocked fhop in Hounfditch."

In imitation of fo laudable an example, I too fhall expect not only pardon, but praife; addrefling my

Reader

Reader in the true fpirit of fuch mo-
deft affurance, οναιο σε ταυ]ης της
ωοικιλομαθιας—I wifh you joy of this
learned mifcellany.

The principal intention however
of this Proæmium yet remains un-
anfwered. I had only in view to introduce to my Readers fuch of my
correfpondents as have obliged and
gratified me by their affiftance; and
whofe permiffión to make my public
acknowledgements to them will confer on thefe pages whatever credit
they may appear to deferve.

By the indulgence of my valuable
friend the Rev. Mr. Kett, of Trinity
College, Oxford, I am allowed to inform my Readers that I am indebted to
him for thofe numbers figned ℒ. viz.
4, 22, 27, 39, and 42.

For number 30, I am obliged to a Gentleman whofe ftudious retirement has made him better known as the elegant author of Columella, the Spiritual Quixote, and other works of fancy and humour, than as the Rev. Mr. Graves of Claverton near Bath.

For number 16, I have to thank an intimate friend, of whofe tafte and abilities every one has had fufficient teftimony who has fortunately feen Select Beauties of Ancient Englifh Poetry, lately publifhed with Remarks, by Mr. Headley of Norwich.

I am permitted to fay, that for number 20, my work is indebted to Francis Grofe, Efq. F. A. S.

For number 24, to the Rev. Jofeph Pott, Rector of the Old Jewry.

For numbers 32, 37, and 38, to Mr. Berkeley, of Magdalen Hall, Oxford.

For

For number 34, to Mr. Hammond of Merton College.

For a letter, ſigned Viator, to the Rev. Mr. Agutter, Magdalen College.

For number 41, to the Rev. Mr. Mayor.

For three letters, ſigned, John Scribe, John Crop, and Jeremy Cra-zybones, to Mr. Leyceſter of Merton College.

Did I know the author of num-ber 10, I certainly would not omit this opportunity of making him my beſt acknowledgments.

There is yet one other Correſpon-dent, to whom this work is indebted for thoſe numbers which bear the ſignature of $Z$; viz. 7, 9, 12, 13, 17, 23, 26, 29, and 33.

To him I feel myſelf obliged, as to one who has deſcended from the emi-nence

nence of a fuperior ftation to encourage an individual, whofe principal
merit was, the defire of contributing
to the entertainment of others, without difgracing himfelf. The permiffion of faying from whom I have
received thefe favours, involves an
additional obligation. My motive for
not ufing the privilege with which I
am thus indulged, is, that in an-
nouncing fuch a name to the public,
I might feem to have principally in
view the gratification of my vanity.
I might alfo perhaps, by fome awk-
wardnefs in my mode of introduction,
reflect no great credit upon the perfon
introduced.

In thefe pages I have occafionally taken the liberty for which I
ftipulated in my introductory number,
and for which I have the fanction
of many fimilar publications of more

eftab-

eftablifhcd reputation, as in the inftances of Jerry Simple, Cantwell, Polumathes, Snub, and Socrates in Embryo, of addreffing letters to myfelf. If under thefe feigned characters I have added to the ftock of innocent amufement, or if I may in general claim the credit of praifeworthy intentions, I am willing to believe that I may, without any fear of the confequences, avow myfelf to be the original projector and promoter of the OLLA PODRIDA.

THOMAS MONRO, A. B.

*St. M. Magdalen College, Oxford.*

OLLA

# OLLA PODRIDA.

## NUMBER I,

### SATURDAY, *March* 17, 1787.

*Sit down and feed, and welcome to our Table.*
SHAKSPEARE'S *As You Like It.*

EVERY one muſt have obſerved the
unpleaſant ſituation of a baſhful man,
upon his introduction into a room, where
he is unacquainted with the company : his
arms are an incumbrance to him ; when
addreſſed, he heſitates in reply, or anſwers
with confuſion ; his converſation is forced,
and his remarks moſt likely foreign to the
purpoſe,

purpofe, and unnatural. I cannot but
confefs that fuch is my prefent fituation.
While I am utterly unacquainted with the
humours of the perfons I am addreffing,
my converfation muft naturally be expected
to turn upon the weather, the news, and
the common occurrences of the day ; when
we are become more intimate, we fhall be
more communicative; we may then proceed to the difcuffion of various weighty
points of fafhion, honour, pleafure, fometimes perhaps *defcending to literature*, but
never to politics.

Should I unfortunately be detected in addreffing complimentary letters to myfelf,
filled with encomiums upon the elegance
of my ftyle, the purity of my language,
and the verfatility of my genius ; I hope,
with the reafonable number of my readers
(and I cannot expect an unreafonable number), it will be a fufficient excufe, that
cuftom hath made it a neceffary appendage
to a work of this kind.   Such letters muft
be written ; and, if no ingenious friend will
fave me the trouble of tranfcribing them
from dedications addreffed to other great
men,

men, why I muſt e'en go to work my-ſelf.

Upon reviewing the different reaſons which are aſſigned by authors for favouring the world with their publications (or, as the ungrateful world is too apt to call it, for obtruding their nonſenſe on the public), I find, that with ſome it is an alleviation of pain, with others a diverſion from melancholy contemplations; ſome ſcribble becauſe it is cold weather, others becauſe it is hot; ſome becauſe they have nothing elſe to do, and others becauſe they had better do any thing elſe.

To ſome this *cacoethes ſcribendi* is a chronic complaint. I remember a man who had regularly a fit of the gout every September: he was unavoidably confined to the houſe, which as unavoidably produced a fit of reading, and dictating to an amanuenſis (for write he could not), ſo that by ſhaking hands with him, you might diſcover the advance of his poem from the ſize and ſtate of his chalkſtones. Many of thoſe people (who, having been long afflicted with rheumatic complaints, are become

become tolerable chronicles of the weather),
agree in their obfervation, that a rainy feafon is apt to produce an inundation of fcrib-
blers.  Thus I have known the birth of an
epic poem foretold by the fhooting of a
corn ; and an ode to peace prophefied from
a pain in the fhoulder.   The reafon of this
is obvious ; wet weather confines people at
home ;  people confined at home become
fick, liftlefs, fatirical, melancholy.   Now
the fick man muft not fuffer his ideas to
ftagnate, the liftlefs muft have fomething
to diffipate his *ennui*, the fatirical fomething
to vent his fpleen upon, and the melancholy fomething to amufe him ; and each,
to anfwer his particular end—writes.

Mr. Afflatus, who " is now a fcribbler,
that was once a man," caught his diftemper
by the mereft accident in the world.   He
was going out a fhooting, and preparatory
to it employed himfelf in drying his powder by the fire.  A fpark flying out, the
whole magazine was in flames ; and my
friend fuffered fo much in the explofion
from the havock it made in the features of
his face,  that I fcarce knew him.   He

.was

was condemned for a confiderable time to his chamber, and during that confinement firft became acquainted with the Aonian ladies. He was driven by neceffity to read; and chance having flung in his way the energetic poetry of Sir Richard Blackmore, fuch a *furor poeticus* was kindled in his breaft, that he inftantly miftook himfelf for a genius, and communicated his miftake to the publick. I have been informed, that in his firft fit of poetick phrenfy, he was fo confiderably elevated and furious, that after having kicked down a whole fet of china, the fervants were obliged to be called in to hold him. The wet weather ftill affects him, but he is now lefs violent; and his domefticks take no other precaution than when they find the glafs falling, or the fky clouding over, to remove every thing out of his way which might be damaged by a fall.—I can now eafily conceive fome fly female enquiring what, after all this detail of other people's misfortunes, can be the reafon of *thy* fcribbling? To which, as I am a downright kind of a being, I anfwer with more truth than politenefs, becaufe it

C                    happens

happens to be my humour; and, my dear madam, fhould you be half as well pleafed with what you read, as I am with what I write, I fhall find in you a conftant reader, and you will find in me a conftant atten- tive flave. And fince I have indulged the flattering fuppofition, that I may poffibly find a reader or two among the Ladies, I beg leave to inform them, that it is by no means my wifh to call off their attention from their work, to difmal enquiries into the nature of truth and falfehood, to the apophthegms of moralifts, the difcoveries of philofophers, or the difquifitions of the lear- ned. I fhall frequently devote a paper entirely to their fervice; and, as I have none of thofe antiquated prejudices or opi- nions about me, that advice may tend to the reformation of manners, or indeed that mankind ftand in any need of improvement, I fhall ftudy to entertain them without af- fuming the fuperiority of a dictator.

In my attempts to collect materials for this purpofe, I fhall hope to fucceed, not- withftanding " Oxford" (according to the opinion of many) " is fuch a dull, infipid,

" out

" out of the way place, that if it were not
" for the ſtage coaches, it would be difficult
" for a body to pick up news enough in
" the week to furniſh a petit-maitre's
" pocket-book."

There ſtill remains a very large claſs of
readers for whom I confeſs myſelf totally
unable to provide. I mean thoſe who
(from various cauſes which I ſhall not at
preſent ‚enumerate) are entertained with
nothing but anecdotes of the *beau monde*,
gleaned from waiters and unliveried gentlemen, or the ſcurrilities of an infolent buf-
foon, which are unpuniſhed becauſe they
are unworthy of notice.

That my attention has not been engaged
in purſuits which will enable me to gratify
ſuch taſtes, I do not repine.

Cur ego laborem notus eſſe tam pravè,
Cum ſtare gratis cum ſilentio poſſim ?

MARTIAL.

" Why ſhould I labour in vicious induſtry,
" when I may remain without toil in in-
" nocent ſilence ?"

C 2          I ſhould

I fhould in vain endeavour to convey to my readers any very accurate idea of my propofed plan, as that which is in itfelf incomplete, muft be imperfect in defcription. Thus far I can venture to promife them, that however little pleafure they may reap from perufing the produce of a gayer hour, or however little inftruction from the lucubrations of a graver one, they will not have occafion to reproach me with having willingly difleminated error, having made my correfpondence with the publick the vehicle of private calumnies, or miniftered by my pen to the gratification of vice.

I may now perhaps be forgiven if I fay a few words of myfelf; and having entered upon that favourite topic on which the dull can expatiate with brilliancy, and the fterile with copioufnefs, let me obtain the negative praife of not having been prolix. I fhall only then add, that I am in good health, neither fick, liftlefs, fatirical, nor melancholy ; and that I fhall be thankful for the communications of all correfpondents, and object to the publifhing of nothing,

thing, which is not devoid of candour, delicacy, common fenfe, or grammatical correctnefs.

———— pereat mea mufa, dolofum
Si quando ornaret vitium, aut ceciniffe recufet
Virtutemque, artemque, et quicquid carmine
dignum,

## NUMBER II,

---

SATURDAY, *March* 24, 1787,

---

*Laudant illa, fed ifta legunt.* MARTIAL.

THE elegant and juftly-admired author of the Adventurer * cenfures
the practice of our inftructors of youth, for
making their pupils more intimately acquainted with the Iliad than the Odyffey of
Homer. I fear he has done this without
producing, by his arguments, a reformation in the conduct of fome, who ftill per-
fift in the profecution of their plan ; or
conviction in the minds of others, who
may have altered it.—" This abfurd cuftom (fays he), which feems to arife from

* N° 75.

the

the fuppofed. fuperiority of the former
poem, has induced me to make fome reflections on the latter." The cuftom does
not appear to me an abfurd one, but founded on the experience of its utility ; nor can
I think the fuperiority of the Iliad fuppofed,
but real.

" The moral of this poem (fays the Adventurer) is more extenfively ufeful than
that of the Iliad, which, indeed, by dif-
playing the dire effects of difcord among
rulers, may rectify the conduct of princes,
and may be called the manual of monarchs :
whereas the patience, the prudence, the
wifdom, the temperance, and fortitude of
Ulyffes, afford a pattern, the utility of
which is not confined within the compafs
of courts and palaces, but defcends and dif-
fufes its influence over common life and
daily practice." Upon this argument,
namely, that the affairs which the Iliad
treats of, are too far removed from common
life to be of fervice to common readers, is
grounded his principal objection to the
practice before obferved.—Admitting the
pofition to be true, the conclufion does not

necef-

neceffarily follow. It is univerfally allowed, that the doctrine of morality has
never been more forcibly inculcated, or its
practice more ftrenuoufly and fuccefsfully
recommended, than in the lofty tales and
fublime language of Eaftern literature.
They have been fubjects of imitation to an
Adventurer, and a Rambler, and of admiration to all. The tendency of thefe tales
is univerfally an incitement to virtue, by
an unlimited difplay of the workings of
Providence. Yet how far removed are they
from the bufinefs " of common life and
daily practice!"

Infinite merit is certainly due to the fimplicity of the Odyffey. Yet is the Iliad by
no means inferior in this particular. Even
"*inter Reges atque Tetrarchas*" there is frequently room for it, and no opportunity is
loft of introducing it. Whoever recollects
how Andromache was employed, when
from the top of the tower fhe beheld the
fate of her husband, will in vain feek to
find the fimplicity of that paffage which defcribes her employment any where equalled.

— ἄλοχος

— — — ἄλοχος δ᾽ ὕπω τι πέπυϛο
Ἕκτορος· ὒ γάρ οἵ τις ἐτήτυμος ἄϷγελος ἐλθὼν
ἬϷγειλ᾽, ὅτϮι ῥά οἱ πόσις ἔκϮοθι μίμνε πυλάων·
Ἀλλ᾽ ἥγ᾽ ἱϛὸν ὕφαινε, μυχῷ δόμυ ὑψηλοῖο,
Δίπλακα, μαρμαρέην, ἐν δὲ θρόνα πρικίλ᾽ ἔπασσε·
ΚέκλεϮο δ᾽ ἀμφιπόλοισιν ἐϋπλοκάμοις καϮὰ δῶμα
Ἀμφὶ πυρὶ ϛῆσαι τρίποδα μέγαν, ὄφρα πέλοιϮο
ἝκϮορι θερμὰ λοεϮρὰ μάχης ἐκνοϛήσανϮι·
Νηπίη, ὒδ᾽ ἐνόησεν, ὅ μιν μάλα τῆλε λοεϮρῶν
Χερϲὶν Ἀχιλλῆος δάμασεν γλαυκῶπις Ἀθήνη.
ΚωκυϮῦ δ᾽ ἤκυσε κ̀ οἰμωγῆς ἀπὸ πύρϮυ,
Τῆς δ᾽ ἐλελίχθη γυῖα, χαμαὶ δὲ οἱ ἔκπεσε κερκίς.

Il. X. 440.

But not as yet the fatal news had ſpread
To fair Andromache, of Hector dead, &c.

Pope, book 22. line 462, &c.

Criticiſm has no language to deſcribe the
exquiſite tendernefs and ſimplicity of the

ΚέκλεϮο δ᾽ ἀμφιπόλοισιν ἐϋπλοκάμοις καϮὰ δῶμα
Ἀμφὶ πυρὶ ϛῆσαι τρίποδα μέγαν, ὄφρα πέλοιϮο
ἝκϮορι θερμὰ λοεϮρὰ, &c.

Mr. Pope's tranſlation of which paſſage will
give the Engliſh reader a very faint idea of
the beauties of his original. The general
originality of Thomſon will not be im-
peached if I ſubjoin a paſſage from his
Winter,

Winter, which bears a beautiful refemblance
of the foregoing lines in Homer .

> In vain for him th' officious wife prepares
> The fire fair blazing, and the veftment warm ;
> In vain his little children, peeping out
> Into the mingling ftorm, demand their fire
> With tears of artlefs innocence.   Alas !
> Nor wife, nor children more fhall he behold,
> Nor friends, nor facred home.

" If the faireft examples (proceeds the
Adventurer) ought to be placed before us
in an age prone to imitation, if patriotifm
be preferable to implacability, if an eager
defire to return to one's country and family,
be more manly and noble, than an eager
defire to be revenged of an enemy, then
fhould our eyes be fixed rather on Ulyffes
than Achilles.—Unexperienced minds, too
eafily captivated with the fire and fury of
a gallant general, are apt to prefer courage
to conftancy, and firmnefs to humanity."
It is one of the acute Dr. Clarke's obfervations, that Homer has reprefented the character of Achilles, " *qualis fuit, non qualis
effe debuerit.*"  The remark, however obvious it may appear when made, would

not

not perhaps have occurred to the mind of a
common reader. The conduct of the son
of Peleus is related, but not defended; the
caufe of virtue does not fuffer by the exhibition of a character in moft refpects amiable, in all illuftrious, yet fometimes giving
way to the gratifications of luft, and fometimes to an inordinate thirft for revenge.
Its proper ftigma is inflicted upon each deviation from virtue, by placing it in an
odious light. His affectionate lamentation
over his dead friend Patroclus, does not prevent the poet from ftigmatizing the cruelty
he exercifed upon the flain Hector.

From a contemplation of the character
of Ulyffes and Achilles, very different fentiments arife—When we are obferving the
former, the mind is rapt in unwearied admiration, it is fcarce awakened to obfervation from a continued feries of praife-wor-
thy actions, but flumbers in the fulfomenefs of perpetual panegyric.—If we would
examine thoroughly the character of the
latter, the mind muft be ever at work:
There is much to praife, and much to condemn, through a variety of good and bad
cir-

circumſtances; we muſt " pick our nice
way." His well-placed affection, his warm
friendſhip, will create love; his revenge
odium, and his cruelty abhorrence. Doubts
will ariſe, and enquiry muſt be made, whether the one is more to be approved, or
the other more to be avoided. Thus are
we kept for ever on the watch; if our vigilance be for a moment abated, we have
paſſed over ſome leading feature in the character of the Hero, or loſt the recital of
ſome circumſtance, by which we might determine whether the virtues or the vices of
Achilles preponderate. When Ulyſſes
comes forward, the mind is already prepared, and knows what to expect: He is
either the πολυμηΊις διος Οδυσσευς, *the wiſe and
divine Ulyſſes,* or the Θεοις εναλιγκιος αυδην,
*Ulyſſes godlike in voice.*—But upon the appearance of Achilles, we are uncertain
whether he has broken his reſolution of not
going out to battle, or whether he is medi-
tating the deſtruction of the Trojan bul-
wark.

The

The meeting between Achilles and Hector, which is terminated by the death of the latter, is replete with variety fufficient to arreft the attention of every one, and ornament fufficient to pleafe every attention it engages. That defiance which each hurls at the other, marks the bravery of both ; and when the latter falls, the prowefs of the former is confirmed. The fcene now alters. In his fpeech over the dead body of Hector, Achilles affigns to the gods the honour of his victory—επειδη τονδε ανδρα Φεοι δαμασασθαι εδωκαν, &c.

Since now at length the powerful will of heaven
The dire deftroyer to our arm has given.

POPE, book 22. line 275, &c.

Yet this generofity cannot deprecate our abhorrence of the cruelty which follows— Hector is dragged at the wheels of his conqueror's chariot—

—Αμφι δε χαιjαι,
Κυανεαι τσιλναυjο· καρη δ'απαν εν κονιησι
Κειjο παρος χαριεν·

*His hair is clotted, and that countenance, heretofore fo beautiful, is all polluted in the duft.*

Now

Now loft is all that formidable air;
The face divine, the long defcending hair,
Purple the ground, and ftreak the fable fand.

PACK: POPE, book 22. line 505, &c.

This is done amid the lamentations of the
Trojans, and it may be prefumed the filent
acquiefcence of the Greeks.    Yet the diftrefs of this fcene is ftill to be heightened.
Who can bear the appearance and voice of
the old king Priam, without heaping curfes
upon the author of his diftrefs?—λισσομαι
ανερα τȣ]ον α]ασθαλον οϐριμcεϱ]ον, &c.—

I, only I will iffue from your walls,
(Guide or companion, friends I afk ye none)
And bow before the murderer of my fon,

POPE, book 22. line 531, &c.

" The remaining reafons why the Odyffey is equal (fays the Adventurer) if not fuperior to the Iliad, and why more peculiarly proper for the perufal of youth, are
becaufe the great variety of events and
fcenes it contains, intereft and engage the
attention more than the Iliad; becaufe characters and images drawn from familiar life,
are more ufeful to the generality of readers,

5                                              and

and are alfo more difficult to be drawn;
and becaufe the conduct of this poem (confidered as the moft perfect of epopees) is
more artful and judicious than that of the
other." The firft of thefe remaining reafons, namely, that the Odyffey muft intereft and engage the attention more than the
Iliad, I fear is a declaration which will go
near to overturn what was advanced in the
beginning of the critique, "that unexperienced minds, too eafily captivated with
the fire and fury of a gallant general, are
apt to prefer courage to conftancy, and
firmnefs to humanity." The difficulty of
drawing a character is perhaps no where fo
happily furmounted as in the 2d book of
the Iliad, wherein he gives an account of
Therfites.

Φολκὸς ἔην, χαλὸς δ' ἕτερον πόδα, τὼ δέ οἱ ὤμω
Κυρτὼ, ἐπὶ ςῆθος συνοχωκότε· αὐτὰρ ὕπερθε
Φοξὸς ἴην κεφαλὴν, ψεδνὴ δ' ἐπενήνοθε λάχνη.
Ἔχθιςος δ' Ἀχιλῆϊ μάλις' ἦν ἠδ' Ὀδυσῆϊ.
Τὼ γὰρ νεικείεσκε. Τοτ' αὖ Ἀγαμέμνονι δίω
Ὀξέα κεκληγὼς λέγ' ὀνείδεα· τῷ δ' ἄρ' Ἀχαιοὶ
Ἐκπάγλως κοτέοντο, νεμέσσηθέν τ' ἐνὶ θυμῷ.
Αὐτὰρ ὁ μακρὰ βοῶν, Ἀγαμέμνονα νείκεε μύθῳ.

His figure fuch as might his foul proclaim;
One eye was blinking, and one leg was lame:

POPE, book 2. line 263, &c.

This

This may perhaps be called rather a description of his perfon than a delineation of his character. Yet, if with this defcription we take in the few preceding lines, the art of the poet has left us ignorant of nothing which is paffing in the mind of Therfites. Providence has been kindly parfimonious in the production of fuch objects, yet they have come within the notice of moft people. The conduct of the Odyffey may be more reducible to rule, but the Iliad abounds with the fublimer beauties.

Whoever is acquainted with the Ajax and Philoctetes of Sophocles, and the contention between Ajax and Ulyffes of Ovid, will be convinced that Homer's character of Ulyffes is drawn to an excefs *con amore*, and that of Achilles with fidelity. On the one hand, he will obferve the flattering fondnefs of the Painter ; on the other, he will approve the inflexible veracity of the Hiftorian.

N U M-

# N U M B E R  III.

---

SATURDAY, *March* 31ſt, 1787.

---

*Arcades Ambo.*      Vɪʀɢ.

S LAVES aṭ Athens, who had been
guilty of theft, were, in order to pub-
liſh their difgrace and infamy, branded in
the forehead with two letters, and were
thence called γραμμάϳοι or *literati.*

When Iˉacknowledge my obligations to
two diſtinguiſhed *literati,* whoſe letters will
compoſe the ſubſtance. of this paper, I
caution my claſſical readers againſt ſup-
poſing that I uſe the word in its original
Athenian ſenſe.

D          *To*

## To the AUTHOR of the
## OLLA PODRIDA.

DEAR BROTHER,    *London, March,* 1787.

THE familiarity with which I addreſs
you will, I think, be ſufficiently juſtified,
when I inform you, that I am an author
as well as yourſelf. Our lines of buſineſs differ
indeed. Your *care* ſeems to be in *endeavouring* to entertain your readers with produc-
tions of the lighter caſt, while I am engaged
in graver duties ; troubleſome indeed to
myſelf, but of the utmoſt importance to
*mankind.* You muſt know, I am the mouth
from which many of our paſtors and in-
ſtructors deliver their oracles. In ſhort, my
office is to write ſermons for young divines ;
which (ſuch is my zeal for religion) I diſtri-
bute at three pence each, or 2 s. 9 d per
dozen. After the expences of printing, &c.
are defrayed, my gains, as you may ſuppoſe,
are very ſmall.—Yet, ſmall as they are, Sir, I
am ſatisfied, while my conſcience, without
flattering, tells me I have deſerved, if not
obtained, a reputation. One of my ſermons

(it

(it was printed in a type which might be miftaken for hand-writing, price only 1 s.) procured the purchafer of it a lecturefhip in the Borough; to be fure, the gentleman had a main good voice, which he did not poffefs for nothing. But what is the fage without the goofe?

Another gentleman, a doctor, who wrote rather grave fermons, being much fmitten with a young lady, who objected to him on account of his gravity, applied to me for a fermon fuited to his circumftances. I took his cafe into confideration, and provided him with a difcourfe fo lively, that he carried off the lady in triumph in lefs than three weeks.—Nobody flept; the people were very attentive, and ftared a good deal.

While I was bufy in compofing this fermon, a few evenings ago, for the doctor, three young divines, my cuftomers, rapped at my door. Compliments having been on each fide paid and received, they were feated. When I informed them of the bufinefs I was engaged in, from what reafon I know not, I found in all of them a promptitude to laughter, which was irkfome to me; but

as

as every now and then fome obfervation
was made, which was the fpecious caufe of
their merriment, I was unwilling to fuppofe they meant a direct infult. But at
laft I had too manifeft a proof of their intentions to deride me. My candle wanted
fnuffing, the fnuffers were not to be found.
I have no bell in my room, but am accuftomed to fummon my landlady, who lives
under me, by the ftamp of my foot. I now
gave the young rogues occafion to banter
me. One told me, I reminded him of Pompey
the Great, who declared before the fenate,
that he could raife legions by the motion of
his foot; but that I was fuperior, in per-
forming what Pompey found he could not.
Another dryly congratulated me upon the
acquifition of a place in the ftamp-office:
the third (who was determined to have his
fling at me, though what he faid had nothing to do with the prefent bufinefs) begged I would give him my opinion of South's
fermons; and obferved, that he had that
morning turned off his taylor for having
detected him in cabbaging. I difdained to
make any reply to the groffnefs of their

2                                    wit,

wit, nor did I even reproach them with in-
gratitude. I neither reminded the one of
the charity fermon which got him fo much
applaufe; nor the other, of the funeral fermon which fet his congregation a-roaring.
But to me they are obliged for moſt of
their difcourfes, and all their reputation.
To be fure, the flip I made in tranfcribing
South's fermon was unlucky. But am
I for that to be made miferable for ever?
Am I for that to lofe my reputation; and
muſt I return to my old trade of ſtay-
making? Do, good brother, confider the
dignity of our profeffion, and put me in a
way of mitigating the rigour of fome of my
critical cuſtomers, and regaining the favours
of others which I have loſt by an unfortunate cabbage, or the laughter of an audience,
when it was the intention of the preacher
that they ſhould be grave. Render me
this piece of fervice, and I will write your
funeral fermon, which you ſhall infpect,
and, if you pleafe, alter before you die.

  Bound, together with you,
   in the fervice of the publick,
    Believe me yours fincerely,
  HABAKKUK CANTWELL.
       P. S.

P. S.  If any gentleman agrees with me for fermons by the great, I give him my lecture on delivery for nothing, and for my effay on pulpit-oratory charge him only one fhilling and fix pence, which to common cuftomers is two fhillings.  I exchange his old fermons for new at half price.

N. B. My landlady has requefted that I will take every handfome opportunity of informing her neighbours and the public, that fhe fells corn-plafter—and really very good, for I have ufed it.  N° 13, St.—— ftreet, Petty France—To prevent miftakes, a blue lamp over the door.—Mr. Cantwell is always at home, except on Sundays, and then is to be fpoken with at the Admiral Rodney, Iflington.

I am unwilling to quarrel with the familiarity of my brother Cantwell, left, as he in all probability deals in the *proverbs* and the *noverbs*, he fhould remark that I lay myfelf open to the application of the well-known, " *Two of a trade can never agree.*"  His generofity in making a prefent

fent of his lecture to his cuftomers, reminds me of the lame man, who cried, "Come, buy my gingerbread, and I'll give you a dram." 'Tis true he gave his dram, but made you pay fix pence for a gingerbread nut. So the famous Dr. Leo cures his patients *gratis*, and only charges half-a-crown for his box of falve,

---

To the A U T H O R *of the*
OLLA PODRIDA.

SIR,

I herewith fend you a fhort hiftory of myfelf. I did once keep a theme-fhop in an univerfity, which fhall be namelefs, where I ferved undergraduates with exercifes of every kind, having men under me whom I employed in the different branches of the trade. Thefe were not your handicraftfmen, your Starvelings, and your Nick-bottoms; but, as I may fay, they were *eruditi togati homines*, learned men, men of . the gown. To each I allotted their differ-

ent

ent departmemts; here were your tranfla-
tors, your declamation-fpinners, and your
weavers of Lent-epigram. By the labours
of thefe gentry, whom I paid by the piece,
I got a decent livelihood ; but as I thought
my talents confiderably improved by habitual commerce with books and bookifh men,
I refolved to fhake off all incumbrance, and
feek a place where I might give play to my
abilities, and obtain a fhare of reputation
as well as a livelihood. It is now about a
twelvemonth fince, that, in conformity to
this refolution, I opened a neat and convenient fhop, not far from the bottom of the
Haymarket, where I deal out to cuftomers
of all forts whatever they may want in the
literary way, at the loweft prices.

I have by me, in the poetic line, every
thing that can be named, from an acroftic
to an epic poem. I have fun-rifings and
fun-fettings for all perfons, places, and
feafons. Not, like Mr. Bickerftaff's, confined to this or that condition. But I have
the milk-maid's fun-rife, the cobler's fun-
rife, the politician's fun-rife, the poet's
or common fun-rife, with proper fun-fets

to

to match them. I have ftorms for feamen, and ftorms for landfmen ; not to mention a few hailftorms, fqualls of wind, &c. &c. I have fimiles from Aracadia for paftoral writers ; metaphors for people of quality, in Joe Miller's true fenfe of the word, fuch as you never *met-a-fore*; and a bundle of tropes unforted, confifting of metonomy, apofiopefis, fynecdoche, &c. for epic poets and fonneteers. I have a fine foliloquy, fuppofed to have been uttered by Nahum Tate upon his death-bed. It is not in a ftrain of rant, but fo tender—it would do your heart good to hear how my fhop-boy does roar when I read it to him.

In the way of profe, I have jokes for disbanded ftatefmen, elegantly-turned compliments fuited to all occafions, and panegyrics applicable to all people, provided they are high in the world ; an effay on the baneful effects of intemperance and charcoal ; a loofe parcel of fentences for mottos ; a few knowing phrafes to be ufed at races, with a file of conundrums to make

the

the ladies laugh—the latter are well adapted to the mouth of any gentleman who
has a remarkable good set of teeth. Of the
graver kind, I have two sermons, which
smack pretty well of the high church.    A
two-shilling pamphlet upon the rise and
fall of the tucker.   This is in black letter,
and treats of an invention of our anceftors,
which has been unhappily loft.    I have
looked in Pancirolus, and all the books of
that fort, and can find no mention of it;
it is therefore a confiderable curiofity.

I have fpeeches fuited to members of
parliament in all trying fituations ; whether
they are about to confult their conftituents
through the medium of a hogfhead of cla-
ret, or to defcant upon an infringement of
the game laws.   Some pithy farcafms upon
country members, who have been often
ridiculed, but never properly handled.  An
effay on matrimony, and an elaborate treatife on the ufe and abufe of the parenthefis
in modern compofition.   Who knows,
Mr. ———, but I may be able to ferve you
one of thefe days, when you have been idle,

or

or are put to it for a joke! I fay nothing,
but there is nobody I would fooner oblige.
I will fend you fome fpecimens of the different works I have mentioned ; and fhall
hope at leaft to meet with your approbation,
if not your cuftom.

I am, Sir, yours, &c. &c.

POLUMATHES.

NUMBER

# NUMBER IV.

*/ : / ' ' / / :*

---

SATURDAY, *April* 7th, 1787.

---

*Deferar in vicum vendentem thus & odores*
*Et piper & quicquid chartis amicitur ineptis.*
        HORACE.

Perhaps in the fame open bafket laid,
Down to the ftreet together be convey'd ;
Where pepper, odours, frankincenfe are fold,
And all fmall wares in wretched rhimes un-
   roll'd.        FRANCIS.

IT is melancholy to reflect on the unhappy circumftances which have frequently attended the deaths of authors. If
we turn over the pages of literary hiftory,
we fhall find that although many have en-
          joyed

joyed the gratification of hearing their own praifes, and fome have even bafked in the funfhine of opulent patronage, yet their deaths have been often obfcure, and fometimes difaftrous. Cicero fell a victim to party-rage ; Sidney expired in the field of battle ; Crichton fell by affaffination ; and Otway perifhed by famine.

The fate of books is oftentimes fimilar to that of authors. The flattery of dedications, and the teftimony of friends, are frequently interpofed in vain to force them into popularity and applaufe. It is not the fafhion of the prefent day to indulge the hangman with the amufement of committing books to the flames ; yet they are in many inftances condemned to a more inglorious deftiny. The grocer, the chemift, and the tallow-chandler, with " ruthlefs " and unhallowed hands," tear whole libraries in pieces, and feel as little compunction on the occafion, as the Thracian ladies did, when they difmembered Orpheus. The leaves are diftributed among their cuftomers with fundry articles of trade that have little connection with claffical frag-

ments,

ments, whilſt the tradeſman, like the
Sibyl, cares not a farthing what becomes of
them.

*Nunquam deinde cavo volitantia prendere ſaxo
Nec revocare ſitus aut jungere carmina curat.*

VIRGIL.

I was led into this train of thought by
receiving a pound of ſugar from my neighbour *Tim Tear-title*, the grocer, wrapt up
in a ſheet of letter preſs. Tim deals ſo
largely in books, that he has many more
than are ſufficient for his own uſe, with
which he very bountifully obliges the literati in foreign parts. I remember, juſt
before the American war broke out, my
curioſity was excited to know what a large
hogſhead, which ſtood at his door, contained. I found, on cloſe examination,
that it was filled with old pamphlets, moſt
of them on ſubjects of liberty, non-con-
formity, and whiggiſm, which Tim was
going to ſhip off for a Yankee ſhop-keeper
in New-England. Whatever ſage politi-
cians may have ſaid to the contrary, it is
not at all to be doubted, that the impor-

7

tation

tation of this cargo fpread the wild-fire of rebellion among the Boftonians, and was the fole caufe of the late bloody and expen- five war.—Although my neighbour *Tim* is no fcholar by profeffion, yet it is aftonifh- ing what a progrefs he has made in books. He has finifhed a compleat fet of the *Ge- neral Councils*, and is now hard at work upon the *Ante-Nicene Fathers*, whom he cuts up with greater expedition than Dr. Prieftley himfelf. Perhaps more logick and metaphyficks have paffed through his hands than Lord Monboddo ever faw. He would have been a long time in difpatching a fet of *French Reviews*, had he not begun upon them when the price of coffee was reduced. The other day fome young fparks, who belong to a celebrated academy, where every thing is taught, brought him a par- cel of Latin clafficks. He tore off the co- vers with as much *fang-froid* as a Nymph of Billingfgate ftrips an oyfter of its fhell, and bought Horace and Virgil for three- halfpence per pound. He obferved, with a fapient look, " That as for your *Virgilii's* " tranflation into Latin, I reckon it no better " than

" than wafte paper ; but if it had been *Mr.*
" *Dryden's Hiftory of the Trojan Horfe*, I
" would have kept it for my own read-
" ing."

I have been told by learned men, that
it is a queftion much debated in the Univerfities, whether or no the *place ought to
agree with the thing placed.* Now after all
that ferious meditation, which fo abftrufe
a point requires, I am determined to decide
in the affirmative. For who cannot fee
the propriety, or rather (as ~~Parfon~~ *Square*
would fay) the fitnefs of things, in wrapping
up a cheefe-cake in a paftoral, fugar-candy
in a dedication, or gunpowder in a fermon
on the fifth of November?

There never was a time when learning
forced itfelf fo much into notice as it does
at prefent. You can no more walk a hundred yards in any ftreet, or go into any
houfe, without feeing fome difplay of it,
than you can turn a corner in London
without feeing a beggar, or hear a failor
talk without fwearing. A man of fafhion
imperceptibly keeps up his acquaintance
with his alphabet, by playing at the noble
game

game of Te-totum, or rifquing his fortune at an E O table. Book-ftalls furnifh hiftory; the walls of houfes poetry; handbills medicine; fire-fcreens geography, and clocks morality. Thefe are the channels which convey to the porter the knowledge of the conftitution, to the apprentice the art of rhiming, to members of Parliament an acquaintance with our India fettlements, and to the fat alderman, wife fayings.

For my own part I am not fatisfied with fuch vulgar means of growing learned, but love to follow literature into her more fecret receffes. Fortunately, chance has furnifhed me with the means of doing this, without being driven to the immenfe *bore* of poring over books, which would only produce the effects of a dofe of opium. I have a trunk, which, like the dagger of Hudibras, may be applied to more purpofes than one. It is lined with feveral fheets of the Royal Regifter, and of courfe contains much edifying information. During my travels, I watch my trunk with the fame fond anxiety which Sancho ufed to feel for his beloved Dapple. On my arrival at an

E                            inn,

inn, after having ſtudied the moſt curious
manuſcript in the houſe, the bill of fare,
I unlock my magazine of linen and learning, and feaſt upon delicious ſcraps of characters, until more ſubſtantial food is ſet
upon the table.   When I travel in company, my aſſociates complain of my taking
an unreaſonable time to equip myſelf.
They are not aware, that frequently whilſt
they think I am fluctuating between boots
and ſhoes, I am conjecturing what the ini-
tial letters of my fragment ſtand for, and
that, inſtead of changing my linen, I am
ſhifting from the Duke of Marlborough to
Lord Chatham.

   To thoſe who wiſh not to forget all that
their ſchool-maſters taught them, this ſort
of light reading is to be recommended.   It
would be no bad plan if all genteel people
would furniſh their trunks, portmanteaus,
caravans, and band-boxes with the beauties
of ſome author that ſuits their taſte.   If
the Beau Monde ſhould be afraid of injuring their eyes, by theſe ſtudies, Mademoi-
ſelle Abigail, or Monſieur Valet de Chambre, had better be deputed to read trunk-
                              lectures

lectures to them. Hoyle on whiſt will an-
ſwer extremely well for old ladies ; Tom
Jones or Joſeph Andrews for boarding-
ſchool miſſes ; Eſton's Theſaurus, or the
Art of ſhooting flying, for parſons ; Paterſon's book of roads for lawyers on the
circuit ; and Phillidore on cheſs for the
gentlemen of the army.

Pedants may object, that if the above
plan ſhould become general, the works of
the learned will be no longer treaſured up
in the libraries of the great. But let them
not be alarmed ; for they may be certain,
that whilſt books are conſidered by a refined
age as a ſpecies of ornamental furniture,
and ſupply the place of the *claſſics in wood*,
they will not be driven from their preſent
poſts. There is, it muſt be confeſſed, great
reaſon 'to be alarmed at the deſtruction
which threatens ſome branches of literature. Innumerable enemies are conſtantly
on the watch, to annihilate inſipid novels,
ſcurrilous ſatires, party pamphlets, and in-
decent ſongs. If they chance to attract
the publick eye for a week or two, they
cannot eſcape that deſtiny which their au-

E 2                                   thors

thors were too much dazzled with their own *charming* productions to forefee. As weeds by their decay fertilize the foil from which they fprung, fo thefe flimfy and noxious publications do great fervice to fociety, by lighting a pipe, embracing a tallow-candle, or forming the bafis of a minc'd-pie.                              Q.

# NUMBER V.

SATURDAY, *April* 14th, 1787.

Μισω σοφιςην ὁςις ἐκ αὐτῳ σόφει.

GR. PROV.

THERE is no fpecies of fcience whofe utility is more generally allowed than that which is called Knowledge of the World, the fafeguard of the prudent, the manual of the cunning, and fometimes the inftrument of virtue. It has been often remarked,·that men of acknowledged abilities and great literary merits, have been in general found more deficient in this kind of knowledge than the illiterate and the vulgar. ·Some have ranked, this acquifition

E 3                           fo

fo low, as to to have fuppofed it unworthy
fuch men's attention ; others have, perhaps, erroneoufly conjectured, that it was
too high for their' attainment; and others
again, with more fhadow of reafon, have
afcribed their want of it to the imperfec-
tion of human nature.

Since the excellence and fuperiority of
this attainment is acknowledged by all, it
is not to be wondered at, if the acquifition
of it engages the attention and purfuit
of all.

It may not be improper to afcertain, as
near as poffible, the meaning of the term
Knowledge of the World, which with
every different clafs of men has a different
acceptation. With fome people it means,
what has been called *a knavifh form of underftanding*, abounding in tricks of low
cunning, and pregnant with ftratagems, by
which a perfon advances his own intereft,
without regard to the ruin of the unwary,
or the contempt of the upright. The man
of trade, whom his own arts or his own
induftry have enriched, is fufficiently convinced, that to his *knowledge of the world*
he is indebted for his prefent exemption
from

from bufinefs, for the enjoyment of his
villa, and the envy of his neighbourhood.
In his great veneration for this kind of
knowledge, he forgets that the fame arts
which expedite the acquifition of wealth,
frequently fupply temptations to impair honefty.

Some arrive at this knowledge, by living
with an opera-finger at Paris, bringing
home the name of a noted Italian ballet-
mafter, or wearying out the attention of
their yawning friends with indefinite and
unfatisfactory accounts of the Efcurial. To
fome a more eafy path toward the acquiring knowledge is open; they may learn,
without leaving London, with what eafe
the ace of fpades will convey an eftate from
one honourable family to another; of how
*little moment* it is when compared with a
rational amufement of a *ferious* game of
whift, whether a wife be made unhappy,
or a family ruined,

Some, who are not fond of parting with
their money without any gratification, have
been prudent enough to ftipulate for *fport*
in exchange; well fatisfied they repair to

E 4                          that

that repofitory of the arts and fciences, Newmarket, and are handfomely recom‐ penced by a good gallop for the lofs of their whole fortune.

It is *knowledge of the world* which di‐ rects the cheefe-monger's wife in her choice of a gown, and the putting up of her pickles; it determines whether her cap fhall be like Mrs. Chefhire's or Mrs. Tape's; whether her Sunday's ride fhall convey her to the Angel at High-gate, or to the Pack‐ horfe at Turn-ham-green. *Knowledge of the world* perfuades the Spendthrift, that in expence alone confifts the *fcavoir vivre*; and teaches the Ufurer to withhold his loan, till the premium is doubled. The increafe of this knowledge begets that comfortable contempt which each clafs entertains for the other; it fupports the man of fub‐ ftance in his condemnation of poverty, and inftructs the man of pleafure to defpife the fons of mechanifm and tallow.

It is *knowledge of the world* by which the man of fafhion acquires a readinefs in the different forms of falutation; the proper referve with which he treats an inferior; and

and the fkilful adulation with which he approaches the fool greater than himfelf.

To his *knowledge of the world* the clerical folicitor is obliged; while he evades the penalties incurred by fimoniacal contracts, flies from the vigilance of epifcopal enquiry, and is mean enough to fhear the flock, which he is too proud to feed.

The fceptic in religion difcovers his *knowledge of the world* by afferting a natural right to think for himfelf; by fearching with eager enquiry after what muft be for ever before his eyes; and doubting the truth of that which nature infifts upon " through " all her works."

It is forfooth an accurate *knowledge of the world* which prompts the Atheift to inform his hearers, that the duties of religion are impofitions upon the weak and credulous, the contrivances of ambition, the clogs and impediments to the progrefs of real merit.

It is this falutary *knowledge of the world* which affifts the Libertine in his career, and gives vigour to the arm of the fuicide.

This

This boaſted wiſdom then, by which the tradeſman acquires wealth, the minion of faſhion the notice of his peers, the ſceptic reputation, and the libertine encouragement, is too high for the attainment only of men of abilities, ſcience, and literature ! This is ſurely a poſition to which no logical fallacy can give the appearance of truth. Is it probable, that the ſame man, who can ſuccefsfully combat the inſidious arguments of ſchiſmatic theologiſts, ſhould become the dupe of a low-minded and deſigning mechanic ? Or ſhall He, who can with accuracy examine the claims of the impoſtor Mahomet, bow down before the ſuperior wiſdom of a tricking pedlar ?

It is from an honeſt benevolence of heart, the peculiar concomitant of an enlightened mind, which neglects to fortify itſelf againſt attacks it has never provoked, and diſdains to ſuſpect the injury it has never felt, that men of ſuperior talents frequently fall into the ſnares of theſe ſagacious ſons of prudence.

It is not to be wondered at, that they whoſe attention has been diverted from the

concerns

concerns of the world to objects of a higher nature, fhould perform thofe offices which are neceffary to fociety with lefs fkill than others, whofe lives have been confumed in the conftant intercourfe with mankind, and the noife and buftle of bufinefs. In the performance of thefe offices, the frequent fuperiority of ignorance over learning is evident and confeffed. The former oftentimes effects with eafe what the latter in vain attempts, with aukwardnefs and timidity; aukwardnefs, arifing from a bafhful mind, and timidity from the confcioufnefs of its own defects.

Yet let thofe who excel in worldly wifdom bear their triumph with moderation, when they are reminded, that wealth, which only gratifies the avarice of its poffeffor, without being the inftrument of his benevolence, is neither honourable nor ornamental; and that power, for which ambition pants, only fhews itfelf illuftrious, when it is exerted to fupprefs injuftice, and to protect innocence.

NUM-

## NUMBER VI.

---

SATURDAY, *April* 21ft, 1787,

---

*Credula turba 'fumus.*

THE character of the late king of Pruffia, together with the refidence of Dr. Katterfelto, and other heroes of that country in England, have contributed to raife in the minds of many of our countrymen a very high and fplendid idea of that nation of philofophers, warriors, and phyficians.

I was

I was paffing, not long ago, through Holborn with a friend, whom I had all my life miftaken for a man of fenfe, when a printed bill of Dr. Katterfelto's was put into our hands, and foon after the Doctor himfelf, in a fhabby kind of chariot, whifked by us :— Is that, exclaimed my friend, an equipage fuitable to the character and condition of a brother to a colonel in the king of Pruffia's life-guards? Ought he' to be reduced to the neceffity every day of reminding the publick of his fituation, his dignity, and his quality? Is it not fcandalous, that he who has done fuch fignal fervices to all the princes and potentates of Europe, fhould be fuffered in this humiliating manner to fupplicate the attendance of gentlemen and ladies upon his exhibition at only one fhilling each?—Oh, Mr. ——, I am forry to fay it, we are an envious nation, and willing only to favour thofe whom we defpife. The French fend over their Veftris, their dancing-dogs, and wheedle us out of our money, an dthen fkip off with it; the Italians,—but we will not talk of them, for I fhall be in a paffion

—while

—while this honeſt Dr. Katterfelto can
with difficulty obtain a livelihood.   There's
Dr. Leo again, who has performed ſuch
and ſo many extraordinary cures in moſt of
the king of Pruſſia's camps, to ſay nothing
of his table in Covent-garden, where I
myſelf have felt the ſalutary effects of his
advice.   I am really aſhamed, ſir, ſuppoſe
theſe gentlemen ſhould ever go back, as
they have often threatened, to their own
country, what muſt become of our national reputation?   The wonderful Doctor
would take away his cats with him, and
the tall regiment would laugh at us.

My friend was ſo ſerious in his harangue,
that I would not hazard offending him by
ridicule; but I could not help hinting my
doubts as to the truth of the aſſertions,
which theſe gentry are very apt to make.

Upon my return home, I immediately
diſpatched a meſſenger to the ſhop of my
ingenious and valuable friend and corre-
ſpondent Mr. Polumathes, requeſting that
he would ſend me by the bearer a ſhort eſ-
ſay on that benevolent credulity, by which
our friend John Bull is ſo diſtinguiſhed,
and

and fo deceived; with which I purpofed
to conclude this paper. My meffenger
brought back the following anfwer, replete
with that candour and good fenfe for which
Mr. P. is fo juftly celebrated.

*Dear Sir*,　　　　　　*Friday Morning.*
　　THE commiffion you have
been fo kind as to favour me with, highly
flatters me. It raifes my idea of your dif-
cernment, and my own abilities: But the
reafon why I cannot execute it fo faithfully
as I could wifh, is briefly as follows: Some
time ago, it was, I know not by what enemies to the ftate, induftrioufly ftrewed in the
common ear, and was believed by the herd,
that the lake of Geneva was filled with Gin.
Now this I knew to be a vulgar error, and
to prevent its evil confequences by emigra-
tion, and to put a little money in my
own pocket, I gave the world a pamphlet
on the fubject. Herein I fufficiently pointed
out to my honeft countrymen thofe inconveniences, into which they were too eafily
led by their credulity; I affured them the
　　　　　　　　　　　　　　report

report was a falfe one ; and, moreover,
that they might get as good gin at the
Two Brewers, or the White Horfe Cellar,
as Geneva could produce. You will not be
furprifed if I add, that in this pamphlet I
exhaufted on the fubject all the rhetoric I
had in my fhop, and indeed left myfelf fo
bare of argument, that I had not enough
by me to anfwer a trifling fquib which was
written in ridicule of my work.

Receive my thanks for the honour you
have done me, and believe me on this, and
all other occafions, your fervant at command,

MICHAEL POLUMATHES.

Such being the anfwer of my friend Mr.
Michael Polumathes, my intention of giving to the world a treatife upon fo interefting a fubject, is fruftrated ; and I have room
left to recommend to their notice the letters of two other correfpondents.

*To*

*To the* A U T H O R *of the*

O L L A P O D R I D A.

DEAR SIR,

I fhould be very much obliged to you or any perfon who would define to me the meaning of a very common phrafe, " He's a dry fellow." It is a mode of expreffion which all people ufe, and many, I dare fay, underftand : I own, I do not. As I was coming out of Whitehall, a few Sundays ago, I met a friend at the door, who afked me what the Doctor had been preaching a-bout ; I told him, as near as I could guefs, about twenty-five minutes. He immedi-ately put me down, as he faid, for a dry fellow. It was in vain that I affured him I was not dry. He infifted upon it I was, and he fhould reckon me fo as long as I lived. I was fome time after relating to him what I thought a *bon-mot* of a man, who, being advifed to enlarge his houfe, becaufe (as his advifer obferved) he had not room to fwing a cat, fimply replied, " I don't want to fwing a cat." He heard

F                          my

my ftory, and then affirmed, that I had a
fet of the *drieft* acquaintance of any man
he knew.   I repeatedly endeavoured to
bring him to an explanation, but to no purpofe : all I could get from him was, " a
curfed dry fellow—a dry dog indeed."
Now if this phrafe has no meaning, it
fhould be abolifhed ; if it has any, I fhould
take it as a great favour if it might be no
longer concealed from the vulgar ; of which
I confefs myfelf one.

JERRY SIMPLE.

## To the A U T H O R of the
## OLLA PODRIDA.

SIR,

Sauntering along the road the other day,
I came to a fmall Inn, where all was buftle
and confufion by the arrival of fome great
family, with their numerous retinue ; but
what claimed moft attention was the accident of a favourite dog, who was trod on
by one of the horfes turning fhort ; whether

it

it was by chance, or whether it again proved, that a favourite has no friends, was not
for me to decide : a glafs of brandy was
called for, a common gill, enough to warm
a poor man in a cold morning, was re-
jected, as infufficient ; and nothing would
do but a tumbler full, to bathe Pero's foot
in : it was afterwards rubbed with friar's
balfam, bound up with rags, and committed to the care of Mrs. Betty, to travel
in the coach with her. I admire compaffion wherever I fee it exerted through the
wide fphere of fenfitive life; but our refinement may be carried too far, and that
fympathizing attention which humanity
demands, be fquandered on the brute creation. I knew an old maiden lady, whofe
tears could tenderly flow at the relation of
the fufferings of a cat, but who did not exhibit any active benevolence at the call of
the wants of her poor or fuffering neighbours. Yet fhe could readily excufe herfelf by unremitting attention to her favourite animals. Let them be provided for according to their condition ; yet we muft

re-

remember that there are duties of humanity belonging to a higher clafs ; and we fhall find but fmall excufe in the judgment of enlightened reafon, if we urge our regard to inferior obligations, while thofe of a fuperior kind are neglected.

I am, Yours, &c.

VIATOR.

NUMBER VII.

—————

SATURDAY, *April* 28, 1787.

—————

*Servatâ femper lege et ratione loquendi.*

.JUVENAL.

THE different writers, who have obliged the world with memoirs of Dr.
Johnfon, all agree to inform us, that he
efteemed converfation to be the comfort of
life. He himfelf, indeed, in an *Idler*, has
not fcrupled to compare it to a bowl of that
liquor, which, under the direction of
Mr. Brydone, fo defervedly engaged the
attention of the Sicilian clergy ; and in the
compofition of which, while the fpirit is

F 3                   duly

duly tempered by water, and the acid fufficiently corrected by fugar, the ingredients
wonderfully confpire to form the moft delicious beverage known among mortals.

But whether it be that the requifites for
producing converfation, like thofe for making punch, are not always to be had, or
are not good in their kind, or not properly
mixed, certain it is that in the former cafe,
as in the latter, the operation does not at
all times fucceed to the fatisfaction of the
company; nothing being more common
than to hear perfons complaining, that after many hours paffed in this way, they
have found neither improvement nor entertainment.

Without ftudy, or method, I fhall fet
down fuch thoughts as may occur to my
mind, on this moft interefting fubject.

That converfation may anfwer the ends
for which it was defigned, the parties, who
are to join in it, muft come together with
a determined refolution to pleafe, and to be
pleafed. If a man feels that an eaft wind
has rendered him dull and fulky, he fhould
by all means ftay at home till the wind
3                                         changes,

changes, and not be troublefome to his friends; for dulnefs is infectious, and one four face will make many, as one chearful countenance is foon productive of others. If two gentlemen defire to quarrel, it fhould not be done in a company met to enjoy the pleafures of converfation. Let a ftage be erected for the purpofe, in a proper place, to which the jurifdiction of the Middlefex magiftrates doth not reach. There let Martin and Mendoza mount, accompanied by Ben and Johnfon, and attended by the *Amateurs*, who delight to behold blows neatly laid in, ribs and jaw-bones elegantly broken, and eyes fealed up with delicacy and addrefs. It is obvious, for thefe reafons, that he, who is about to form a converfation party, fhould be careful to invite men of congenial minds, and of fimilar ideas refpecting the entertainment of which they are to partake, and to which they muft contribute.

With gloomy perfons, gloomy topics likewife fhould be (as indeed they will be) excluded, fuch as ill health, bad weather, bad news, or forebodings of fuch, &c. &c. To

preferve

preferve the temper calm and pleafant, it is
of unfpeakable importance, that we always
accuftom ourfelves through life to make
the beft of things, to view them on their
bright fide, and fo reprefent them to others,
for our mutual comfort and encouragement.
Few things (efpecially if, as Chriftians,
we take the other world into the account)
but have a bright fide: diligence and practice will eafily find it.  Perhaps there is no
circumftance better calculated than this, to
render converfation equally pleafing and
profitable.

In the conduct of it, be not eager to interrupt others, or uneafy at being yourfelf
interrupted; fince you fpeak either to
amufe or inftruct the company, or to receive thofe benefits from it.  Give all,
therefore, leave to fpeak in turn.  Hear
with patience, and anfwer with precifion.
Inattention is ill manners: it fhews contempt; and contempt is never forgiven.

Trouble not the company with your
own private concerns, as you do not love
to be troubled with thofe of others. Yours
are as little to them, as theirs are to you.
You will need no other rule, whereby to
judge of this matter.                      Con-

Contrive, but with dexterity and propriety, that each perfon may have an opportunity of difcourfing on the fubject with
which he is beft acquainted. He will be
pleafed, and you will be informed. By
obferving this rule, every one has it in his
power to affift in rendering converfation
agreeable : fince, though he may not chufe,
or be qualified to fay much himfelf, ·he can
propofe queftions to thofe who are able to
anfwer them.

Avoid ftories, unlefs fhort, pointed, and
quite *à-propos*. He who deals in them,
fays Swift, muft either have a very large
ftock, or a good memory, or muft often
change his company. Some have a fet of
them ftrung together like onions : they
take poffeffion of the converfation, by an
early introduction of one ; and then you
muft have the whole *rope*, and there is an
end of every thing elfe, perhaps, for that
meeting, though you may have heard all
twenty times before.

Talk *often*, but not *long*. The talent of
haranguing in private company is infup-
portable. Senators and Barrifters are apt

to be guilty of this fault; and Members, who never harangue in the houſe, will often do it out of the houſe. If the majority of the company be naturally ſilent, or cautious, the converſation will flag, unleſs it be often renewed by one among them, who can ſtart new ſubjects. Forbear, however, if poſſible, to broach a ſecond, before the firſt is out, leſt your ſtock ſhould not laſt, and you ſhould be obliged to come back to the old barrel. There are thoſe who will repeatedly croſs upon, and break into the converſation, with a freſh topic, till they have touched upon all, and exhauſted none. Oeconomy here is neceſſary for moſt people.

Laugh not at your own wit and humour: leave that to the company.

When the converſation is flowing in a ſerious and uſeful channel, never interrupt it by an ill-timed jeſt. The ſtream is ſcattered, and cannot be again collected.

Diſcourſe not in a whiſper, or half voice, to your next neighbour. It is ill breeding, and in ſome degree a fraud; converſation-ſtock being, as one has well obſerved, a joint and common property.

In

In reflections on abfent people, go no farther than you would go, if they were prefent. " I refolve," fays Bifhop Beveridge, " never to fpeak of a man's virtues " before his face, nor of his faults behind his " back ;" a golden rule ! the obfervation of which would, at one ftroke, banifh flattery and defamation from the earth.

Converfation is effected by circumftances, which, at firft fight, may appear trifling, but really are not fo. Some, who continue dumb while feated, become at once loquacious when they are (as the fenatorial phrafe is) *upon their legs.* Others, whofe powers languifh in a clofe room, recover themfelves on putting their heads into frefh air, as a fhrovetide cock does when his head is put into frefh earth. A turn or two in the garden makes them good company. There is a magic fometimes in a large circle, which fafcinates thofe who compofe it into filence; and nothing can be done, or, rather, nothing can be *faid*, till the introduction of a card-table breaks up the fpell, and releafes the valiant knights and fair damfels from captivity. A table indeed, of any kind,

con-

confidered as a centre of union, is of eminent fervice to converfation at all times ;
and never do we more fenfibly feel the
truth of that old philofophical axiom, that
nature *abhors a vacuum*, than upon its removal.    I have been told, that even in the
*blue-ftocking* fociety, formed folely for the
purpofe of converfation, it was found, after
repeated trials, impoffible to *get on*, without
*one* card-table.    In that fame venerable fociety, when the company is too widely extended to engage in the fame converfation,
a cuftom is faid to prevail—and a very excellent one it is--that every gentleman,
upon his entrance, felects his partner, as he
would do at a ball ; and when the conver-
fation-dance is *gone down*, the company
change partners, and begin afrefh.    Whether thefe things be fo, or not, moft certain it is, that the lady or the gentleman
deferves well of the fociety, who can devife any method, whereby fo valuable an
amufement can be heightened and improved.

Z.

NUM-

[ 77 ]

## NUMBER VIII.

---

SATURDAY, *May* 5, 1787.

---

*Cui dicas fæpe video.*

THERE are many perfons in the world, whofe wit and whofe judgment, like two parallel lines, never meet; who are ftill neither deficient in wit, nor deftitute of judgment. An improper ufe of the former, or a temporary abfence of the latter, ufually renders both ineffectual. To what purpofe is judgment employed in making proper obfervations, and forming proper opinions; or wit called forth to illuftrate thofe obfervations, or difplay thofe opinions in all the ornament of well-turned language,

language, or elegant allufion ; if they are,
perchance, exhibited before an audience,
prejudiced againft the fpeaker, unwilling to
attend to him, or incapable of underftanding
him ? In fuch a cafe, the judgement muft
have been lulled to .fleep, and the wit
thrown away.

To my reflections upon this fubject I
was led by a circumftance which not long
ago happened to myfelf. An ingenious
friend, with whom I was converfing, addreffed to me fome ftrictures upon a periodical publication, which, he obferved, was
then carrying on in Oxford, called the *Olla
Podrida*. After expatiating for fome time
in general terms upon the fmall probability
of fuccefs attendant on fuch a plan, owing
to the political diftraction of the nation, the
exhaufted ftate of materials neceffary for
fuch a work, and in fhort the general decay
of readers and writers ; he defcended to be
more particular in his criticifms; he could
not help obferving, that the characteriftic
of the firft number was an affectation of
modefty, and of the fecond an affectation of
learning. Why elfe, added he, was not
the full tranflation of each paffage in Homer

mer admitted from Mr. Pope ? He then concluded his critique with fome happy farcafms upon Monfieur l'Auteur, at which he laughed violently, and I accompanied him as well as I could. I avoided entering into a minute defence of the gentleman at whofe expence we had been fo agreeably entertained, left I fhould difcover myfelf to be too much interefted in his behalf; but was content to obferve, that it might be more difficult to write an introductory paper than we were aware of, and, with regard to the admiffion of Mr. Pope's tranflation of each paffage, that the paper appeared fo full, as neceffarily to exclude either that or the original.

Befides, added he (recovering himfelf from the convulfion of merriment, into which his own friendly ideas had betrayed him), upon fuch a fubject as the Iliad or Odyffey, who cares what the Adventurer has faid, or what the Olla Podrida has to fay ? Every body knows that each is a model of different excellence, that the former is the work of genius in the full and vigorous exertions of all its powers, and the

latter

latter bears evident marks of the poet's having arrived at a maturity of judgement,
though, at the fame time, he difcovers
the decay of age. I acquiefced more with
filence than fatisfaction in what I heard my
friend advance. Had he known me for the
author, while his confcientious adherence,
to truth might have extorted the fame opinions from him, he would have been prevented from triumphing in the infolence
of wit. This tribute he would have paid
to delicacy. When he reads the eighth
number of the Olla Podrída, he will probably agree in opinion with me, that thofe
thoughts have been conceived in an unlucky moment, which are exprefled in an
improper one. He will likewife be reminded, that people are inclined to entertain little opinion of that judgment which
controverts their own fentiments, and little relifh for that wit by which themfelves
become ridiculous.

I fhall folace myfelf with the affurance
Mr. Addifon has given us, " That there is,
and ever will be, juftice enough in the
world to afford patronage and protection
for

for thofe who endeavour to advance truth
and virtue, without any regard to the
paffions and prejudices of any particular
caufe and faction *."

But left I fhould feem to dwell too long
upon a fubject neither interefting nor entertaining to my readers, I fhall fubjoin the
following letter:


*To the* C O O K *of the*
O L L A  P O D R I D A.


*Xanthe retro propera.*                 OVID.

Mr. TARATALLA, *or whatever your Name is,*

THERE is at prefent, in this little
ifland of Great Britain, fo much hurry,
buftle, and confufion, that nothing is in
its proper place. O'Kelly has been taken
in, the Bath butcher has been beaten, and
no progrefs is made toward finding out the
longitude. We are in the fame ftate in
which Rome was during the Catilinarian

* Spectator, No. 445.

G                        confpiracy;

confpiracy ; no man knows upon whom he may depend ; honeft men are afraid of each other ; and thieves are betrayed by their affociates. The honourable fraternity of Black-legs cannot follow their calling, becaufe the management of the Faro-table is in the hands of nobility. The women of fafhion are at my Lord Mayor's dinner ; Royalty is gone to a Barnet Boxing-match ; and the Parfon of the parifh lives an hundred miles from his flock, becaufe his preferment is a finecure.

Not three days ago, I met my fhoe-maker airing himfelf and his houfhold, between Hampftead and Kentifh town, in a jobb-coach, all duft, and fweat, and belly. The gentility of this notable tradefman's equipage induced me to make fome enquiry into the ftate of his bufinefs and circumftances. He was candid enough to inform me (for that was his phrafe, " I will candidly inform you"), that conftant attention for years to his fhop had enabled him to go *thus a pleafureing* every Saturday. And, thank God, he had been able to educate his family genteelly ; two daughters

were

were then at the boarding fchool at Old
Brentford, and two fons at the Latin college at Knightfbridge. This honourable
fhoe-maker's trade, being left to his journeymen, is, like the Parfon's, a finecure:
And he would willingly, no doubt, take
the hopes of his family from the college, if
he could be fo fortunate as to procure him
a finecure place in the cuftoms; nor would
it be improper, or unentertaining, to fee
Mrs. Laft accommodated with the Ranger-
fhip of fome foreft; a genteel finecure, like
religion, charity, matrimony, honefty,
and benevolence, which are become all, all
finecures !

Mr. Laft, and his family, are neither
particular in the end they have in view,
nor in the means they ufe to acquire that
end. Yet let them remember, that though
the trouble of their fhop may be carried on
by proxy, and their bufinefs by thofe
means become a finecure, they will find
ruin not to be the finecure they willingly
aim at, and that they cannot die by proxy;
the former of which muft as inevitably

be the portion of the tradefman above his bufinefs, as the latter muft of all mankind.

The prevalent fafhion feems to be, for every one to fhine confpicuoufly, where no one expects to fee him. If this total derangement of the order of things continues to fpread through all ranks of people, we fhall perhaps fee the fpirit of the Chevalier D'Eon, or the Bruifer Ben, diffufed among our fair countrywomen, or the Bench of Bifhops huzzaing a ham-ftrung Ox from Cripple-gate to Fleet-market.

If you call at your coachmaker's in a morning, he is trying a pair of horfes for his own chariot; if in an evening, you cannot fee him, for he is at the Opera: your hair-dreffer refufes to fhave you for he is a *ploco cofmift*, and not a barber: the barber fends his boy to do it, obliged himfelf to attend one of the company's dinners. A waiter will not buckle on your fpurs, becaufe it is the office of Mr. Boots, who calls his deputy; and your gentleman's gentleman, inftead of pimping for his mafter, is intrigueing for himfelf.—If we go

on.

on at this rate, who the Devil is to do the bufinefs of world? Who will cry the peas and beans about the ftreets this fpring? Who will fell oranges at the Abbey? Who will fweep the ftage, fnuff the candles, fhift the fcenes, make thunder and lightning, play Scrub, or dance a hornpipe? All which things are fo neceffary to the welfare of mankind, that without them life is a joke, and this world a vale of tears.

Ten years hence, I fhall not be furpriz-ed to find this nation fo thoroughly poffeff-ed by the refolution to be all Gentlemen, that Houfe-breakers will be pardoned at the gallows, upon condition of their fubmitting to become Pedlars, Brewers, Conveyancers, or Lord Chief Juftices, for the reft of their lives: while the man, who is to be tranf-ported, may perhaps be tempted to ex-change his infamy for the drudgery of a foreign Bifhopric. Many an induftrious Handicraftfman, who has been condemn-ed to the floating Academy at Woolwich for life, will be difmiffed on pain of fitting nine years at the Helm of Great Britain, giving proper fecurity for his good behaviour. Nor will the place of Mafter of the Ceremonies at Court be unprofitably filled by fome well-bred Lawyer from the pillory.

Of trade and profeffion we fhall be thus radically cured. No man can then call another Apothecary ! No Common-council-man's heart will burft with fpleen at the grandeur of a Lord Mayor's Shew. No Wine-merchant need be at the trouble of committing adultery with a cargo from Portugal. No Epitaph-writers will be con-ftrained to pun on the death of the Cobler. No Taylor will be troubled to turn the Author's Breeches. Veniet felicius ævum, *the happier day will come* when we fhall be all on a level ; every Man his own Coach-man, his own Tobacconift, his own Gentle-man, his own Man-midwife, and, as I know who would fay, his own Wafher-woman.

I am, Mr. TARATALLA, yours, &c.

SNUB.

NUMBER

## NUMBER IX.

---

SATURDAY, *May* 12, 1787.

---

*Mane falutantum totis vomit ædibus undam.*

VIRGIL.

AMONG the grievances of modern days, much complained of, but with little hope of redrefs, is the matter of receiving and paying *Vifits*, the number of which, it is generally agreed, "has been increafing, is increafed, and ought to be diminifhed." You meet frequently with people, who will tell you, they are worn to death by vifiting; and that what with morning vifits, and afternoon vifits, dining

G 4                          vifits,

vifits, and fupping vifits, tea-drinking vifits,
and card-playing vifits, exclufive of balls
and concerts, for their parts, they have not
an hour to themfelves in the four and
twenty.—But they muft go home and drefs,
or they fhall be too late for their vifit.

Nor is this complaint by any means peculiar to the times in which we *have the
honour to live.* Cowley was out of all patience on the fubject above an hundred
years ago. " If we engage, fays he, in a
" large acquaintance, and various familiari-
" ties, we fet open our gates to the invaders
" of moft of our time : we expofe our life
" to a *quotidian ague* of *frigid impertinences,*
" which would make a wife man tremble
" to think of."

But as Cowley was apt to be a little out
of humour between whiles, let us hear the
honourable, pious, and fweet-tempered Mr.
Boyle, who, among the troubles of life,
enumerares as one " the bufinefs of receiv-
" ing fenfelefs vifits, whofe continuance, if
" otherwife unavoidable, is capable, in my
" opinion, to juftify the retirednefs of a
" hermit."

Bifhop

Biſhop Jeremy Taylor is clear, that "men " will find it impoſſible to do any thing ". greatly good, unlefs they cut off all fu- " perfluous company, and viſits."

If we confult the ladies (as indeed we ought to do upon all occaſions), we find it recorded by Ballard of the very learned and excellent Mrs. Aſtell, that " when ſhe " faw needleſs viſitors coming, whom ſhe " knew to be incapable of converſing on " any uſeful ſubject, but coming merely " for the fake of *chat* and *tattle*, ſhe would " look out of the window, and jeſtingly " tell them (as Cato did Naſica), *Mrs. Aſtell* " *is not at home* ; and in good earneſt kept " them out, not ſuffering fuch triflers to " make inroads upon her more ferious " hours."

And now what ſhall we fay to thefe things? For, after all, nothing can be more certain, than, whatever learned or unlearned folk may pretend to the contra- ry, viſit we muſt, or the world will be at an end ; we may as well go ſupercargoes to Botany-bay at once.

I                                        Diſtinction

Diftinction is the parent of perfpicuity. Suppofe, therefore, we take in order the different forts of vifits above-mentioned, and confider them (as a worthy and valuable author phrafes it) " with their roots, reafons, and refpects."

And firft of the firft, namely, morning vifits. It is evident, that, as things are now regulated amongft us, all vifits of bufinefs muft be made at this feafon ; for we dine late for this very purpofe ; and no *Gentleman* does any thing after dinner, but— drink. In the days of our forefathers, under Elizabeth, and her fucceffor James, it was otherwife ; for Bifhop Andrews, we are told, entertained hopes of a perfon who had been guilty of many faults and follies, till, one day, the young-man happened unfortunately to call in a *morning*. Then the good bifhop gave him up.

Mrs. Aftell herfelf would not have difdained to take her fhare in a little *chat* and *tattle*, over the tea-table. They may be ftyled correlatives, and go together as naturally as ham and chickens.

If

If it be afked, what number of friends it is expedient to collect, in order to make a vifit comfortable, I muft confefs myfelf unable to anfwer the queftion, fo diverfe are the opinions and cuftoms that have prevailed in different ages and countries. Among ourfelves, at prefent, if one were. to lay down a general rule, it fhould be done, perhaps, in thefe words, — *The more, the merrier.*

Some years ago, thefe multitudinous meetings were known by the various names of affemblies, routs, drums, tempefts, hurricanes, and earthquakes. If you made a morning vifit to a lady, fhe would tell you very gravely, what a divine rout, a fweet hurricane, or a charming earthquake, fhe had been at, the night defore.

To have difcuffed all thefe fubdivifions of vifits, and diftinguifhed properly the nature of each, as confidered in itfelf, would have been an arduous tafk, from which I find myfelf happily relieved by the modern very judicious adoption of the term PARTY, which is what the logicians ftyle an *univerfal,* and includes every thing of the kind. A com-

A company of twelve at dinner, with a reinforcement of eighteen at tea and cards, may, I believe, be called a *small* party, which a lady may attend, without any af-fiftance from the hair-dreffer.

There is one maxim never to be departed from; namely, that the fmallnefs of the houfe is no objection to the largenefs of the party. The reafon is, that, as thefe meetings are chiefly holden in the winter, the company may keep one another warm.

But this will not in every inftance be the cafe, after all the care and pains upon earth. For, when the other apartments were full, I have known four perfons fhut into a clofet at Chriftmas, without fire or candle, playing a rubber by the light of a fepulchral lamp, fufpended from the cieling.

At another time, the butler, opening a cupboard, to take out the apparatus for the lemonade, with the nice decanters, to prevent mifchief, in cafe of weak ftomachs, found two little miffes, whom the lady of the houfe, ever anxious to promote the happinefs

pinefs of all her friends, had fqueezed and
pinioned in there, to form a fnug party at
cribbage.

An accident happened, laft winter, at
one of thefe amicable affociations, from
a contrary caufe, where the fluids in
the human frame had fuffered too great
a degree of rarefaction. A gentleman,
making a precipitate retreat, on finding
himfelf inflated, like a balloon, with a
large dofe of gas, or burnt air in him,
tumbled over a card-table, which (that no
room might be loft) had been fet upon a
landing place of the ftairs. The *party*, with
all the implements of trade, table, cards,
candles, and counters, and the unfortunate
perfon who had brought on the cataftrophe,
rolled down together. No farther mifchief,
however, was done ; and two gentlemen
of the party, as I have been well informed,
found time to make a bet on the *odd trick*,
before they got to the bottom.

But thefe are trifling circumftances, and
no more than may be expected to fall to
the lot of humanity. I do not mention
them, I am fure, as conftituting any objection.

tion to a PARTY, or as affording any reafon why *one* fhould deprive *one's* felf of the pleafure *one* always has in *feeing one's friends about one.*                                                    Z.

---

After the remarks of my kind and inge-nious correfpondent Z, the lucubrations of Mr. Taratalla will, I fear, afford little en-tertainment; however,

> *Edita ne brevibus pereat mea charta libellis,*
> *Dicatur potius* τον δ' απαμειβομενος.
>
>                                        MARTIAL.

> Rather than leave my page half-filled, I'd fcrawl,
> " A Cobler their was, and he liv'd in his " ftall."

ALL periodical writers are, by their pro-feffion and place, cenfors of the public manners; and, that their office may be difcharged with fidelity and fkill, they fhould poffefs a certain degree of that virtù and connoiffurefhip which pervades all things from the tying of a cravat to the demon-ftration of the *pons afininus.* They claim

a right

a right to be believed in every thing
they may advance; to be admired for
that ingenuity which they undoubtedly
poſſeſs ; and to be patronized and encouraged by the diſcerning *many.*—Should
they ſometimes relate adventures they may
have met with in a ſtage-coach, in the
lobby of a play-houſe, or among the triflers
of the drawing-room, their readers are
bound in honour to believe that they have
not all their life long been actuated by that
high-minded ſpirit which uſually excites
authors to mount the top of a coach, to
ſoar into the twelve-penny gallery, and to
leave the ſplendour of the drawing-room to
" low ambition, and the pride of kings."

Unfortunately for myſelf, and my readers, I do not unite in my own perſon all
thoſe qualifications which ſhould adorn a
profeſſor of painting, dancing, muſick, elec-
tricity, horſemanſhip, and half a ſcore
more things of the ſame nature, all of
which, in the courſe of my buſineſs, I
ſhall be expected to deal out to my cuſtomers. In order to ſupply thoſe deficiencies
in myſelf, which I ſincerely lament, I have

ſettled

fettled a regular correfpondence with fome honeft gentlemen of the quill, of great credit and great ftock in trade, from whofe kind affiftance I hope to give univerfal fatisfaction.  When I firft hinted my propofal to the literati, mentioning the terms .upon which I purpofed employing any two or three hands, who might be out of work, I recieved, among others, the following anfwer to my advertifement.

### To the AUTHOR of the OLLA PODRIDA.

SIR,   I am an excellent fcholar, a man of great abilities, extenfive knowledge, and of infinite wit and humour.  I have written twelve effays, which will do very great honour to, and very much encreafe the reputation of your work; all which I will let you have for half a Guinea, and will throw you half a fcore epigrams into the bargain.  I would have waited upon you myfelf with them; but, Sir, my fhirt is wafhing, and my coat is gone to be mended.

I am Sir,

your moft obedient humble fervant,

JOHN SCRIBE.

*I haf-*

*I haſtened to Mr. Scribe's Lodgings, at Paddington.*—I ſhall not here give a very minute deſcription of the different modes of ſalutation with which two authors come together, left ſome of my readers, who are diſpoſed to turn the graveſt things into ridicule, ſhould be inclined to laugh, particularly as my friend before ob-ſerved, that his ſhirt was with his laundreſs, and his coat with the taylor. Suffice it therefore to ſay, that, after a mutual inter-change of compliments, he celebrating my liberality, and I his talents, we proceeded to diſcuſs the buſineſs which had occaſioned our meeting. The engagement entered into between us was ſoon concluded upon, and produced a confidential intimacy, which excited Mr. Scribe to favour me with ſome inſight into his own character, opinions, and adventures. But as in the ardour of a new-formed friendſhip I promiſed to give his compleat life to the world, in two vo-lums octavo, price fourteen ſhillings, to be ſold by all the bookſellers in town and country, I will not anticipate the pleaſure my readers will have in the peruſal of my

H                           work,

work, by mutilated and imperfect sketches of that history, which will soon be presented to them whole and uncorrupt.

Upon taking leave of my Paddington friend, as he followed me down stairs, he very obligingly offered his assistance in the framing of any advertisements which might be necessary or conducive to the sale of my work. He then shewed me, as specimens of his talents in this species of writing, an essay on leather breeches, made upon mathematical principles, and a recommendation of the concave razor. These, he observed, were works of a lighter kind, and such as he called ἔπεα πτοικιλά, *or the amusements of Paddington.* I thanked him, but declined the acceptance of his offer.

Upon my return home, I found three or four visitants had called upon business similar to Mr. Scribe's. Amongst whom an Hibernian stay-maker, from the Borough, wished to enlist in my service, and in testimony of his abilities had left a parcel of dreams of his own composing, which are ushered in by complaints of his inability to sleep. A French Marquis, to whom
the

the air of Great Britian had been recommended by his phyſicians, left word, that,
having nothing elſe to do, he had conde-
ſcended, during his reſidence in this iſland
purely from his *penchant* for the ſcience,
and *pour paſſer le temps*, to inſtruct the
nobleſſe in dancing. This courſe of life,
he very properly obſerved, gave him many
opportunities of furniſhing me with intelligence from the beau monde, and accordingly my readers will frequently *ſee how
things go on* from the authentic information
of the Marquis.

NUM-

# NUMBER X.

SATURDAY, *May* 19, 1787.

*Vivite felices, quibus eſt fcrtuna peraĉta*
*Iam ſua* ——.         VIRGIL.

IN expatiating upon the tranſient brevity
of all ſublunary happineſs, moraliſts of
every age and climate have ſhewn themſelves deſirous of indulging in the flights of
their imaginations. Human life has been
ſeverally compared to a race, to the gliding
courſe of a river, to a moveable proceſſion,
and to many other fleeting appearances, of
which each part exiſts by the ceſſation or
non-commencement of exiſtence in the reſt.

It

It is upon the same principles that, by phi-
losophers of more abstrufe speculation, time
from its succeflive continuity has been de-
monstrated never to be present. To make
the proper ufe then of thefe demonstrations,
one might eafily prove the abfurdity of repofing our happinefs upon prefent time
which has been allowed to have no exiftence, and of attempting to build a real fu-
perftructure upon the imaginary bafis a
non-entity. But if our felicity cannot originate from fenfation or the enjoyment of
the prefent moment, it muft of courfe be
derived either from a *fpeculative anticipation
of futurity*, or a *foothing remembrance of
pleafures already enjoyed*. To contraft then
thefe two original fources, fhall be the fubject of the following paper, that we may be
enabled to difcriminate which of the two is
more defirable, from the permanency of
thofe pleafures it beftows, and their inde-
pendency of external fupport.

In the contemplation of future life, our
thoughts muft of neceffity be agitated by
the moft powerful paffions inherent in our
H 3                         frame.

frame. Hope and Fear, which have always been found to have most influence
upon human actions, are the passions which
give a tincture of themselves to all our
views, whilst we look forward into futurity. If the prospect before us appear chearful and serene, Hope communicates to us a
pleasure as lively in the view of it, as Sen-
sation could in the enjoyment; and though
a disappointment of our expectations may
deprive us of this *imaginary* bliss, and convince us of the error which we have been
cherishing in our bosoms; yet it is that
kind of error *(mentis gratissimus)* from
which it gives us *real* pain to be separated.
On the contrary, whatever good fortune
may await us, if we have no reason to
flatter ourselves with the expectation of
it; if, as far as human eye can penetrate,
the prospect before us appear a dark and
dreary waste, the fear of incumbent misfortunes renders our sufferings more painful, than if we actually laboured under
the evils which we only apprehend, and
sinks us in all the " misery of fancied
" woe."

5                                    We

We fee then, that in the anticipation of life we frequently make ourfelves miferable by the apprehenfion of evils which we never experience; and that the pleafures which are derived from Hope, though acute and brilliant, are neither permanent, nor independent of external fupport. Their duration, indeed, muft inevitably be deftroyed by the revolution of Time, which brings with it the object that we have in view: and if our hopes then prove to have been ill grounded, the chagrin of fruftrated expectations is a confequence too obvious to need being mentioned; but if we are even fortunate enough to meet with a full completion of our wifhes, it does not equally follow, that we fhould enjoy the happinefs propofed: perhaps after all we fhall find a kind of difappointment even in the gratification of our defires, for appearances of Happinefs fill the eye with fancied grandeur at a diftance, but, contrary to other objects of fight, gradually diminifh upon the nearnefs of our approach. But the Idea of felicity being derived from Hope, will appear ftill more groundlefs if we con-

fider

fider the uncertainty which muft neceffarily
attend it. When we rely upon events
which are yet to come, we fubmit ourfelves
to the direction of an arbitrary and capricious Fortune; and fhall, perhaps, to
our misfortune experience, that the beft
concerted fchemes, and moft probable expectations, are eafily fruftrated by innumerable cafualties, which it is not in our power
to forefee, nor, if we forefee, to prevent. It
is not, however, requifite to enlarge upon
that moft trite of all topics, the inftability
of human events; enough, I think, has
been faid to prove, that whatever blifs we
may propofe to ourfelves in contemplating
the bright appearances of our future life,
and " in Fancy fwallowing up the fpace
between," it cannot poffibly be either permanent or felf-derived; which qualities,
though they be not of themfelves able to
form a compleat fyftem of Happinefs, are
yet fo far neceffary, as to render any fyftem
incompleat which is without them.

I fhall now take a view of thofe pleafures
which arife from a retrofpect of our paft
lives, and endeavour fo to contraft them

with

with thofe already confidered, as may make them appear with additional Beauty from the comparifon.

It muft, however, be allowed that, fituated as we are in this world, fubfervient to the fmiles and frowns of Fortune, a ferene tranquillity is the higheft happinefs we have reafon to expect, and that that fubtle pleafure, which is purfued with fo much avidity by the gay and the diffipated, is a mere Phantom, without any other exiftence than in the imaginations of its eager votaries. Hence the pleafures which originate from a cool and difpaffionate ufe of our reafon, muft be more fatisfactory than thofe which we derive from the violent emotions of our moft forcible Paffions. But in no exercife can we employ our reafoning faculty to greater advantage, than when we conjecture with fuperior certainty upon future events, by well confidering and reflecting upon thofe which we have already experienced.

We have before feen that, in our views of futurity, we are liable to be made miferable by the dread of bad fortune, as well

as

as happy by the fanguine pre-occupation of good—Here then the pleafures of reflection evidently prove themfelves fuperior; for the review of paft happinefs does not convey to us any higher fatisfaction, than the remembrance of difficulties which we have furmounted. It is here at laft, that, freed from the fhackles of Fortune, and every other external power, which may have before entangled us, we make all our happinefs centre within ourfelves; and, like the induftrious Bees that produce honey as well out of bitter Herbs as fweet, even out of the evils of life we extract the choiceft and moft refined blifs. Indeed, in the midft of our misfortunes we may be confoled by the confideration of being at fome future period entertained with the thoughts of what now gives us pain ; as Æneas is reprefented fupporting his dejected companions by a fimilar confolation :

*Forfan et hæc olim meminiffe juvabit.* Virg.

And as this Blifs is felf-derived and independent of any thing external, fo is it alfo durable: for, as it is drawn from thofe
tranf-

tranfactions which we are confcious have already taken place, it is evident that nothing can put a period to its exiftence but the annihilation of that confcioufnefs and faculty of remembering whence it was originally derived. From this confideration, it is plain, that a life of activity and exertion is fo much the more preferable to a life of indolence and repofe, as it affords more room for the exercife of this faculty. Our happinefs, we have before feen, arifes from the recollection of paft pleafures, proportionably chequered with the remembrance of hardfhips which we have furmounted. Now the engagements of Society fo interfperfe an active life with the anxious viciffitudes of Hope and Fear, that we muft unavoidably meet with many difficulties unknown in the ftill path of Retirement, which, though difagreeable when encountered, neverthelefs convey a fecret fatisfaction to the mind in reflecting on them when fubdued. The man, indeed, who fecludes himfelf from the cares of the world, remains at the fame time unroufed by the pleafing emotions which

others

others enjoy; and in the decline of age
will look back upon the continued famenefs
of his paft life with a liftlefs indifference;
for if in the funfhine of youth his happinefs
glow with a warmth fcarcely vital, how
can the remembrance of it as faintly reflected by a lukewarm imagination cheer
his drooping fpirits in the winter of old
age? In oppofition to this languor of a life
worn out in inaction, it may, perhaps, be
needlefs to inftance with what lively fpirits
the aged votaries of ambition or wealth
indulge themfelves in eafe after the toils
of a long and laborious purfuit after their
refpective objects; with what pleafure the
Soldier dwells upon the narrative of his
honourable though dangerous exploits; how
the Sailor rejoices whilft he recounts the
rocks and tempefts which he has fo peri-
loufly furmounted.

*—— Gaudent ut vertice rafo*
*Garrula fecuri narrare pericula nautæ.*

Juv.

But as all human happinefs muft inevitably be alloyed by fome mixture of evil,
and as the above view of the pleafure of
reflec-

reflection may feem to imply a fpecies of happinefs more perfect than is confiftent with our prefent ftate, after having feen the joys which attend it, let us now ex-amine into its concomitant evils ; let us confider whether the debauchee, when the decay of his faculties prompts him to in-dulge in an indolent repofe, looks back with folid fatisfaction upon thofe viciffi-tudes of Pleafure and Pain, the former of which he is confcious of having purchafed at the expence of his innocence, the latter of having merited by his guilt; whether the remorfe, arifing from a confcioufnefs of having violated every principle of juftice and generofity, be compenfated to the Mi-fer, by confidering with what labour he has amaffed his accumulated hoards : and, if upon this enquiry we find that the review of his paft conduct ferves rather to encreafe than to alleviate his prefent pains, we fhall be led to infer, that the teftimony of a good Confcience is another requifite towards compleating that happinefs which we have in view. He, who by his worldly wifdom is enabled to withftand the moft violent

attacks

attacks of fortune, if he poffefs not this chearful companion within his breaft, will ftill be a ftranger to any true peace or comfort ; he will view even the fmiles of Profperity without fatisfaction, and, finding nought but a turbulent confufion in his own bofom, will fhrink back with horror from himfelf.—It appears then, that though many accidental circumftances may contribute to heighten the beauties of this review; the effential requifite is a mind confcious of unerring rectitude ; and, as this is entirely dependent upon ourfelves, that we have it in our power, by our own conduct, to provide for the decline of age, when our natural infirmities require an additional confolation, a never-failing fource of true and placid enjoyment.

I have feen it fomewhere recommended; that, in order to enjoy the pleafures of the imagination in our nightly dreams, we fhould be able to reft upon our pillow, and reflect coolly upon the tranfactions of the preceding day : In the fame manner I fhould recommend it to every one fo to regulate his conduct through the active fcenes of

focial

focial life, that he may lie down in the evening of old Age, and review them with unruffled fatisfaction : and, as we have obferved that the happinefs derived from Hope, though inferior to that of Reflection, is not however trivial, I would alfo recommend him fo to extract and mingle the joys of each, as to make the *foothing remembrance of paft pleafures*, a folid foundation for a *fpeculative anticipation* of thofe to come.

N U M-

---

*—Smiles from reafon flow, to Brutes deny'd.*
MILTON.

IT has been the bufinefs of philofophers in all ages to invent an appofite and charaƈteriftic term by which Man may be diftinguifhed from the brute creation in his exclufive right to fome peculiar faculty. The deep penetration and vigorous refearches of an illuftrious Heathen have enabled him to inform us, that man is an *animal bipes implume,* a two-legged animal without

without feathers.  And Philofophers of later ages have difcovered, that he is a laughing animal, a rational animal, a tool-. making animal, a cooking animal.

It is my prefent intention to confider him as the laughing animal; and that faculty, though it fhould refolve itfelf into as many fubdivifions as a lecture upon heads, or branch forth into ramifications like a Welfh pedigree, I fhall purfue thro' all its degrees, from the *rifus fardonicus* of the ancients, to the *Tee Hee* of the modern drawing-room.

When I infift upon the gravity of the fubject I am about to handle, left I fhould be accufed of extravagance of opinion, I fhall endeavour to fhew by a brief narrative of facts, that the confequences which flow from the ufe and abufe of this our diftinguifhing faculty are of the moft ferious nature.  I have feen a whole battalion of militia men, as valorous and as red-coated as a regiment of guards, difconcerted and put into confufion in the midft of their manœuvering and tobacco-chewing, from the broad-fhouldered ferjeant of the grena-

I

dier

dier company to the duck-legged corporal
of recruits, by the horfe-laugh of a bye-
ftander. I was once prefent *(credite dicen-
ti)* in the pit at the Opera, during the re-
prefentation of Macbeth—On my right
hand fat an unthinking Englifhman, who,
forgetful that he was a fpectator of a ferious
performance, burft into a horfe-laugh, juft
at the very time when Lady Macbeth and
her *caro fpofo* were conjuring up all the
horror that heads and heels were capable of
exciting. Her Ladyfhip, confcious that
fhe brandifhed her dagger in tune, and that
fhe rubbed off the "damn'd fpot" from
her hand moft harmonioufly, without ex-
hibiting to the audience any of that *difagree-
abilità* of countenance for which Mrs. Siddons has been condemned, was very highly
as well as very juftly enraged. The curtain fell, and the Signora declared fhe
would never appear again before an Englifh
audience. In vain did the diftreffed manager reprefent to her, that the tafte, the
judgement, the every thing of this unhappy nation, were infinitely beneath her notice; heaping at the fame time upon poor
John

John Bull a profufion of epithets, all end-
ing in *iffimo*. In vain was he preffing in
his folicitations, that fhe fhould give them,
at leaft, one more trial ; fhe ftill perfifted
in her cruel threats, that fhe would leave
them, and return to her own country. At
laft, however, the kind interference of a
noble frequenter of the Opera-houfe produced a reconciliation. He could not but
confefs the headftrong vulgarity, and unreafonable prejudices of his countrymen,
who confidered every competition with
their favourite poet as a burlefque and an
infult. Yet, he hoped, the ignorance and
the infolence of a few would not be a fufficient reafon for the punifhment of the
great body of *cognofcenti*. He, moreover,
fpiritedly declared, that he would call any
perfon to a very fevere account, who fhould
dare to laugh, when on the printed bills of
the night was written, in large characters,
" *a ferious Opera.*"

The refentment of Signor Macabet himfelf was carried to a ftill higher pitch. He
who but the day before had been compli-
mented with the Thanefhip of Cawdor, be-

caufe

caufe he had ftood a minute and an half longer, by the manager's watch, upon one leg, than any Macbeth or Artaxerxes who had ever appeared upon any ftage, was actually found the next morning hanging in a pair of embroidered garters, with taffels of filver twift. The Signor made a vacancy in the opera lift, and his garters were entirely fpoiled, having been fo much ftretched as to be unfit for the ufe of any future Macbeth, Rinaldo, Artaxerxes, or, in fhort, any body with a decent leg.

This tragical after-piece was entirely occafioned by the Horfe-laugh, the ufe of which is fometimes allowable, but the two frequent repetition of it I cannot but confider as a difeafe. This difeafe is very prevalent in the city, it is often found at a fitting of the Quorum, and, in fhort, at moft places where the company meet *to be merry*; the fymptoms attending it are violent convulfions, and a bloated habit.

This diforder, among the men, I believe to have originated from the falfe philofophy of a few fmatterers in fcience, who conceived, that as Man was diftinguifhed from

the

the brutes by laughter, the more he laughed, the farther he was removed from the
lower fpecies. Yet they fhould in their,
philofophical refearches have recollected,
that *extremes meet*, and for that very reafon
this fpecies of laughter, which being too·
much indulged was confidered as unbe-
coming *Mankind*, has been degraded by the
title of the *Horfe-laugh*. With the ladies,
this complaint has a different origin. The
Venus of the Greeks, from whom we derive all our notions of the elegant and beautiful, when reprefented by the poets in
her moft bewitching attire, is called the
φιλομειδης, a term expreffive of that rational
chearfulnefs of countenance, which com-
prehends all that is lovely in the female
face. The poverty of our language has
been obliged to tranflate this " the laugh-
" ter-loving ;" and to that caufe alone are
owing all thofe fhrill yet violent fallies of
mifinterpreted Gaiety, which frighten our
horfes in the park, give us the head-ach at
old Drury, and, worfe than all, diftort the
features of the faireft women in the world.

I 3                    Of

Of Grinning, which I do not confider as a fpecies of laughter, I fhall treat upon fome future occafion, and endeavour to defcribe the different modifications of it, as it is at prefent practifed by thofe Profeffors, who exercife their faculty through a horfe-collar at a country fair, by that ufeful animal in the Kitchen, the Turnfpit, and by the illuftrious Affiftant and Partner of Mr. Aftley—General Jackoo.

I fhall proceed therefore to the *rifus in angulo* of the ladies, or giggle in the corner. This fpecies of merriment has many different ends in view. It fometimes hunts down a man of bafhfulnefs, fometimes ridicules a hump-back, or a red nofe, and fometimes becomes an affignation of gallantry. The two former of its qualities are particularly called forth, when a bevy of beauties, huddled up into one corner of a room, monopolize the wit of a whole company, and exercife all the cruel artillery of ftolen glances, and half-ftifled laughs, to the great difquiet of any man who is not as ferene amidft difficulties as Fabricius was in the tent of King Pyrrhus.

That

That the giggle in the corner is fome-times an affignation of gallantry, my male readers, who have no authority upon which they can with more confidence rely, will find fufficiently demonftrated {in Horace. My female readers are reminded of a ma-nœuvre of this kind, by fome lines in the firft paftoral of Mr. Pope :—He there makes a fhepherd give the following account, which by the bye I think hardly fair :

- Me gentle Delia beckons from the plain,
  Then, hid in fhades, eludes her eager, fwain,
  But feigns a laugh, to fee me fearch around,
  And by that laugh the willing fair is found.

The *Tee-Hee* is that gentle relaxation of the mufcular fyftem which proceeds from no inward impulfe, and is vulgarly though not improperly denoted the affected laugh. This is a term of great latitude, and com-prehends the laugh of all thofe who are called, by the Guardian *, the Chians, the Ionics, and the Megarics.   The Tee-Hee is the tribute generally paid to any ftory which is fuppofed to be a witty one, but not perfectly underftood ; it is the chorus of a fcandalizing tea-table, the condefcen-

---

* Number 29.

fion

fion of a great man, and the pride of a little one ; the refource of dulnefs, and the ornament of a good fet of teeth.

To difcover the origin of this, I have toiled through all the chronological books I could think of, but to no purpofe :— However, from the oral tradition of an old weather-wife gentleman, who is accuftomed to note remarkable occurrences, I learn that it came into this country with Lord Chefterfield, upon his return from his travels. It was at firft confined entirely to his Lordfhip's fuite ; it then diffufed itfelf, by degrees, through St. James's and its environs ; and laft of all became the common property of thofe who were diftinguifhed by the appellation of good company. Still, however, the practice of Tee-Heeing was far from general ; citizens were unacquainted with it, for my Lady Mayorefs had no routs ; and though it once rode to Rumford with a gentleman out of livery, and was there dropped, yet, as no one underftood it, no one thought proper to pick it up.—The happy improvement of our manners has now made that fcience
universal,

univerfal, which for a long time was partial : —Good company, refinement, and Tee-Heeing, are now as common and as cheap as hack-parfons, or Welfh mutton ; —we may dine with them at a fhilling ordinary on Sundays ; are over-run with them at a mafquerade ; elbowd to death by them in the little hell at Newmarket ; lofe our handkerchiefs to them in the lobby of the play-houfe; and get trampled under their feet at a bull-baiting in Moorfields.—About five weeks ago, I fell in with a Tee-Heeing Highwayman in Epping foreft. He was too accomplifhed and too well mounted for me to think of keeping fuch company long ; and we parted, after I had depofited with him five pennyworth of half-pence, a metal watch-chain, and an ode to the fpring, which, after fome trouble, I convinced him was as good as the Bank.

- After all that can be faid on this fubject, we may as well think of feparating wit from the firft of April, or goofe from Michaelmas-day, as that we can live at eafe without laughter, " the chorus of converfation," and the union of focial intercourfe.

The

The raptures of poetic imagination have extended this faculty to every part of the creation in a ſtrain of metaphorical alluſion, adopted by all poets, in all ages and countries ; in Milton we find,

> ――― all things *ſmil'd*
> With fragrance, and with joy my heart
>   o'erflow'd.

And in that higher ſpecies of poetry, it is ſaid of the vallies, they ſhall ſtand ſo thick with corn, that they ſhall *laugh* and fing.

It is not then the thing itſelf of which we can complain, but the abuſe and miſmanagement of it. He is no object of imitation or envy, who can moroſely withhold his laughter, when he may indulge it, without incurring the charge of folly ; nor is that man much to be eſteemed, who, with ignorance, affectation, arrogance, and illnature, uſurps the privilege of laughing upon all occaſions, without regard to ſituation, circumſtance, or decorum.

NUMBER.

[ 123 ]

NUMBER XII.

---

SATURDAY, *June* 2, 1787.

---

I MADE an entrance, in a former paper,
on the important fubjeȼt of *Vifiting*,
and diftinguifhed the different kinds of vifits now in vogue amongft us, with their
excellences and defeȼts.

It is hard, indeed, to guefs at the *plea-*
*fure* of affembling in very large parties.
There is much heat, hurry, and fatigue,
to all who are concerned. The effence of
the entertainment feems to confift in a
*crowd*, and none appear to be perfeȼtly
happy, while they can ftir hand or foot.
At leaft, this is the cafe with the lady of
the

the houfe, whofe fupreme felicity it is, to be kept *in equilibrio,* by an equilateral pref-fure from all quarters. Fixed in her orb, like the fun of the fyftem, fhe difpenfes the favour of her nods and fmiles on thofe bo-dies, which—I wifh I could fay—*move* around her ; but that they cannot do. .

But though pleafure be not obtained, trouble perhaps, it may be faid, is faved, by receiving a multitude at once, inftead of being fubject to their perpetual incurfions in feparate bodies; and when the polite mob has been at my houfe, I am at reft for fome time.—True ; but then there is a *reciprocity* ; and as others have affifted in making your mob a decent and refpectable one, you muft do the fame by them, and every evening will pafs in this *rondeau of delights* ; a vortex, out of which none can emerge, and into which more and more are continually drawn, for fear of being left in folitude ; as all who wifh to vifit will very foon be obliged to vifit after this method, or not at all. From the metro-polis the fafhion has made its way into provincial towns, all the vifitable inhabi-

tants

rants of which will be affembled together at one houfe or other, through the winter; and this, though perhaps there is not a fingle perfon among them, who does not diflike and complain of the cuftom, as abfurd and difagreeable.

For the conduct of *thefe* vifits no directions can be laid down; but concerning others (while any fuch fhall remain) where a moderate company of neighbours meet, to pafs a little time in converfation, fome obfervations may be offered.

They are ufeful, and indeed neceffary, to maintain a friendly and focal intercourfe, without which we are not in a capacity to give or receive help and affiftance from each other.

They are ufeful to cheer and refrefh the fpirits after bufinefs, and may render us fitter to return to it again.

They are ufeful, when they are made with a view of relieving and comforting fuch as are afflicted and diftreffed; and that, not only in great and fignal troubles, but the common cares and concerns of life; of advifing, exhorting, and confoling fuch

**as,**

as, having weak and low fpirits, are op-
preffed by anxiety and melancholy; of
which in England the number always has
been, and always will be, very confiderable. Time is well employed in thefe and
the like good offices, where a friend is the
beft phyfician. The very fight of a cheerful friend is often like the fun breaking
forth in a cloudy day. A melancholy
perfon is at leaft as much the object of charity as a fick one. The cheerful owe this
duty to thofe who are otherwife; and enjoy, themfelves, the moft refined and exalted kind of pleafure, when they find their
endeavours to fucceed.

Vifits are ufeful, when they become the
means of acquiring or communicating
ufeful knowledge, relative to the conduct
of life, in concerns either perfonal or do-
meftic; or, even when no fuch knowlege
is obtained, if by innocent mirth, pleafant
tales, &c. people are brought into good
humour, and kept in it. No recreation is
more truly ferviceable and effectual than
this: and it is faid of Archbifhop Williams,
that, " the greater the performance he was

I                                    " about

" about to undertake (whether a fpeech, a
" fermon, or a debate), the more liberty
" and recreation he firft took, to quicken
" and open his fpirits, and to clear his
" thoughts."

By vifiting, opportunities are offered of
introducing occafionally matters literary and
religious, new publications, &c. For
though, perhaps, this is not fo often done
as it might be, when people meet ; yet it
cannot be done at all, unlefs people do
meet.

To render vifits lively and agreeable,
where the company is fmall, and it can be
managed conveniently, the converfation
fhould be general. The ladies, by their
fprightlinefs, fhould animate the gentlemen ; and the gentlemen, by their learning, inform the ladies. Inftead of this,
the gentlemen too often lay their heads together, on one fide of the room, and talk
on fubjects of literature or politics ; leaving
the ladies to fettle the articles of caps and
gowns, blonds and gauzes, on the other ;
which is hardly fair, efpecially in thefe
days, when fo many of the other fex are
qualified

qualified to join in a conversation on more important topics.

The end of a visit is frustrated, if it be made too long ; as when the same company sit together from three in the afternoon till twelve at night, or nine hours ; for then, that which was designed for a recreation becomes itself a burden, unless there be some particular business or amusement in hand.

Live not in a perpetual round and hurry of visiting. You will neglect your affairs at home ; you will by degrees contract a dislike to home, and a dread of being alone ; than which nothing can be more wretched and pernicious. You will acquire a habit of being idle, of gossiping, dealing in slander, scandal, &c. and of inducing others to do the same.

In a small party, as also in a single family, the work-basket and a book agree well together. While the ladies work, let one person read distinctly and deliberately, making proper pauses for remarks and observations ; these will furnish conversation

for

for a while; when it begins to flag, let the reader go on, till frefh matter fupply frefh converfation. A winter - evening paffes pleafantly in this manner; and a general wifh will be expreffed, that it had been longer. The mind becomes ftored with knowledge, and the tongue accuftomed to fpeak upon profitable fubjects.

Rouffeau afferts, that every perfon in a company fhould have *fomething to do*. I fee not how this can well be contrived; but his reafon is curious, and deferves confideration. " In my opinion," fays he, " idle-" nefs is no lefs the peft of *fociety*, than of " folitude. Nothing contracts the mind, ".nothing engenders trifles, tales, back-"biting, flander, and falfities, fo much as " being fhut up in a room, oppofite each ".other, and reduced to no other occupa-" tion than the neceffity of continual *chat-" tering*. When all are employed, they " *fpeak* only when they have fomething to " *fay*; but if you are doing nothing, you " muft abfolutely talk inceffantly, which " of all conftraints is the moft trouble-
K                          " fome,

" fome, and the moſt dangerous. I dare
" go even farther, and maintain, that to
" render a circle truly agreeable, every one
" muſt be not only doing ſomething, but
" ſomething which requires a little atten-
" tion."

Should this plan of Rouſſeau be favourably received, and a notion be entertained
of carrying it into execution, the chief difficulty will be to provide proper employment for the *gentlemen*. My readers will
turn the matter in their minds. The only
caſe in point, which I can recollect of at
preſent, is that of a friend, who, when
young, amuſed himſelf with making par-
tridge-nets. On a viſit, he would take his
*work* out of the *bag*, hitch one end of the
net upon a ſconce, and proceed to buſineſs.
His example militates powerfully in favour
of the plan ; for his converſation, while
ſo employed, was remarkably free and eaſy.

Under the above regulations we can never
be the worſe, and, if we keep tolerable
company, ſhall generally be the better, for
a viſit. Something muſt occur, which is
worth

worth remembering, and noting down. A reflection at the end of a visit will soon shew, whether it comes properly under the denomination of those condemned by casuists, as *useless and impertinent*; since that is *useless*, which tends to no good purpose; and that is *impertinent*, which claims your time and attention, and gives nothing in return.                                        Z.

# NUMBER XIII.

---

### SATURDAY, *June* 9, 1787.

---

WHEN a friend told Johnfon that he was much blamed for having unveiled the weaknefs of Pope, " Sir," faid he, " if one man undertake to write the life " of another, he undertakes to exhibit his " true and real character: but this can be " done only by a faithful and accurate deli- " neation of the particulars, which difcri- " minate that character."

The

The biographers of this great man feem confcientioufly to have followed the rule thus laid down by him, and have very fairly communicated all they knew, whether to his advantage, or otherwife. Much concern, difquietude, and offence, have been occafioned by this their conduct in the minds of many, who apprehend, that the caufe in which he ftood forth will fuffer by the infirmities of the advocate being thus expofed to the prying and malignant eye of the world.

But did thefe perfons then ever fuppofe, or did they imagine that the world ever fuppofed, Dr. Johnfon to have been a perfect character? Alas, no: we all know how that matter ftands, if we ever look into our own hearts, and duly watch the current of our own thoughts, words, and actions. Johnfon was honeft, and kept a faithful diary of thefe, which is before the publick. Let any man do the fame for a fortnight, and publifh it: and if, after that, he fhould find himfelf fo difpofed, let him " caft a ftone." At that hour when the failings of all fhall be made manifeft,

the

the attention of each individual will be
confined to his own.

It is not merely the name of Johnson
that is to do fervice to any caufe. It is his
genius, his learning, his good fenfe, the
ftrength of his reafonings, and the happinefs of his illuftrations. Thefe all are
precifely what they were: once good, and
always good. His arguments in favour of
felf-denial do not lofe their force, *becaufe
he fafled*; nor thofe in favour of devotion,
*becaufe he faid his prayers.* Grant his *failings* were, if poffible, ftill greater than
thefe: Will a man refufe to be guided by
the found opinion of a counfel, or refift the
falutary prefcription of a phyfician, becaufe
they who give them are not without their
faults? A man may do fo; but he will
never be accounted a wife-man for doing it.

Johnfon, it is faid, was fuperftitious.
But who fhall exactly afcertain to us, what
fuperftition is? The Romanift is charged
with it by the Church-of-England man;
the Churchman by the Prefbyterian; the
Prefbyterian by the Independent; all by the
Deift; and the Deift by the Atheift. With
                                        fome

some it is superstition to pray ; with others,
to receive the sacrament; with others, to
believe in revelation; with others, to believe in God. In some minds it springs
from the most amiable disposition in the
world—" A pious awe, and fear to have
"offended," a wish rather to do too much,
than too little. Such a disposition one
loves and wishes always to find in a friend;
and it cannot be disagreeable in the fight of
him who made us. It argues a sensibility
of heart, a tenderness of conscience, and
the fear of God. Let him, who finds it
not in himself, beware left, in flying from
superstition, he fall into irreligion and
prophaneness.

That persons of eminent talents and attainments in literature have been often
complained of as — dogmatical, boisterous,
and inattentive to the rules of good breeding, is well known. But let us not expect every thing from every man. There
was no occasion that Johnson should teach
us to dance, to make bows, or turn compliments. He could teach us better things.
To' reject wisdom because the person of

him

him who communicates it is uncouth, and
his manners are inelegant—what is it, but
to throw away a pine-apple, and affign for
a reafon the roughnefs of its coat? Who
quarrels with a botanift, for not being an
aftronomer; or with a moralift, for not
being a mathematician? As it is faid in
concerns of a much higher nature, " every
" man hath his gift, one after this manner,
"and another after that." It is our bufinefs
to profit by all, and to learn of each that
in which each is beft qualified to inftruct
us.

That Johnfon was generous and charita-
ble, none can deny. But he was not always
judicious in the felection of his objects : diftrefs was a fufficient recommendation, and
he did not fcrutinize into the failings of the
diftreffed. May it be always my lot to
have fuch a benefactor! Some are fo nice
in a fcrutiny of this kind, that they can
never find any proper objects of their benevolence, and are neceffitated to fave their
money. It fhould doubtlefs be diftributed
in the beft manner we are able to diftribute
it ; but what would become of us all, if
he,

he, on whofe bounty all depend, fhould
be "extreme to mark that which is done
" amifs?"

It is hard to judge any man, without a
due confideration of all circumftances.
Here were ftupendous abilities, and fuitable
attainments, but then here were hereditary
diforders of body and mind reciprocally
aggravating each other; a fcrophulous
frame, and a melancholy temper; here
was a life, the greater part of which paffed
in making provifion for the day, under the
preffure of poverty and ficknefs, forrow
and anguifh. So far to gain the afcendant
over thefe, as to do what Johnfon did,
required very great ftrength of mind indeed.
Who can fay, that, in a like fituation, he
fhould long have poffeffed, or been able to
exert it?

From the mixture of power and weaknefs in the compofition of this wonderful
man, the fcholar fhould learn humility.
It was defigned to correct that pride which
great parts and great learning are apt to
produce in their poffeffor. In him it had
the defired effect. For though confciouf-

nefs

nefs of fuperiority might fometimes induce
him to carry it high with man (and even
this was much abated in the latter part of
life), his devotions have fhewn to the whole
world, how humbly he walked at all times
with his God. T

i. His example may likewife encourage
thofe of timid and gloomy difpofitions not
to defpond, when they reflect, that the
vigour of fuch an intellect could not preferve its poffeffor from the depredations of
melancholy. They will ceafe to be furprized and alarmed at the degree of their
own fufferings : they will refolve to bear,
with patience and refignation, the malady
to which they find a Johnfon fubject, as
well as themfelves : and if they want
words, in which to afk relief from him
who alone can give it, the God of mercy,
and father of all comfort, language affords
no finer than thofe in which his prayers
are conceived. Child of forrow, whoever
thou art, ufe them ; and be thankful, that
the man exifted, by whofe means thou haft
them to ufe.

His

His eminence and his fame muſt of courſe have excited envy and malice : but let envy and malice look at his infirmities and his charities, and they will quickly melt into pity and love.

That he ſhould not be conſcious of the abilities with which Providence had bleſſed him, was impoſſible. He felt his own powers; he felt what he was capable of having performed ; and he ſaw how little, comparatively ſpeaking, he had performed. Hence his apprehenſions on the near proſpect of the account to be made, viewed through the medium of conſtitutional and morbid melancholy, which often excluded from his ſight the bright beams of divine mercy. May thoſe beams ever ſhine upon us! But let them not cauſe us to forget, that talents have been beſtowed, of which an account muſt be rendered; and that the fate of the " unprofitable ſervant" may juſtly beget apprehenſions in the ſtouteſt mind. The indolent man, who is without ſuch apprehenſions, has never yet conſidered the ſubject as he ought. For one perſon

who

who fears death too much; there are a
thoufand who do not fear it enough, nor
have thought in earneft about it. Let us
only put in practice the duty of felf-exami-
nation ; let us enquire into the fuccefs we
have experienced in our war againft the
paffions, or even againft undue indulgence
of the common appetites, eating, drinking,
and fleeping : we fhall foon perceive how
much more eafy it is to form refolutions,
than to execute them ; and fhall no longer
find occafion, perhaps, to wonder at the
weaknefs of Johnfon.

On the whole—In the memoirs of him
that have been publifhed, there are fo many
witty fayings, and fo many wife ones, by
which the world, if it fo pleafe, may be
at once entertained and improved, that I
do not regret their publication. In this,
as in all other inftances, we are to adopt
the good, and rejeƈt the evil. The little
ftories of his oddities and his infirmities in
common life will, after a while, be over-
looked and forgotten ; but his writings
will live for ever, ftill more and more ftudied

died and admired, while Britons fhall continue to be characterized by a love of elegance and fublimity, of good fenfe and virtue. The fincerity of his repentance, the
ftedfaftnefs of his faith, and the fervour
of his charity, forbid us to doubt, that his
fun fet in clouds, to rife without them:
and of this let us always be mindful, that
every one who is made better by his books,
will add a wreath to his crown.        Z.

# NUMBER XIV.

## SATURDAY, *June* 16, 1787.

BETWEEN the Sloven and the Cox-comb there is generally a competition which shall be the more contemptible, the one in the total neglect of every thing which might make his appearance in public supportable ; and the other in the cultivation of every superfluous ornament. The former offends by his negligence and dirt, the latter by his airs and perfumery. Each entertains a proper contempt for the other ; and while both are right in their opinion, both are wrong in their practice. The

dress

dreſs of a man is almoſt invariably an indi-
cation of his habit of mind : I do not mean
to aſſert, that by a red coat you can poſi-
tively ſwear to his valour, or by a black
one to his integrity ; but from his general
manner of adorning his perſon, you may
diſcover the general train of his thinking.
He who has never been ſeen in diſhabille
but by his hair-dreſſer, or his valet de
chambre, I am inclined to ſuppoſe has never known the luxury of mental relaxation.
Not that his mind is occupied in abſtruſe
ſpeculations ; but, being ever ſolicitous for
the welfare and ornament of his perſon, he
cannot deſcend to take a ſhare, in thoſe
concerns of the world, which, if they
gained poſſeſſion of his mind, might diſ-
compoſe the features of his face. He has
no conſolation for the afflicted*, for care
produceth wrinkles ; he ſhuns laughter, leſt

* He is one of that uncomfortable ſpecies, ſo happily delineated in the learned preface to Bellendenus :

Ψυχραν εχει σαις καρδιαν θερμοις επι·
Ύδαρις τι πυξ και λιπλον αίμ· απ· τετραν)·
Νηφων τ' απιστιν τ' αχθρα τα βια λιγω,
Λοιπον, αγελασος, απροσηγορον τραξ·

he

he fhould fhake the powder from his curls;
he cannot fmoke left his coat fhould fmell
of tobacco; and he is prevented from the
moderate ufe of wine, for it would endan-
ger, if not ruin, his complexion.

Thefe well-dreffed advocates for virtue
avoid gluttony, not that they may practife,
abftinence, but left they fhould injure their
fhapes; they fly from drunkennefs, not
becaufe it is a vice, dangerous in itfelf, and
deftructive in its confequences, but that
they may preferve their faces from pimples.
Reafons of equal moment regulate all their
actions, concerns, and opinions. The man
of drefs is, perchance, a diffenter, becaufe
the path-way which leads to the meeting-
houfe is cleaner than that to the church;
or he is a churchman, becaufe his pew is
lined with green bays.

There is an equivocal fpecies of beings,
called *petites maitres*, who are owned by
neither fex, and fhunned by both. They
are a race not peculiar to * any nation, or
clime,

* They are evidently alluded to in the following
Epigram of Aufonius:

Dum dubitat natura marem faceretne puellam,
Factus es, oh pulcher, pœne puella puer.

Give

clime, or country. Ancient Rome had many of them; Modern Rome, has, I fufpect, more. They flourifh among our pacified friends in France; nor are we in England entirely without them. We may foon, perhaps, hear of their exiftence among our colonifts at Botany-bay; that they have fprung up in the fafhionable part of Lapland, or are gaining ground with the paper money in North America.

To this part of the creation is almoft entirely confined that violent extravagance of drefs which fixes a man's head between twocapes or promontories, like an attorney in the pillory, and cuts away the fkirts of his coat, as if he had narrowly efcaped from a fire. Among thefe whimfical innovators in drefs, I have found all my conclufions refpecting the ftate of their minds, built upon unfound foundations: The fame fpirit of innovation, which was continually varying the pofition of the

Give me, ye Gods, the Hufband cries, an Heir,
The teeming Wife demands a Daughter fair;
The Gods too kind, nor that deny, nor this,
Forth comes an Heir, half Mifter and half Mifs.

sleeve-button, or the pattern of the stock-
ing, might, I thought, render them un-
quiet members of the community, and dangerous to the state. But I am happily miftaken. They are harmless citizens; and
those minds which in my patriotic zeal I
was too fearful might be plotting against
my country, I have, upon a closer examination, discovered to be a perfect blank.

Somewhat of a man's mind may, perhaps, be discovered by his promptitude or
backwardness to comply with what is term-
ed the Fashion of Dress. He who can be
content to follow fashion, with all her mutability, through all her revolutions, must
have imbibed some of that fickleness which
such a pursuit inspires. The same uncertainty which makes him fluctuate between
Mr. Rag the taylor, and Mr. Blossom the
habit-maker, will mark his conduct in the
more serious concerns of life.

He on the contrary, who is ridiculously
precise in dress, nothing varying according
to the fashion of the times, will be generally found overbearingly dogmatical in opinion. The same bigotry which condemns

L                                       him

him to one pair of buckles, will chain him down likewife to one fet of opinions. He would contend for the propriety of his dialect, though he were educated within a mile of the Lake of Windermere; he would defend his tafte, though he brought it from the ifle of Sky; and he would dogmatife in religion, though he had his unftable principles from Birmingham.

It is a common cuftom from the drefs and appearance of a man to guefs at his trade or profeffion. The decency of the round curl, the gravity of the black coat, and the emblematic orthodoxy of everlafting waiftcoat and breeches, are fufficient to mark a man for a Defender of the faith. The laying out of the " gravel-walk and grafs-plat" in a citizen's green and gold waiftcoat, will evince to an accurate obferver the ftreet in which he lives, and whether his warehoufe contains the goods of an eminent Shoemaker, the right pigtail of a Tobacconift, or the ventures of a Turkey Merchant. When we fee thofe unaccountable combinations of ill mixing colours, which are fometimes difplayed in the

coat,

coat, waiſtcoat, and breeches, we cannot help ſuſpecting, that the wearer of them is by profeſſion a Fidler, not much in repute, or by trade a Taylor, with no other uſe for his patterns than to make " a motley ſuit" for himſelf.

It requires no great penetration to diſcover, that the ſhort man with the anchor on his button, who contends for the liberty of the preſs, is the midſhipman of a man of War; or that the fat Laughter-loving dame, all pink ribbons and ſmiles, makes ſauſages in Fetter-lane, or diſpenſes cakes and ale at the bar of the Croſs Marrowbones, near Mile-end Turnpike.

What, after all, it may be aſked, is the ſtandard of propriety in dreſs ?—There is, perhaps, none. His own judgment and underſtanding muſt be the guide of every one. And it may not be uſeleſs to remember, that from the outward appearance people form opinions of the inward man; that he will excite indignation, whoſe whole mind is viſibly laid out upon his dreſs, as certainly as the profeſſed drunkard will diſguſt, whoſe face is like the

south

fouth afpect of a garden-wall, hung with ripe fruit. He who, perhaps, owes the poverty of his underftanding to his own neglect, will in vain endeavour to repair his confequence and dignity by the affiftance of the Graces and the Taylors; all they can do for him is, to render his folly more apparent, and himfelf more ridiculous.

Moderation is, perhaps, no where a more pofitive virtue than in drefs, to which no man of fenfe will devote the whole of his time, and no reafonable man will refufe fome portion of it.

## NUMBER XV.

### SATURDAY, *June* 23, 1787.

—— *Nimis alta fapit,*
*Bellua multorum capitum.*

IN a Society, inftituted for the purpofe of amicable difputation, to which I once found means to obtain admittance, the following queftion was propofed for difcuffion :—Which circumftance would be more irkfome to a gentleman of delicate feelings, the reflection that he had killed another in a duel, or had been himfelf pulled by the nofe from Penzance in Cornwall, to our Town of Berwick upon Tweed, by way of London :

London :—That his audience might have as clear a comprehenſion as poſſible of the ſubjeĉt to be diſcuſſed, the leader of the debate thought it neceſſary to ſpecify to them the diſtance between the two places mentioned, in which his accuracy was queſtioned by a gentleman with his hand-kerchief under his wig : The conteſt was carried on with violence and acrimony, but was at length ſomewhat appeaſed by means of a third perſon, who, upon bringing the parties to explain, diſcovered that they had made their calculations upon different prin-ciples, the one having conſulted Paterſon's book of roads, the other Ogilby's.

It was on all ſides ſagaciouſly concluded upon, that one muſt be wrong ; but it was impoſſible to aſcertain which, without ex-amining the comparative excellences of Meſſrs. Paterſon and Ogilby, each of whom was extolled by either party as a literary Coloſſus. This gave the debate another in-tereſting turn ; and as I found the heat of the room and the conteſt likely to endan-ger my welfare, and produce ſomething more than a war of words, I made as pre-

cipitate

cipitate a retreat as the nature of the cafe would admit; but before I could gain the door, I found the amicable difputants had laid afidé their rhetoric and their coats, and exchanged the fanciful and ideal fhafts of wit for the material weapons of pewter pots and oaken fticks. Never was that happy comparifon of the Grammarians more thoroughly illuftrated, by which they liken logic to the clenched fift! My efcape from thefe Logicians was a fource of comfortable contemplation, yet I could not lay afide all my fears for the fafety of thofe I had left behind; however, I had the fatisfaction to find, the next morning, that no material injury had been fuftained. Upon turning into a fhop, I bought a pair of gloves of the Paterfonian; and foon after difcovered the follower of Ogilby mending the club-room windows.

Thefe and a few other circumftances, which I need not, perhaps, enumerate, have induced me to offer to my patient readers a few obfervations on that great love of refinement and *fentimentality* which is daily gaining ground among the lower orders of

our

our fellow-countrymen, of which nothing can I believe radically cure them but a Dutch war. The grand caufes of this mif-chief, I am inclined to fuppofe, are the above-mentioned pewter-pot fpouting clubs, and thofe rhapfodies of nonfenfe which are fo liberally poured upon the publick, under the title of Sentimental Novels, utterly fubverfive of common fenfe, and not very warm friends to common honefty; There is a fafcinating power in nonfenfe, which may fometimes afford relaxation, if not amufement, to a man of fenfe; but which always meets with fomething congenial to itfelf in meaner capacities. For fuch capacities fuch compofitions are well adapted; and for thefe the furrow is left unfinifhed, and "the hammers mifs their "wonted ftroke."

Some of my readers may, perhaps, be not only readers of novels, but writers of them. Though I do not confider myfelf as qualified in any particular to dictate to fo refpectable a part of the community, yet I cannot forbear offering a few, perhaps erroneous, remarks upon them and their productions.  While

While the writers of novels have fo many admirable models, upon which their ftyle might be formed, it is not without regret that we turn over the infipid pages which are thruft into our fight in every bookfeller's fhop. They feem to have forgotten that there are writers better than themfelves; that if we wifh for delicate and refined fentiment, we can recur to Grandifon and Clariffa; if we would fee the world more perhaps as it is, than as it fhould be, we have Jofeph Andrews and Tom Jones; or that we can find the happy mixture of fatire and moral tendency in the Spiritual Quixote and Cecilia.

I cannot help noticing the glaring impropriety they are guilty of, who make their nobility and their peafants fpeak the fame language: They defend themfelves, no doubt, by the authority and example of Virgil's Shepherds, Sanazarius's Fifhermen, and the ruftics of Mr. Pope. But when they are told, that to copy the deformities of good writers will be no embellifhment to bad ones, they may perhaps ceafe to overwhelm us with the fentimentality of

their

their Abigails, the heroic gallantry of their Footmen, and the rhetorical flourishes of their Shoemakers. Thefe are more particularly the characters which do a material injury to that part of the nation, who, when they have fhut up fhop, wet their thumbs and fpell through a novel. A love-fick Chambermaid is enough to ruin half the fifterhood; an intrigueing Apprentice is the torment of Mafter Tradefmen; and the high-flown notions of honour, which are inculcated by " Johnny with his fhoulder-knot," will fet a couple of taylors a duelling. If the rapid courfe of thefe grievances be not checked, we fhall have the Epicure juftly complaining, that he can get no lamb to eat with his afparagus, from the fenfibility of the Leadenhall-butchers; or that the melting tendernefs of the Cooks prevents the eels from being fkinned, or the lobfters boiled alive. Should delicacy of thinking become too common, we may drive the lawyers from their quibbles, and how, then are we to get thofe little odd jobbs done for ourfelves, and our eftates, fo convenient for our families, and fo beneficial

to

to our landed interefts? Suppofe, moreover, the Jews (I do not mean particularly
thofe to whom Dr. Prieftley's invitation is
directed, but) the money-lenders and the
proprietors of the crucible, fhould be in-
fected with this growing fenfe of honour;
the gaming-table muft be deferted; there
would be no market for ftolen watches; and
the triumph of fentiment would be the
downfall of the nation.

There is much perhaps to be complained
of in other publications which tend to dif-
feminate the glare and tinfel of falfe fentiment; I mean the works of thofe imita-
tors of Sterne, whofe pages are polluted
with ribbaldry and dafhes; and thofe
compilers of modern tragedies at which no
man weeps, unlefs in pure friendfhip for
the author.

If I in the playhoufe faw a huge black-
fmith-like looking fellow blubbering over
the precious foolery of Nina, I fhould immediately take it for granted he came in
with an order, and look upon his iron tears
as a *forgery*. Indeed, might I be allowed
to dictate upon fuch an occafion, no man
fhould

fhould be permitted to moiften a white handkerchief at the *obs* and the *abs* of a modern tragedy, unlefs he poffeffed an eftate of feven hundred a year, clear of mortgage, and every other incumbrance. Such people have a right to fling away their time as they pleafe ; the works of the loom receive no impediment from their idlenefs, and it is at leaft an innocent though infipid amufement.

While I feem endeavouring to harden the hearts of my country againft thofe attacks which are made upon them from the ftage, I am far from wifhing to rob them of that pompt benevolence which is a leading feature in our national charaƐter. But I am afraid of refinement even in our virtues. I am afraid left the fame eye which is fo prone to give its tributary tear to the well-told hiftory of fancied woe, fhould be able to look upon real mifery without emotion, becaufe its tale is told without plot, incident, or ornament. I would only therefore remind thofe fair ladies, and well-dreffed gentlemen who frequent our theatres becaufe they have nothing elfe to do, or

that

that they may enjoy the luxury of ſhedding tears with Mrs. Siddons, that if they will look round among their fellow creatures they will find their time rather too ſhort, than too long, for the exerciſe of their compaſſion in alleviating the diſtreſſes of their neighbours: and they may, by theſe means, be ſupplied with luxuries, which will never reproach them with time ſquandered away, or miſ-ſpent in idleneſs or vice.

NUMBER

## N U M B E R  XVI.

SATURDAY, *June* 30, 1787.

*Gaudetque viam feciffe ruinâ.*  LUCAN.

WITH a View, no doubt, of more deeply interefting our attention, it feems the practice of modern Tragedy Writers to aim at exciting terror by a general yet indifcriminate recourfe to the bowl and the dagger; whilft, after exhaufting the whole armory of the Property Room, the fifth act is frequently accelerated from the mere want of furviving perfonages to fupport the Play. The modern Hero of the

Drama

Drama feems as it were profeffionally to
confider killing as no murder; the rout of
armies, the capture of thoufands, and the
downfall of empires, forms the naufeous
yet perpetual chit-chat of the narrative.
However grofs may be the deficiencies of
plot, character, ftyle, and language, incident pregnant with devaftation and blood-
fhed is deemed a receipt in full for every
excellence; and in proportion as the ordinary ftandard of human actions is exceed-
ed, the nearer in the opinion of the author
the piece approaches to perfection. Such a
conduct, however, betrays the greateft poverty of expedient, and not infrequently
defeats its own end, by exciting difguft inftead of approbation. Nature deals in no
fuch hyperboles; to the credit of herfelf,
and the comfort of her creation, fhe as rarely fhews in the moral world, a Nero, a
Borgia, a Cromwell, or a Catiline; as fhe
does in the natural, a Comet, or an Hurricane, an Earthquake, or an Inundation.
Whoever has curforily turned over the
Dramatic Works of Lee and Dryden, will
acknowledge the juftnefs of this charge.

With

2

With uniform and unexampled characters either of vice or virtue in the extreme,
the aggregate of mankind are little affected;
as they cannot come under their obfervation
in real Life, they have few claims to their
notice, and none to their belief, in fictitious
reprefentations. Mixed characters alone
come home to the minds of the multitude.
The angelic qualities of a Grandifon, or an
Harlowe, are reflected but by the hearts of
a few folitary individuals, whilft thofe of
Jones finds a never failing mirrour in the
greater part of mankind. At all events, if
it is impoffible to avoid verging to one extreme or the other, the fide of Virtue, it is
hoped, is the moft probable, and therefore
the moft proper of the two; and wherever
we are tempted by a ftory, peculiarly adapted to the tragic Mufe (carrying with it, at
the fame time, a fufficiency of the terrible),
it is the bufinefs of the Poet, to be moft
cautious in the felection, and to deal out
death and deftruction as reluctantly and as
feldom as the nature of the incidents will
admit; for I cannot help concurring with
Jonathan Wild in opinion, that mifchief is

M                    much

much too precious a commodity to be
fquandered.

The judicioufly blending the lights and
fhades of a character, fo as to make the one
neceffarily refult from, and fall into, the
other, conftitutes one of the moft difficult
branches of the Art; and in the works of
common writers it is in vain we look for
an effect of the kind. To delineate with
exactnefs the temporary lapfe of the Good
from Virtue to Vice, or thofe peculiar fituations in which the wicked man faulters in
his career, and blufhes to find himfelf
"ftaggering upon Virtue," demands the
hand of a Mafter. A character of uninterrupted deteftation can fcarcely exift;
and when it is obtruded upon us, we have
a right to queftion the abilities of him who
drew it. The Satan of Milton, though
with a heart diftended with pride, and re-
joicing in difobedience, when marfhalling
his troops (all of whom had forfeited Heaven in his caufe) for the exprefs purpofe
of confronting the Almighty, betrays emotions almoft incompatible with his nature.
They are fingularly affecting :——

—— cruel

—— cruel his eye, but caſt
Signs of remorſe, and paſſion to behold
The fellows of his crime, the followers rather,
(Far other once beheld in blifs) condemn'd
For ever now to have their lot in pain ;
Millions of ſpirits for his fault amerc'd
Of Heav'n, and from eternal ſplendours flung
For his revolt ——

Mark the effect :

—— he now prepar'd
To ſpeak ———
Thrice he aſſay'd, and thrice, in ſpite of ſcorn,
Tears, ſuch as Angels weep, burſt forth —

1ſt Book, 604, &c.

Nor has Virgil ſuffered the unnatural
and abandoned Mezentius, equally the Con-
temner of the Gods, and the Enemy of
man, to leave us without exciting ſome
pity, however undeſerved. The grief with
which he hears the death of his amiable
ſon Lauſus announced, and the eagerneſs
with which he inſtantly haſtens to revenge
it, the magnanimity he diſcovers in his
laſt words, in reply to the taunts of Æneas,
afford a fine relief to that horror and deteſtation which the former part of his charac-

ter

ter had previously excited : The whole is a
mafter-piece in its kind *.

In the Medea of Euripides, one of the
firft Performances Antiquity has left us, it
is the aim of the Poet throughout to make
Medea an objeƈt of commiferation ; and to
this end, he has made a tender and unre-
mitted folicitude for the fate of her children·
the leading feature of her charaƈter : and
on comparing the provocation on the one
fide with the revenge on the other, we
fhall find them by no means difpropor-
tioned. High-born, impatient, and ardent
in her attachment, with a fenfibility trem-
blingly-alive to feel her wrongs, and a fpirit, to the utmoft, to revenge them, fhe is
ftill a tender mother, though no longer a
fond wife, and in every refpeƈt perfeƈtly
human. For Jafon, fhe had forfaken and
betrayed her father and her country, killed
her brother Abfyrtus. Through his means
fhe had been infulted by Creon, and banifhed his kingdom ;—Creon, the very
man whofe daughter Creufa had ufurped

* See from line 833 to the conclufion of the 10th
Æneid.

her

her bed, and alienated the affections of her hufband. Yet every writer, who has employed himfelf on this fubject fince the Greek bard, feems widely to have miftaken, or wilfully to have departed, from what fhould have been their model. Seneca, with fome few flight exceptions, has divefted her of every claim to pity ; Corneille has done the fame ; and Glover, a Poet of our own, has left the blunder as he found it.—Whoever is defirous of being made acquainted with fome of the moft poignant ftruggles between the defire of revenge, and maternal affection, is more particularly referred to this Play *.

It may not be amifs to conclude thefe remarks with a few extracts from a moft excellent modern performance, where the Author has committed an errour (of which he was probably fenfible at the time), in order to avoid exceeding, what he feems to have confidered, the regular boundaries of Human depravity.

In the laft Scene of the Revenge, where the dreadful unravelment of the Plot takes place through the immediate agency of

* See Medea, 1021, 1069, 1244, &c. &c.

M 3　　Zanga

Zanga himſelf, the following circumſtances
are thus forcibly unfolded :

> Thy wife is guiltleſs, that's one tranſport to
>   me ;
> And *I*, *I* let thee know it, that's another :
> *I* urg'd Don Carlos to reſign his miſtreſs,
> *I* forg'd the letter, *I* diſpos'd the picture ;
> *I* hated, *I* deſpis'd, and *I* deſtroy.

By theſe aggravations of malevolence,
the deteſtation of the Audience is worked
up to the higheſt poſſible pitch ; in the
ſubſequent part of the ſcene, Alonzo is
racked with a ſtill farther diſcovery of the
reaſons that incited Zanga to Revenge from
Zanga himſelf ; in an agony of deſpair, he
ſtabs himſelf, and dies ; and the Poet concludes the Piece with endeavouring to draw
a ſhade over the character of the Moor before
he leaves him to the mercy of the ſpectator ;
and by one ſpeech aims at an atonement for
him in oppoſition to the deteſtation and diſguſt he had previouſly ſo ſucceſsfully excited. Zanga approaches the body, and thus
ſpeaks :

> Is this Alonzo ? where's his haughty mien ?
> Is that the hand which ſmote me ?   Heavens !
>   how pale !                                    And

And art thou dead? So is my enmity,
I war not with the duft: the great, the proud,
The Conqueror of Afric was my foe.
A Lion preys not upon carcafes.
This was the only method to fubdue me;
Terror and doubt fall on me; all thy good
Now blazes; all thy guilt is in the grave.
Never had man fuch funeral applaufe;
If I lament thee, fure thy worth was great.
O *Vengeance! I have follow'd thee too far* ;
And to receive me Hell blows all her fires —

Zanga might here with propriety retort upon Young the very words which were put into his mouth in addreffing Alonzo: " Chriftian, thou miftak'ft my character."

For thefe fymptoms of repentance and regret which he here difcovers in acknowledging his having gone too great lengths in his purfuit of Revenge, and that he had followed Vengeance too far, are totally out of place, and unnatural; they are againft the tenets of that religion which he is fuppofed to profefs, and the practice and example of his country, which confider a contrary conduct as eminently meritorious.

The

The plain rule of Horace fhould certainly,
to have compleated the Piece, have been
here ftrictly adhered to ;

—— *Servetur ad imum*
*Qualis ab incepto procefferit, aut fibi conftet.*

C.

NUMBER

NUMBER XVII.

SATURDAY, *July* 7, 1787.

*Eſt natura hominum novitatis avida.*

THAT with reſpeᴄt of news, as well
as of liquors, Man is a thirſty foul;
we are taught, in the words of my motto,
at the very firſt entrance on our elemen-
tary ſtudies. Curioſity is the appetite of
the mind. It muſt be ſatisfied, or we
periſh.

Among the improvements, therefore, of
modern times, there is none on which I
find more reaſon to congratulate my countrymen, than the increaſe of knowledge by
the multiplication of newſpapers.

With

With what a mixture of horror and commiſeration do we now look back to that period in our hiſtory, when, as it is ſaid, a written letter came down once a week to the coffee-houſe, where a proper perſon, with a clear and ſtrong voice, was pitched upon to read it aloud to the company aſſembled upon the occaſion! How earneſtly did they liſten! How greedily did they ſuck down every drop of intelligence that fell within their reach! Happy the man who carried off but half a ſentence! It was his employment, for the reſt of the evening, to imagine what the other half might have been. In days like theſe there was indeed (if we may uſe the expreſſion) "a famine in the land;" and one wonders how people contrived to keep body and ſoul together.

The proviſion at preſent made for us is ample. There are morning papers for breakfaſt; there are evening papers for ſupper;—I beg pardon—I mean dinner; and leſt, during the interval, wind ſhould get into the ſtomach, there is, I believe—I know there *was*—a paper publiſhed by way

of

of luncheon, about noon. That fanaticifm may not overwhelm us, and that profane learning may be duly mingled with facred, there is alfo a Sunday gazette; which removes one objection formerly urged, and furely not without reafon, againft the obfervation of the day.

Some have complained, that to read all the newfpapers, and compare them accurately together, as it is neceffary to do, before a right judgement can be formed of the ftate of things in general, is grown to be a very laborious tafk, which whoever performs properly can do nothing elfe. And why fhould he? Perhaps, he has nothing elfe to do; perhaps, if he had, he would not do it; or, perhaps, if he had not this to do, he would be in mifchief. The complaint fprings from a very criminal indolence, the child of peace and wealth. No man knows what may be done, within the compafs of a day, till he tries. Fortune favours the brave. Let him buckle to the work, and defpair of nothing. The more difficulty, the more honour. The Athenians, we are told, fpent their time only

only " in hearing or telling fome new thing." Would he wifh to fpend his time better than the Athenians did ?

It has been thought, that tradefmen and artificers may fpend too much of their time in this employment, to the neglect of their own refpective occupations. But this can be thought only by fuch as have not confidered, that to an Englifhman his country is every thing. Self is fwallowed up, as it ought to be, in patriotifm: or, to borrow ecclefiaftical language, the conftitution is his diocefe; his own bufinefs can only be regarded in the light of a *commendam*, on which if he caft an eye now and then, as he happens to pafs that way, it is abundantly fufficient.

The fpirit of defamation, by which a newfpaper is often poffeffed, has now found its own remedy in the diverfity of them; for though a gentleman may read, that he himfelf is a fcoundrel, and his wife no better than fhe fhould be to-day, he will be fure to read, that both of them are very good fort of people to-morrow. In the fame manner, if one paper, through miftake,

miftake, or defign, kill his friend, there is another ready to fetch him to life ; nay, if he have good luck in the order of his reading, he may be informed that his friend is alive again, before he had perufed the account of his death.

The expence of advertifing in fo many different newfpapers may, perhaps, be deemed a hardfhip upon authors. But then they have, in return, the comfort of refledting, what benefadtors they are to the revenue. 'Befides, how eafy is it for them to balance the account, by printing with a large type, due fpace between the lines, and a broad margin ? Great advantage may be obtained by throwing their compofitions into the form of letters, which may be as fhort as they pleafe ; and a reader of delicacy thinks, the fhorter, the better. A letter of fix lines is a very decent letter. It may begin at the bottom of one page, and end at the top of the next, fo that eight parts in ten of what the reader purchafes confift of blank paper : his eye is agreeably relieved ; and if the paper be good

for

for any thing, he has, upon the whole, no bad bargan.

That the vehicles of intelligence, numerous as they are, yet are not too numerous, appears, becaufe there is news for them all, there are purchafers for all, and advertife-ments for all : thefe laft not only afford aid to government, and are pretty reading, but fometimes have an influence upon the important affairs of the world, which is not known, or even fufpected.

No event of latter times has more aftonifhed mankind, than the fudden downfall of the Jefuits; and various caufes have been affigned for it. I am happy, that it is in my power, by means of a correfpondent at Rome, who was in the fecret, to furnifh my readers with the true one—an anecdote, which, I believe, has never before tranfpired.

It was owing, then, to an advertifement in an Englifh newfpaper, which paffed over to the continent, and, by fome means or other, found its way to the Vatican. I remember perfectly well to have read the advertifement at the time, and to have noted it down in my adverfaria, as I am

wont

wont to do, when any thing ſtrikes me in a particular manner. It ran thus : —

" John Haynes, of St. Clements, Ox-
" ford, begs leave to inform the public,
" that he alone poſſeſſes the true art of
" *making leather breeches fit eaſy.*"

As the newſpaper containing the adver-
tiſement came from Oxford, his Holineſs
and their Eminences immediately ſaw, that
in theſe laſt words was conveyed a keen
though covert ſatire upon the *looſe caſuiſtry*
of the ſons of Loyola. A conſiſtory was
called, and Ganganelli formed his reſolution. What followed, all the world knows.

I thought it but juſtice to my worthy
friend Haynes, to mention thus much : and
as, by the introduction of fuſtian, his trade
has long been upon the decline, I would
hope that every good proteſtant will forth-
with beſpeak a pair of leather breeches
(and pay for them when brought home) of
a man who has given ſuch a blow to Pope-
ry, and had the addreſs to effect what the
*Provincial Letters* attempted in vain.

From this inſtant it is evident, that we
ought to read all newſpapers, country as
well

well as town, on which we can lay our
hands ; for we know not what we may
have loft, by miffing any one of them.
This enlarges the fphere of our refearches,
and the imagination riots in the delicious
profpect. The journals printed at the two
univerfities muft always have an efpecial
claim to our attention.

I was feized, a few years ago, at a confiderable diftance from our Alma Mater,
with a violent fever. James's powder
ceafed to be of fervice ; the phyfician of
the place, who had been called in, fhook
his head ; and I began to think I fhould
never more behold St. Mary's fpire, and
Radcliffe's libary. I was almoft fpeechlefs,
but endeavoured, from time to time, as well
as I could, to articulate the word JACKSON.
My attendants concluded me delirious, and
heeded not what I faid : till a lad, who
travelled as my fervant, coming acciden-
tally into the room, exclaimed eagerly, that
he would be hanged if his mafter did not
mean the Oxford newfpaper. It was fetched
by exprefs, and I made figns, that it fhould
be read. The effect was a kindly perfpira-
tion,

tion, followed by a gentle fleep, from which I awoke, with my fever abated, and felt myfelf greatly refrefhed indeed. I continued mending. On the Saturday following, " the julep, as before," was re-peated; and on Monday I arofe, and pur-fued my journey.

There is one argument in favour of a multiplicity of newfpapers, which I do not remember to have met with; namely, that no man is ever fatisfied with another man's reading a newfpaper to him; but the mo-ment it is laid down, he takes it up, and reads it over again. It is abfolutely necef-fary, therefore, that each fhould have a newfpaper to himfelf, and fo change round, till every paper fhall have been read by every perfon.

A queftion has fometimes been debated concerning the beft time for reading newf-papers. But furely the proper anfwer to it is, Read them the moment you can get them. For my own part, I always dry my paper upon my knees, and make fhift to pick out a few articles during the ope-ration. It has been fancied, that by read-

N                                    ing

ing of this kind in a morning (the feafon marked out for it, fince Mr. Palmer's regulation of the poft), the head of a young academic becomes fo filled with an heterogeneous mixture of trafh, that he is fit for nothing.   But—*bona verba*,—Fair and foftly, my good friend. Why fhould we not take up the matter at the other end, and fay rather, his mind is fo expanded by a rich variety of new ideas, that he is fit for—any thing?

I fhall conclude this fpeculation with obferving, that we have juft caufe to be thankful for the number of newfpapers difperfed among us; fince, in a little time, nothing elfe will be read; it being nearly agreed by all perfons of the ton, that is, by all men of fenfe and tafte, that religion is a *hum*, virtue a *twaddle*, and learning a *bore*.                                   Z.

---

SATURDAY, *July* 16, 1787.

---

*Tempus edax rerum veteres cecinere Poëtæ,*
*At noſtrum tempus quis negat eſſe bibax?*

ANONYM.

Of *Eating* time, old Poets rhyme,
But ours is ſurely *Drinking* time.

AGAINST Drunkenneſs there are, perhaps, no arguments ſo ſtrong as thoſe which may be collected from the ſongs of Bacchanals. We are diſſuaded from it by the moraliſt, who repreſents it as the faſcination of a Siren, which wins us over to vice, by ſubduing our reaſon;

N 2                          and

and we are invited to it by the fong of the
Bacchanal, as fomething which will footh
our cares, infpire us with joys vehement,
if not permanent ; and banifh from our
minds the evils and the troubles of life.
The former feems to think, that this vice
has fo many allurements, as to require his
cautions againft our being feduced by it ;
and the latter, that it has fo few, as to
ftand in need of his recommendation of it.

*Fœcundi calices quem non fecere difertum ?*
*Contraŏlâ quem non in paupertate folutum ?*
HORACE.

Wine can to poverty content difpenfe,
Or tip the ftammering tongue with eloquence.

In reafoning, thefe words will go no
farther than to prove, that he who is
poor may, by drinking, become in imagination rich ; or that he who ftammers may,
by the fame expedient, find the temporary
ufe of his tongue. The man who is not
poor then will recollect, that he ftands in
no need of fuch a receipt ; and he who
does not ftammer will think that remedy
unneceffary which was intended to cure a
difeafe by which he is not afflicted. I can,

4
more-

moreover, inform them, upon pretty good·
authority, that this medicine has made
many a rich man poor, and deprived many
an orator of his fpeech.

Drunkennefs is further recommended to
us as the infpirer of courage,—*In prælio
trudit inermem,*—it thrufts the unarmed
man to battle.—That it has this effect is, I
believe, very true, and fo much the worfe
for the unarmed man.  The teftimony of
a black eye, or a bloody nofe, the frequent
offsprings of a drunken frolic, are ftriking
proofs, that to go unarmed to battle is no
great mark of wifdom or defirable courage.

There are many perfons in the world
who meafure a man's qualities by his capacity to hold wine ; the religion of thefe
good people is a bottle of port, their wit a
thump on the back, and their jokes upon
the whole no laughing matter.  They are,
however, fo honeft, and fo difagreeable,
that a reafonable man will do any thing to
ferve them, and any thing to avoid their
company.  I may, perhaps, incur the charge
of being envious, when I declare, that I
have very little fatisfaction in the prefence

N 3                                  of

of him whofe only boaft is, that he is a
better man than myfelf by two bottles.
Wine, however, infpires confidence, wit,
and eloquence ; that is, it changes modefty
to impudence, ingrafts the art of joking
upon dulnefs, and makes a ftory-teller of a
fool. While thefe qualifications are worth
attaining, I would have fobriety confidered
as a vulgarity, if not ftigmatized as a
vice ; but when that ceafes to be the cafe,
I hope the liberal fpirit of tolerating principles, which is fo much the fafhion of the
age, will allow a moderate man, without
infamy, to fay, "I would rather not get
very drunk to-day." Indeed, I have reafon
to believe this might be brought to pafs,
having feen a gentleman, with great politenefs, excufed from taking his wine, upon
his producing a teftimony from his phyfician, that he then laboured under a vio-
lent-fever ; or a certificate from church-
wardens of the parifh, properly authenti-
cated, to teftify that his aunt was dead.

I have often fuppofed, that there muft
be fome difgrace or impropriety in habitual
drunkennefs, from the many excufes which
are

are framed by perfons who indulge themfelves in it. I know a fond couple (fond I
mean of liquor) who are continually, " from
" eve to morn, from morn to dewy eve,"
deluging their thirfty fouls in gin and
water.—Mr. Morgan excufes himfelf becaufe he has loft money in the alley; and
poor Mrs. Morgan complains of a perpetual
coldnefs at her ftomach. Some people find
an excufe for drinking in the lofs of their
wives, in which they are happily aided by
the proverb, that " Sorrow is dry." Others
drink to diffipate the cares and folicitudes
of matrimony ; and others, becaufe they
cannot be admitted to a portion of fuch-
cares and folicitudes. Sufficient argument
therefore may be found, to make a notable
and legitimate drunkard of the bachelor,
the married man, or the widower. It is
difficult to afcertain amongft what clafs of
people this accomplifhment is in the higheft repute. A firft minifter muft have
hours of relaxation, and a firft minifter's
footman thofe of entertainment : To ac-
complifh which, the former has a right if
he pleafes to get " drunk as a piper," and

N 4                                    the

the latter, by the fame rule, " drunk as a lord."

From the proverbial phrafe, which I have had occafion to quote, " drunk as a piper," and other circumftances, I am led to conjecture, that the fcience of drinking has been cultivated with particular fuccefs among muficians,

> *Quels* liquidam *pater.*
> *Vocem cum cithará dedit.*

To whom Apollo has given,

> *To wet their whiftle, and handle the lyre.*

The great man, whofe mufical talents are annually noifed in Weftminfter Abbey, was no lefs the votary of Bacchus than of Apollo; and from a late newfpaper we learn, that Mr. Abel, the celebrated performer, amidft the joys of wine, either being little fkilled in our language, or having drunk until he was unable to fpeak any, caught up his *viol de Gamba*, and with great execution and good humour obliged the company with the ftory of Le Fevre. Such a ftory fo told to a man of quick apprehenfion, a good ear, and tolerably drunk, muft,

no

no doubt, have proved a recreation interefting and entertaining. Yet I cannot but
rejoice, that there are many people in the
world who ftill continue to ufe the old way
of telling ftories by word of mouth, and
who can join in a converfation without
thinking it neceffary to have recourfe to
*F fharp.*

I am, however, no judge of thefe matters, and think it right to confefs that I am
no mufician ; and that the enthufiaftic raptures of a drunken fidler convey to my
mind no ideas of the true fublime.

Thofe great geniufes who are not
thoroughly fatisfied with being vicious, unlefs they can find precedents for their vice,
may drink on under the fanction and authority of Alcæus, Ariftophanes, and En-
nius. Dulnefs may ftill plead a right to
this indulgence, becaufe the unfteady principles of heathen morality did not ftigmatize it in Cato. I have already produced
examples, under which all muficians, poets,
fatirifts, and great wits, may fhelter themfelves ; and I will undertake to furnifh the
fame kind of licenfe for the barbers, the
                                        dentifts,

dentifts, the carpenters, the glaziers, or any other order of men who will depute an embaffy to call upon me :—! fhall only re-queft, in return, that they will allow me a trifling confideration, in their refpective branches. I fhall ftipulate for a triple bob-major, becaufe Demofthenes fhaved his head ; and to have my teeth drawn, becaufe that orator had an impediment in his fpeech ; I muft have a wooden leg, becaufe Agefilaus was lame ; and a pair of glafs eyes, becaufe Homer was blind. I fhall at leaft be fupplied with as rational apologies for my deformity, as they will for their drunkennefs ; and, in procefs of time, I have no doubt, but it will be confidered as high-ly ornamental to be bald-pated, fluttering, limping, and blear-eyed.

To fay nothing of the immorality of drunkennefs, I cannot look upon it as the accomplifhment of a gentleman. It feems to me to be in the fame clafs of polite fci-ences with quoits, cock-fighting, tobacco-chewing, and quarter-ftaff.

If we examine the character of Falftaff, in whom all the bewitching qualities of a

profeffed

profeffed drunkard are exhibited, we fhall find it fuch a one as few would willingly think like themfelves. He has not only wit himfelf, but is the caufe of it in other men. He manifefts much good humour in bearing the raillery of others, and great quicknefs in retorts of his own. He drinks much; and, while he enumerates the qualities of your true fherris, he fkilfully commends what he drinks. Yet the fame character is as ftrongly reprefented to us, a parafite, an unfeafonable joker, a liar, a coward, and a difhoneft man.

There are, perhaps, fome few circum-ftances under which the liberal ufe of wine may be more eafily excufed ; but, while we furnifh palliatives for vice, we only multi-ply the means to cheat ourfelves.

I fhall conclude this paper with a few remarks on the character of the drunkard, from a pleafant * writer of the laft cen-tury : —

" A drunkard (fays he) is in opinion a " good fellow, in practife a living conduit ; " his vices are like errata in the latter end

* John Stephens, the younger, of Lincolnes Inne, 1615.

" of

" of a falfe coppie, they point the way to
" vertue by fetting downe the contrary.
" There is fome affinity betwixt him and
" a Chamelion ; he feeds upon ayre, for-
" he doth eate his word familiarly. He
" cannot run faft enough to prove a good
" footman : for ale and beere (the heavieft
" element next earth) will overtake him.
" His nofe, the moft innocent, beares the
" corruption of his other fenfes folly ;
" from it may bee gathered the emblem of
" one falfely fcandal'd, for *it* not offending
" is colourably punifh'd. A beggar and
" Hee are both of one ftocke, but the
" beggar claims antiquity. The beggar
" begs that he may drink, and hath his
" meaning ; the other drinks that he may
" beg, and fhall have the true meaning
" fhortly," &c.

## NUMBER XIX.

---

SATURDAY, *July* 21, 1787.

---

*Rudis indigeſtaque moles.*

MANY of my readers will, perhaps, compare this day's proviſion to the Saturday's dinner of a notable houſewife, compoſed of beef-ſteaks, and the fragments of the week. 1 wiſh them rather to con-ſider it as an entertainment, to the furniſh-ing of which the preſents of my friends have principally contributed, and. wherein it only remains for me to place the diſhes on the table.

*To*

## To the AUTHOR of the
## OLLA PODRIDA.

DEAR SIR,

I BE a baker's daughter, and to tell you the truth, fo much in love you can't think. Now, Sir, as you feems to be a grave fort of gentleman, I dares to fay you can read the hand, caft nativities, tell fortunes, and all that,—what now do you think, Sir, I will give you, if fo be that you will tell me for certain whether or no I fhall have Dick? why fourteen kiffes, and that's a baker's dozen you know, and fo no more from yours, till I'm married,

PATTY PENNYLESS.

To this fair lady the author of the Olla Podrida has only to reply, that he is not a conjuror, nor indeed does he wear a wig. However, by cofulting his books, he has difcovered a few negative maxims, by the obfervance of which his Correfpondent may *have Dick* if Dick be worth her having.—
Should

Should he be extravagant in the praife of her beauty, fhe is advifed not to believe him. Should he offer her a green gown, not to accept it. In the difpofal of her baker's dozens, not to be profufe; and, moreover, not to be any perfon's till fhe is married, not even her well-wifher's, and fo no more. TARATALLA.

## To the A U T H O R of the OLLA PODRIDA.

GOOD SIR,

I AM an old Soldier, and though I fay it, have feen and felt as much hard fervice as any man, and have actually fought as long as I had limbs to fupport me. My legs, Sir, which at this prefent writing are no lefs than fourteen hundred Englifh miles afunder, are buried (for aught I know) in two different quarters of the Globe, and will, alas! never crofs each other again. I have a hand, Sir, in two great kingdoms, whofe names, for politic reafons, I think proper at prefent to conceal, and only add,

that it is no impoffible thing for a man to
be in one country, and at the fame time
to have a hand in another. Such is my
fituation, Sir, that I am cropt clofe like a
Buckinghamfhire pollard, and have hardly
a twig left upon my trunk. Now, Sir,
there is a knot of merry gentlemen in our
neighbourhood, who, forfooth, having legs
and arms of their own natural growth, are
pleafed to be confiderably witty on what
is left of me, and not infrequently extend
their pleafantry to the afcititious branches
which are engrafted upon me. I requeft,
through the medium of your paper, Sir,
that you will inform thefe wags, that my
arms and legs are formed from the fame
piece, and not of different kinds of timber,
as they have malicioufly reported; and that
although I wear my common crab-trees
on common occafions, I have a pair of beft
mahogany fupporters for red-letter days
and Sundays. I am the more defirous of
their being informed of thefe particulars,
as I pay my addreffes to a well-favoured
middle-aged lady of fome fortune in the
village : and I would have you, her, them,

and

and all the world to know, that I never was fo ill bred as to pay her any compliment on my common legs, nor did I ever venture upon a falute but upon mahogany. I am informed by my man who takes me to pieces, and puts me together again every night and morning, that thefe merry men ftick at nothing to ridicule me. If you would take my part againft the fad dogs, you would very much oblige an old General, who hath, you find, long fince laid down his arms, and is no longer able to lift up a hand againft any coward who prefumes upon his incapability to affront him.            JOHN CROP.

I hope I have taken the moft effectual method to remedy Mr. Crop's grievances, by ftating his account of them.

To

*To the* AUTHOR *of the*
OLLA PODRIDA.

SIR,

IT has pleafed Providence to build this
veffel of mine of fuch crazy materials, that
a blaft or two of wind from the eaft north-
eaft quite overfets me.  No fooner does the
weather-cock, which is erected on the cu-
pola of my pigeon-houfe, point at eaft, but
the rheumatic pains, pins and needles,
cramps, joint achs, pinches, contractions,
twinges, and the fciatica, attack me in all
my quarters.  Whether our bodies, which,
I cannot help fometimes thinking, are made
for many ends, defigns, and purpofes,
whereof we are at prefent ignorant, may
not ferve as inns and baiting-places for
fwarms of infects which are at fuch times
on their journey to unknown regions, or
whether thefe piercing blafts bring down
upon us wretched mortals numberlefs invi-
fible fpears, arrows, knives, and fwords,
which, acted upon by the force of the wind,

fheath

fheath themfelves deep in our mufcles, bones, and joints, I muft leave Sir to you and the learned world to determine. Thefe ills very frequently put my thoughts, as well as limbs, to the rack, to difcover their real fprings and caufes, and I often medi-tate upon this matter, until conceits of no very common fhape and form are moft equi-vocally generated in my pericranium. Sometimes I fancy that thefe guefts bring with them on their wings a very peculiar fpecies of animalcula, which, lighting on this our flefhly habitation, creep in like bats and jack-daws into old caftle walls through unnumbered and imperceptible chinks, fif-fures, and crannies of our rimofe and rim-peled carcafes, where, when they have got in, they keep a great ftir-about in quarrel-ling, fighting, and making love; in build-ing nefts, and depofiting eggs, the produc-tions of which, after we have been fome time buried in the earth, leave us without an ounce of flefh to cover us. Thefe are ftrange chimæras, Sir, and make me trem-ble from head to foot in my great chair. But, Sir, while I know my houfe is to be

fwallowed

fwallowed down by an earthquake, the certainty of my being out of it, with all my treafures and valuables fafe and found, when this accident happens, gives me an unfpeakable pleafure, and a comfort at my very heart.

I am, Sir, your humble fervant,

JEREMY CRAZYBONES.

The whimfical philofophy of Mr. Crazybones feems to me to border on that pleafant melancholy humour which fober rationality fometimes denominates madnefs. When it is properly afcertained, that he is harmlefs, and in good bodily health, I fhall endeavour to prefcribe a medicine for him which may ferve to diffipate thofe chimæras which make him tremble fo in his arm chair.

To the AUTHOR of the
OLLA PODRIDA.

DEAR SIR,

THE Spectator and others have always thought proper to furnifh the public with
fome

fome defcription of their perfons and domeſtic qualities. I wiſh you likewife would
communicate to your readers, whether you
are a tall or a ſhort man; an horfe-back-
breaker, or a pantaloon; whether you wear
a wig, or your own hair, and talk much
or little; with fuch other intereſting particulars, defcriptive of your character and
appearance. I fuppofe you are neither a
floven nor a coxcomb.—Pray, Sir, are you
a batchelor or a married man?

Yours, &c.  MINUTIUS.

For information in all thefe intereſting
particulars, I ſhall refer Minutius to a view
of myfelf. If he has any ſkill in phyfiog-
nomy, he will difcover every thing he
wifhes, when I inform him, he may fee
me any morning, between five and fix,
going toward Joe Pullen's tree.—He will
know me by my red waiftcoat, and a pipe
in my mouth.

To *the* AUTHOR *of the*
OLLA PODRIDA.

SIR,

I HAVE a ftrong defire to fee my writings in print, though at prefent I have nothing to fay.—I wifh, however, you would infert this in fome corner of your paper, and you will much oblige,

RICHARD BRIEF.

NUMBER

# NUMBER XX.

*To the* AUTHOR *of the-*
OLLA PODRIDA,

*Falsus honos juvat.*

SIR,

SO prevailing is the love of superiority
in the human breast, that the most
strange and ridiculous claims are set up for
it, by those who have no real merit to offer. It is, indeed, absurd enough to value
oneself for bodily perfections, or mental
powers, both being totally the gift of the

O 4                    Supreme

Supreme Being, without the leaſt merit on
our part.  Nor is that confequence, arrogated from illuſtrious birth, at all juſtifi-
able, ſince the proof of poſſeſſing it cannot ariſe higher than probability:  All
ladies are not Suſannahs, nor all ſervants
Joſephs.    But fuppoſe it allowed ; a good
man does not want that addition ; and to
a bad one, the virtues of his anceſtors are
a ſtanding reproach.    A lower kind of importance is frequently aſſumed from the excellence of one's domeſtic animals, ſuch as
a fine pack of hounds, ſtaunch pointers, or
fleet horſes, when the arrogator of their
merit has neither bred, choſen, nor taught
them ; and has had no other concern with
them, than ſimply paying the purchaſe-
money.    How excellently does Dr. Young,
in his Univerſal Paſſion, draw and expoſe a
character of this kind !

> The 'Squire is proud to ſee his Courſer ſtrain,
> Or well-breath'd Beagles ſweep along the
>     plain.
> Say,  dear Hippolitus (whoſe drink is ale,
> Whoſe erudition is a Chriſtmas Tale,
> Whoſe miſtreſs is faluted with a ſmack,
> And friend receiv'd with thumps upon the
>     back,)                              When

When thy fleek' gelding nimbly leaps the
  mound,
And Ringwood opens on the tainted ground,
Is that thy praife, let Ringwood's fame
  alone ;
Juft Ringwood leaves each animal his own,
Nor envies when a Gypfy you commit,
And fhake the clumfy bench with country
  wit,
When you the dulleft of dull things have
  faid,
And then afk pardon, for the jeft you made.

But of all the ridiculous pretenfions to
pre-eminence, that arifing from the place of
one's refidence feems the moft foolifh, and
nothing is more common, and that not limited to countries, provinces, or cities, but
is regularly extended to the different parts
of this town of London, and even to the
feveral ftories of a houfe. The appellation
of country-booby is very ready in the mouth
of every citizen and apprentice, who feels
an imaginary fuperiority from living in the
metropolis ; and any one who has feen
London ladies of the middling order, in a
country church, muft have obferved, that
there they failed not to difplay a contemp-

tuous

tuous confequence founded on their coming from that town.

London is divided into the Suburbs, City, and Court, or as it is ftyled, Eaft of Temple Bar, and *To'ther End of the Town*; and again fubdivided into many degrees and diftricts, each in a regular climax conferring ideal dignity and precedency. The inhabitants of Kent Street, and St. Giles's, are mentioned by thofe of Wapping, Whitechapel, Mile-End, and the Borough of Southwark, with fovereign contempt; whilft a Wappineer, a Mile-ender, and a Boroughnian, are terms proverbially ufed, about the Exchange and Fenchurch Street, to exprefs an inferior order of beings; nor do the rich Citizens of Lombard Street ever lofe the opportunity of retailing the joke of a White-chapel fortune. The fame contempt is expreffed for the cits inhabiting the environs of the Royal Exchange, or refiding within the found of Bow Bell, St. Bennet's, Sheer Hog, Pudding Lane, and Blow-bladder ftreet, by the inferior retainers of the law in Chancery-Lane, Hatton Garden, and Bedford Row; and
thefe

thefe again are confidered as people living
totally out of the polite circle by the dwel-
lers in So'ho, and the afpiring tradefman
fettled in Bloomfbury, Queen's, and Red
Lion Squares, in the firft flight from their
counting houfes in Thames Street, Billingfgate, and Mark Lane. The new
Colonies about Oxford Street fneer at
thefe would-be people of fafhion, and are
in their turns defpifed by thofe whofe
happier ftars have placed them in Pall Mall,
Saint James's, Cavendifh and Portman
Squares. Thus it is, taking this criterion
of pre-eminence in a general view ; but to
defcend to a fmaller fcale, the Lodger in
the firft floor fcarcely deigns to return the
bow of the occupier of the fecond in the
fame houfe, who, on all occafions, makes
himfelf amends by fpeaking with the utmoft contempt of the Garretteers over head,
with many fhrewd jokes on *Sky Parlours.*
The precedency between the Garret and
the Cellar feems evidently in favour of the
former, Garrets having time out of mind
been the refidence of the literati, and facred
to the Mufes ; it is not therefore wonderful
that

that the inhabitants of thofe fublime regions fhould think the renters of Cellars, independent of a pun, much below them.

Befides the diftinctions of Altitude, there is that of *forward* and *backward*: I have heard a lady, who lodged in the fore room of the fecond ftory, on being afked after another who lodged in the fame houfe, fcornfully defcribe her by the appellation of " the Woman living in the back room."

Polite fituations no only confer dignity on the parties actually refiding on them, but alfo, by emanations of gentility, in fome meafure ennoble the Vicinity; thus perfons living in any of the back lanes or courts near one of the polite fquares or ftreets, may tack them to their addrefs, and thereby fomewhat add to their confequence. I once knew this method practifed with great fuccefs by a perfon who lodged in a court in Holbourn, who conftantly added to his direction, *oppofite the Duke of Bedford's, Bloomfbury Square.*

To prevent difputes refpecting the fuperiority here treated of, I have with much impartiality, trouble, and fevere ftudy, laid
down

down a fort of table of precedency, and marfhaled the ufual places of refidence in their fucceffive order, beginning with the loweft. Firft, then, of thofe who occupy only a part of a tenement, ftand, the holders of ftalls, fheds, and cellars, to them fucceed the refidents in garrets, whence we gradually defcend to the fecond and firft floor, the dignity of each ftory being in the inverfe ratio of its altitude ; it being always remembered, that thofe dwelling in the fore part of the houfe take place of the inhabitants of the fame elevation renting the back rooms ; the ground floor, if not a fhop or a warehoufe, ranks with the fecond ftory. Situations of Houfes, I have arranged in the following order : Paffages, alleys, courts, ftreets, rows, places, and fquares. My reafon for thefe arrangements, I may, perhaps, give on a future opportunity.

As a comfort to thofe who might defpond at feeing their lot placed in an humiliating degree, let them confider, that all but the firft fituations are capable of promotion ; and that an inhabitant of a Yard or Court may, without moving, find himfelf a dweller in a ftreet. Many inftances

of

of this have very lately occurred. Does any one now hefitate to talk of Fludyer and Crown Streets, Weftminfter ? and yet both were, not long ago, fimply Axe Yard and Crown Court, from which they have been raifed to their prefent dignity, with-out paffing through the intermediate rank of lanes. In the fame manner Hedge Lane is become Whitcombe Street; and Cum-berland Court takes the title of Milford Place; and Cranbourn Alley has experien-ced a fimilar elevation; and any one, that fhould chance to call it lefs than Cranbourn Street, would rifque fomething more than abufe from the ladies of the quilting-frame, and fons of the gentle craft refident there. Tybourn Road has been created Oxford Street; and Leicefter Fields honoured with the rank, ftyle, and title, of Leicefter Square.

NUM-

# NUMBER XXI.

---

SATURDAY, *August* 4, 1787.

---

'Οςις δε διαβολιαις πειθεται ταχυ
Ητοι πονηρος αυτος εςι τ᷈ς τροπ᷈ς
Η παντ᷈απασι παιδαρι᷈ γνωμην εχει.

MENANDER.

He who willingly extends his credulity to the belief of calumnies, is a wicked man or fool.

THAT sacred weapon, Satire, so seldom falls into hands able to wield it with fortitude and discretion, that if we examine the characters of those who have arrogated to themselves the office of stigmatizing vice, the result of our labours will oftentimes prove disappointment and regret.

Yet,

Yet, as not every difappointment is without fome ufeful leffon, it may not, perhaps, be quite unprofitable to offer a few
curfory remarks upon fome of thofe writers
who have paffed through the world under
the denomination of Satirifts.

To fix a period from which Satire may
be fuppofed to have had its beginning, is
to date the origin of that whofe exiftence is
coeval with the nature of man. The manners of all times have furnifhed materials
for the pen of the Satirift ; and writers of
all nations have difcovered either their integrity in the proper ufe of it, or their
malevolence in the proftitution of it. That
Homer gave fufficient proofs of his abilities
to become a powerful Satirift, we have heard
in his Margites, and we have feen in his
character of Therfites.

The different regulations of the Greek
Comedy have been accurately and frequently ftated to us ; it is therefore unneceffary
to give a very minute account of what every
one is, or may be, fo minutely acquainted
with.—In confequence of the licentious fatire produced into public by Cratinus and
Eupolis

Eupolis, it was decreed that no one should name another on the stage. Under these reftrictions wrote Menander and Philemon, with the chaftity of whose ftyle, and the purity of whose fentiments, we have reafon to lament that we cannot be more intimately acquainted. To them fucceeded Arioftophanes, upon whom his biographical panegyrift has been able to heap no other commendation, than fuch as is due to the mifapplication of abilities which might have been ferviceable to his country, and creditable to himfelf.

Let the reader of Arioftophanes diveft himfelf of his inclination to become acquainted with the cuftoms of the Greeks, and the niceties of their language, and he will find little in that author tending to make him a wifer or a better man. While ribaldry is confidered as the perfection of wit, fo long fhall we look for a model in Arioftophanes; while the malicious exercife of fuperiour abilites be commendable, fo long fhall Arioftophanes be commended. The humour of this writer is generally low, and frequently obfcene; his ridicule,

P

from being mifapplied, rather difgufts his
reader, than vilifies his object; and that
odium, which in the wickednefs of his heart
he would heap upon another, falls with
juftice upon himfelf. When we confider
the reputed elegance even to a proverb of
the Athenians, it is not without aftonifhment that we mark the confequence of his
plays; fcarce lefs than infatuation feems
to have actuated the minds of his audience.
By means of his worthlefs ribaldry the
finger of fcorn was pointed againft Æfchy-
lus, Euripides, and Sophocles; and to his
too efficacious calumny Socrates paid the
tribute of his life. Plutarch, in his comparifon between Ariftophanes and Menander, obferves of the former, " that his lan-
" guage is tumid, full of ftage trick, and
" illiberality, which is never the cafe with
" Menander—The man of fcience is of-
" fended, and vulgarity delighted. He,
" however, obtained popularity by exercif-
" ing his wit againft the tax-gatherers; he
" is remarkable (adds he) for having fo
" diftributed his fpeeches, that there is no
" difference whether a father fpeaks or a

I                                      " fon,

" fon, a ruftic or a deity, an old man or a
" hero. In Menander it is directly oppo-
" fite." But the violence with which Plutarch condemns the writings of Ariftophanes may perhaps difcover that his judgment
was fomewhat biafled by his indignation
againft the Author. Thus far, however,
on all fides will be readily granted, that
could the fate of Menander and Ariftophanes have been reverfed, it is probable, Comedy would have found a ftandard of tafte
inftead of a precedent for licentioufnefs, and,
ufing fuch example, would have proved herfelf the mirror of truth, inftead of the vehicle of calumny. The reader who has dif-
cretion enough to look upon Ariftophanes
as the fkilful advocate in a bad caufe, may
be entertained by his writings, and not prejudiced by his opinions. But we are too
apt to fubfcribe without examination to the
dicta of acknowledged abilities :—There is
little trouble in this, but much danger.

Of the Roman Satirifts we may fpeak
more favourably than perhaps of any fet of
writers, who have adorned any country.
The habits of their lives in general gave a

fanction

fanction to the gravity of their doctrines.
The conduct of Plautus was no difgrace to
his writings ; Lucilius gave no precepts of
virtue to others, which he did not exemplify in himfelf; and to that beft writer of
the moft accomplifhed age, Horace, who
fhall deny the meed of praife, which the
teftimony of his own times declared his
due, and the univerfal confent of fucceeding
ages has ratified and confirmed ? Equal to
him in ftrength of mind, and in virtue by
no means inferior, were Juvenal and Perfi-
us ; yet they had not that art and judgment, the poffeffion of which has made
Horace more read and admired, and the
want of which has made themfelves more
neglected.

The policy of the Gauls, and the terrors
of the Baftile, have, no doubt, while they
curbed the licentioufnefs of a gay and lively
nation, at the fame time depreffed the ardour
of many ingenious Satirifts ;—That this has
been the cafe, the world has little caufe to
lament, fince the few, who have difcovered
themfelves in that country, feem rather
defirous of eftablifhing a reputation for
them-

themfelves, than zealous for the promotion of virtue, They are content to be called good writers, without ambition to be accounted virtuous men.

In order to review fome of the beft Satirifts of our own nation, we muft pafs over the bigotry of one age, in which Milton feems to have prefided, and the profligacy of another, in which this land exchanged the horrors of civil war, and inteftine difcords, for the vicious luxuries of an ill-fpent peace, which were ratified by the countenancs, encouragement, and example of a King, The wits of this age were confiftent in their lives and writings, and immorality was the characteriftic of both. They feem to have agreed as it were with univerfal confent, that " a tale of humour was fufficient knowledge, good-fellowfhip fufficient honefty," and a reftraint from the extremes of vice, fufficient virtue.

If we defcend to what has been called the Auguftan age of Englifh literature, we fhall find the fatirical works of that time will not bear a very near infpection. It is a lamentable truth, that the fame pen

which

which had been fo often and fo fuccefsfully employed in the caufe of virtue;
which had given immortality to the Man
of Rofs, and the compliment of truth to
Addifon, was unwarily led into an attempt
to pluck the laurels from the brow of Bentley, and to gratify an unmanly malevolence in the publication of the Dunciad.

The cenfures of Swift feem to have been
marked by habitual ill-nature; and the compliments of Young, by an habitual want
of difcrimination. And it generally happens, that the cenfures of fuch Satirifts,
and the commendations of fuch panegyrifts,
keep an equal balance, both weighing—
nothing.

Nothing has, I believe, been more frequently an object of ill-placed ridicule than
Learning, which, before it can appear ridiculous, muft be mifnamed Pedantry.
Every Homer has his Zoilus; and every
Zoilus, like Homer's, is remembered only
to be defpifed. Whatever effect the attacks
of Ariftophanes upon the Tragœdians of
his day might have toward vitiating the
tafte of his countrymen, pofterity have
feemed willing to do juftice to thofe works,

in

in the admiration of which the wifeſt and beſt men of all ages have united.

I am inclined to believe that the learning of Dr. Bentley loſt no admirers from the attacks of Pope, or the infinuations of Swift; and an inſtance, taken from times nearer our own, will, perhaps, place the odium of malevolent ſatire in a ſtronger light. To the truth of this every one can bear witnefs, who is acquainted with thoſe attacks which have been made by Churchill and others upon Johnſon. That great writer—who, as he was a man, could not but err, and as he was a wife man, could not perſiſt in error; who was no feeble or time-ſerving moraliſt, but the firm and fyſtematic teacher and practiſer of virtue: He has ſhewn us, that the ſhafts of malevolence may be turned aſide, however keenly pointed, or however deeply em- poiſoned. The reader of Lexiphanes is ex- cited to laugh without approbation; and the attack of Churchill remains a melan- choly inſtance of proſtituted wit. What ſhall we ſay of thoſe, who, offended by no public and growing vice, provoked by no

private

private wrongs, in deliberate wantonnefs
fport with the characters of their neighbours, whom they hold out to unjuft ridicule, and unmerited reproach ? It is but a
weak apology for the bafenefs of their
hearts, that the produce of their pens may
afford amufement to the idle, and gratification to the malevolent. But our reflections upon this fubject will be too applicable to many of thofe publications which
are the difgrace and entertainment of the
times in which we live.—In the commendation of fuch men, let all thofe join who
have learnt, from the writings of Shaftef-
bury, that ridicule is the teft of truth ; or
from the conduct of Voltaire, that calumny
is a cardinal virtue.

N U M-

# NUMBER XXII.

## SATURDAY, *August* 11, 1787.

*The Briton ſtill with fearful Eye foreſees*
*What Storm or Sunſhine Providence decrees;*
*Knows for each Day the Weather of our Fate;*
*A Quid nunc is an Almanack of State.*

YOUNG'S SATIRES.

AMONG the various Employments which engage the Attention of Mankind, it is not unpleaſant to conſider their Topicks of Converſation. Every Country has ſome peculiar to itſelf, which, as they derive their origin from the Eſtabliſhment of Cuſtom, and the Predominance of national Pride, are permanent in their Dura-

tion,

tion, and extenfive in their Influence. Like
ftanding Difhes, they form the moft fubftantial Part of the Entertainment, and are
ferved up at the Tables both of the Rich
and Poor. The Dutchman talks inceffantly of the Bank of Amfterdam, the Italian of the Carnival, the Spaniard of a Bull
Fight, and the Englifh of Politicks and the
Weather.

That thefe laft - mentioned Topicks
fhould gain fo great an Afcendancy over
the Englifhman, is by no Means a Subject
of Wonder. In a Country, where the
Adminiftration may be changed in Half a
Year, and the Weather may alter in Half
a Minute, the quick and furprifing Viciffitudes muft neceffarily roufe the Attention, and furnifh the moft obvious Materials for Converfation. From the Influence
of that Gravity which is remarked by
Foreigners to be the Characteriftick of the
Inhabitants of Britian, they are difpofed to
view thefe endemical Subjects in a gloomy
Light, and to make them the Parents of
fullen Diffatisfaction, and ideal Diftrefs.
John Bull, with a contracted Brow, and
                                    furly

furly Voice, complains that we have April in July, and that the greateſt Patriots are ſhamefully out of Place. All this may be very true ; but, if his Worſhip could be perſuaded to confeſs his Feelings, he would acknowledge, that the Gratification of complaining is far from inconſiderable, and that if theſe Topicks, on which he vents his Spleen, were taken from him, little would remain to occupy his Mind, or ſet his Tongue in Motion.

Let us indulge, for a Moment, the whimſical Suppoſition, that our Climate was changed for that of Italy, and our Government for that of the Turks ; the Conſequences are eaſy to be foreſeen—a general Silence would reign throughout the Iſland, from Port Patrick to the Land's End. We ſhould be all well qualified for the School of Pythagoras. Our Silence, indeed, would ſcarcely be limited like that of his Scholars to five Years. Every Houſe in England would reſemble the Monaſtery of La Trappe, where the Monks are no better than walking Statues. The only Talkers among us would be Phyſicians,

Lawyers,

Lawyers, Old Maids, and Travellers.
The Phyfician might fatigue us with
his Materia medica, the Lawyer with his
Qui tam Actions; the Old Maid with difficult Cafes at Cards, and the Traveller
with the Dimenfions of the Louvre without Fear of Interruption or Contradiction.
We fhould look up to them as Students do
to Profeffors reading Lectures, and like
poor Dido feel a Pleafure in the Encouragement of Loquacity.

" *Iliacofque iterum demens audire labores*
" *Expofcit, pendetque iterum narrantis ab ore.*

" She fondly begs him to repeat once more
" The Trojan Story that fhe heard before ;
" Then to Diftraction charm'd in Rapture
       " hung
" On every Word, and dy'd upon his Tongue."
                                        PITT.

The Game at Whift would be played
with uninterrupted Tranquillity, and the
Cry of Silence in the Courts of Juftice
might be omitted without the fmalleft Inconvenience. In fhort, all the Englifh
who went Abroad would be intitled to the
                                        Com-

Compliment which was once paid a No-
bleman at Paris. A lively French Marquis
after having been a whole Evening in his
Company without hearing him articulate a
Syllable, remarked, *that Milord Anglois
had admirable Talents for Taciturnity.*

Prodigality prevails in Town, and Oeconomy in the Country, in more Inſtances
than may be at firſt imagined. In town,
ſuch is the Number of Newſpapers, that
the Coffee-Houſe Lounger may ſate himſelf, like a Fly in a Confectioner's Shop,
with an endleſs Variety. He may ſee an
Event ſet in all poſſible Lights, and may
ſuit it to the Complexion of his Mind, and
the Sentiments of his Party. Such is the
Advantage of a refined Metropolis, where
Profuſion enlarges the Dominions of Pleaſure in every Direction, and ſupplies the
greateſt Dainties to gratify the vitiated Appetite of Curioſity. In the Country, the Caſe is
widely different. In moſt genteel Families
a ſolitary Paper is introduced with the
Tea-Urn and Rolls, but certain Reſtraints
are laid upon the Manner of peruſing it:
Half the News is read the firſt Morning,
and

and Half is referved for the Entertainment
of the next.  This frugal Diftribution in
the Parlour is, without Doubt,  adopted
from fomething fimilar which  takes Place
in the Store-room.  The Miftrefs of the
Family difpenfes the proper Quantity of
Pickles and Preferves, and then locks the
Door till the following Day.  Our Affairs
in the Eaft are fettled at one Time ; whilft
the Burgomafters and the Princefs of
Orange are left to their Fate till another.
Enough is read to furnifh the Family with
Subjects for Converfation ; and, as Topicks
are not numerous, the Thread of Politicks
is fpun very fine.  Little Mifs wonders,
when fhe hears Papa adjuft the Affairs of
the Nation, that he is not a Parliament
Man, and thinks that, if the King were
ever to hear of him, he would certainly be
made Prime-Minifter.

   There is (if the Expreffion may be allowed) a Refinement in our Fears.  A rational Apprehenfion of impending Evil is
the Mother of Security, but the Mind that
is terrified by remote Dangers is weak and
ridiculous.  The Imagination is like a
                                        Mag-

Magnifying-glafs, which, by enlarging the
Dimenfions of diftant Objects, makes them
appear formidable. It is the Office of Reafon to place them in proper Situations, and
to fuggeft, that we are not expofed to their
Effects. The Neapolitan, who lives at the
Foot of Vefuvius, has juft Caufe for trem-
bling at the Symptoms of an Eruption ;
but, he may depend upon it, his Vines are
in no danger from the Volcanos in the
Moon. The Stock-Holder may well fear
the Confequences of the Belgic Commotions. The Farmer, whofe Hay is fcattered over the Meadows, may, without the
Imputation of Weaknefs, be vexed at the
Torrents of Rain. But why fhould the
Man, who has no Concern but to walk
from Cheapfide to White-Chapel, apply to
his Barometer ten Times before he ventures
out ? or be difturbed in his Dreams for the
Safety of the Grand Signior ?

A Club was once eftablifhed by certain
Gentlemen, whofe Minds were too much
polifhed by their Travels not to banifh
every Thing that is interefting to John
Bull. Among their Rules and Orders it

was

was enacted, That no mention fhould be made of the State of the Weather or Politicks, but that all their Converfation fhould turn upon Literature and Virtû. It happened, that the Prefident of the Club, who was a pretty Petit Maitre of twenty Stone, was attacked by a violent Ague. He was feized with a cold Fit whilft adjufting a Difpute between two Dilettanti, whether the Church of *Santa Maria in Navicelli* was larger than *Santa Maria in Valicelli.* This important Argument was interrupted by the Prefident's Digreffion in Abufe of the Englifh Climate, which he declared was calculated for no Beings under the Sun but Draymen and Shepherds. Some of the Fraternity talked peremptorily of expelling him from the Society, for breaking their firft Rule, and introducing a Subject which ought to be left to the Canaille. After great Animofity, and abundant Altercation, it was finally determined to expunge the Rule, becaufe they could not engage a Party who were fufficiently refined by Liqueurs to be freed from the Grievance of their Englifh Conftitutions.

It

It was once ſeriouſly diſcuſſed by the French Academy, whether it was poſſible for a German to be a Wit. It would be more worthy of the Sagacity of the ſame learned Body to determine, whether it be poſſible for an Engliſhman not to be a Politician. To form a right Deciſion, let them converſe with what Order of Men they pleaſe, and they will find, that the ruling Paſſion is the Regulation of the Political Machine. The Ferocity which is natural to Iſlanders may be the Reaſon of our being more diſpoſed to command than to obey. Hence it is no uncommon Caſe for a Man ſo far to miſtake his Abilities, as to talk of riding the State Horſe, when he is hardly expert enough to ſhoe him. All Perſons of all Ranks harangue as if the Secrets of the State would be beſt entruſted to their Diſcretion, as if their own Addreſs qualified them for the moſt critical Situations, and the Judgment of their Rulers ſhould be ſuſpended until ſuperior Sagacity pointed out the right Path. Whilſt the Barber ſnaps his Fingers among his Cuſtomers, he talks of managing the *Moun-*

Q                                    *ſeers,*

*feers*, and laying on Taxes without Op-
preſſion. The Aldermen, at a Corporation
Dinner, do the ſame over their Turbot and
Veniſon. To compleat the Climax, theſe
are the identical Points which perplex the
Underſtandings of the King and his Counſellors in the Cabinet.

Notwithſtanding the Severity of Military
Law, the different Orders of Society would
ſuſtain no Injury, if, like a well-diſciplined
Army, they neither broke their Ranks, nor
mutinied againſt their Officers. A Family
is a Kingdom in Miniature : In that domeſtic, but important Sphere of Government, every Man of common Senſe is able
to preſide. The Maſter of a well-regulated
Houſe is more beneficial to the State, than
a Hundred political Declaimers. To curb
the Paſſions, to fix religious Principles in
the Minds of Children, and to govern Servants with mild Authority, all ultimately
promote the beſt Intereſts of the Publick.
Obedience branches out into various Rela-
tions. The Debt which we demand from
our Dependants, we owe to our Governors.
Subordination is to a Subjećt, what Reſig-

nation

nation is to a Chriftian. They are both admirably well calculated to filence the Clamours of Party, and adminifter the Cordial of Content. Let the Englifhman reprefs his Murmurs, by refleting that he is a Member of a Conftitution which com-bines the Excellencies of all Governments; and that he breathes in a Climate which permits him to be expofed to the Air more Days in a Year, and more Hours in a Day, without Inconvenience, than any other in Europe.

SATURDAY, *August* 18, 1787.

---

*Quadrupedante putrem sonitu quatit ungula*
*campum.*                                    VIRG.

AMONG the fources of thofe innumerable calamities which, from age
to age, have overwhelmed mankind, may
be reckoned, as one of the principal, the
abufe of *Words*. Dr. South has two admirable difcourfes on the fubject; and it is
much to be wifhed, that a continuation
could be carried on, by fome proper hand,
enumerating the words, which, fince his
time, have fucceffively come into vogue,
and been, in like manner, abufed to evil
purpofes, by crafty and defigning men.

x                                        It

It is well known what ſtrange work
there has been in the world, under the
name and pretence of *Reformation*; how
often it has turned out to be, in reality,
*Deformation*; or, at beſt, a tinkering ſort
of buſineſs, where, while one hole has
been mended, two have been made.

I have my eye, at preſent, on an event
of this kind, which took place in very
early times, and is ſuppoſed to have been
productive of many and great advantages to
the ſpecies; I mean the alteration brought
about in the " œconomy of human *walk-*
" *ing*;" when man, who, according to the
beſt and ableſt philoſophers, went originally on four legs, firſt began to go upon two.
I hope it will be excuſed, if I venture
humbly to offer ſome reaſons why I am led
to doubt, whether the alteration may have
been attended by all the advantages ſo
fondly imagined.

There is ſomething ſuſpicious in the
hiſtory given of this reformation. It is ſaid
to have had the ſame origin with that
aſcribed by Dr. Mandeville to the *moral
virtues*. It was the " offspring of *flattery*,

begot

begot upon *pride.*" The philofophers difcovered, that man was proud : they attacked him in a cowardly manner, on his
weak fide, and by arguments, the fophifm
of which it might be eafy enough, perhaps,
if there were occafion, to unravel and expofe,
prevailed upon him to quit his primæval
pofition ; and, whether fairly or not, they
coaxed him upon *two.* How far any good
is to be expected from a reformation founded on fuch principles, the reader muft
judge for himfelf.

By the account, with which the authors
of it have furnifhed us, thus much is certain, that nothing can be more *unnatural:*
and yet, fay thefe philofophers, at other
times, " Whatever you do, *follow nature* ;"
a precept, which, in general, they feem
very well difpofed to practife, to the beft of
their abilities. A child *naturally* goes on
all four ; and we know how difficult a
matter it is, to fet him an end, or to keep
him fo. He has not even the ftability of a
ninepin, which will ftand, till it be bowl-
ed down. For my own part, I never fee a
child's forehead with a great bump upon it,
or

or fwathed up in a black-pudding, left it
fhould receive one, but I am irrefiftibly
impelled to bewail this pretended reformation, as a moft notorious and melancholy
defection from our primitive condition.

When the two children brought up to
man's eftate, apart from all human beings,
by the command of a king of Egypt, who
imagined, that the language which they
fhould fpeak muft neceffarily be the original language of the world—When thefe
children, I fay, had the honour to be
introduced at court, amidft a circle of
all the learned and wife, and noble perfonages of that celebrated country ; hiftory bears her teftimony, that they proceeded up the drawing-room, and made
their way to the royal prefence, upon *all
four*. I am aware, that fome have thought,
they threw themfelves into that attitude,
from the dread and awe infpired into them
by the fight of Majefty ; others, ftill more
refined, have fuppofed they might have
done fo, to adapt themfelves to the employment of thofe whom they found affembled in that place, and be prepared

either

either to *creep*, or to *climb*, or *both*, as opportunity offered. But I cannot apprehend,
that the course of their education could
have qualified them for speculations so abftrufe as thefe; and, therefore, I muft
take leave to fay, I look upon the fact to be
good evidence, that fuch was the attitude
proper to man.

I am ftill farther confirmed in my opinion, from that ftrong propenfity vifible in
mankind, to return to it again. The pof-
ture, into which we have been feduced, is
productive of conftant uneafinefs. We are
in a fidget from morning to night; to re-
lieve us from which, the expence of chairs
and fophas is a very confiderable tax upon
our property; and, after all, we cannot
compofe ourfelves perfectly to reft, but
when recumbent upon our beds. That
our fole bufinefs is with *earth*, univerfal
practice feems to determine. Why then
fhould we look after any thing elfe? or
why be reproached with, *O curvæ in terras
animæ!* efpecially when we recollect the
fate of the poor aftronomer, who, while
he was gazing at the ftars, fell into a
ditch. It

It deferves notice, that fome of our moft diftinguifhed titles of honour are borrowed from our fellow-creatures, the quadrupeds, whofe virtues we are ambitious to emulate. An accomplifhed young gentleman of family, fortune, and fafhion, glories in the name, ftyle, and title, of a Buck. You cannot pay him a greater compliment, than by beftowing on him this appellation ; and indeed, no one reafon in the world can be affigned, why he fhould walk upon *two*.

The opinion of a great commercial nation, like our own, cannot with more certainty be collected from any circumftance than from the management of the moft important article of finance. Now, we find that article entrufted to the care of Bulls and Bears. And although a Bear, which is a quadruped, by a metamorphofis no lefs fudden and furprifing than any in Ovid, be at times transformed into a Duck, which is a biped, yet it is obferved, that there is a fomewhat aukward about him ever after. He moves, indeed, but his motions are not as they fhould be, and he is from thenceforth faid not to *walk*, but to *waddle*. It

may

may be added, that we never hear of a
*Duck* commencing dancing-mafter ; whereas Captain King informs us, " the Kamt-
" chadales are not only obliged to the *Bears*
" for what little advancement they have
" hitherto made in the *fciences* or *polite arts,*
" as alfo the ufe of fimples both internal
" and external; but they acknowledge
" them likewife for their *dancing-maflers.*;
" the *Bear-dance* among them being an
" exact counterpart of every attitude and
" gefture peculiar to this animal, through
" its various functions. And this dance is
" the foundation and groundwork of all
" their other dances, and *what they value*
" *themfelves moft upon.*"

I could have wifhed, that one of thefe
Siberian teachers had been prefent the other
day, to have beftowed a lecture upon a
friend of mine, who had been inftructed to
marfhal his feet in a tolerably decent way;
to move forward by advancing one before
the other, and backward by fliding one
behind another; in fhort, he had attained
fome proficiency in what Dr. South ftiles,
" that whimfical manner of fhaking the
" legs,

" legs, called *dancing* ;" when, all at once, holding up his hands in an angle of forty-five degrees, with a countenance full of ineffable diftrefs, and a moft lamentable accent, he exclaimed to the mafter, " But, " Sir ! What fhall I do with THESE ?"

Nor is the complaint of my friend at all fingular. For the truth is, (and why fhould I diffemble it ?) that fince we have left off to put our arms to their due and proper ufe of *fore-legs*, they are ever in the way, and we know not what upon earth to do with them. Some let them dangle, at will, in a perpendicular line parallel with their fides ; fome fold them acrofs their bofoms, to look free and eafy; fome ftick them a-kimbo, in defiance ; fome are continually moving them up and down, and throwing them about, fo as to be at variance with their legs, and every other part of their bodies ; as was the cafe with Dr. Johnfon, when Lord Chefterfield had like to have fallen into a *deliquium*, by looking at him, and could confider the author of the Englifh di&ionary in no other light than that of an ill-taught pofture-mafter.

mafter. Some thruft their hands, as far as
they can, into their breeches pockets.
This laft is a bad *habit* enough ; becaufe
they who find nothing in their own pockets
(which perhaps pretty generally happens)
may be tempted to try what they can find
in thofe of others. While fore-legs were
in fafhion, the limbs, which are now the
caufe of fo much embarraffment to us,
had full employment : It might be faid,
"Every man his own horfe:" and when
one confiders the prefent extravagant price
of horfes, one is induced on this account
alfo to wifh, that it had ftill continued to
be fo.

As I am upon the fubject of the *reforma-*
*tions* made in our perfons, I cannot help
mentioning a little dab of one; effected in
an age fo diftant, that no fyftem of chrono-
logy within my knowledge has marked the
æra, much as it deferves to have been
marked. The period is altogether unknown, when our nature was firft defpoiled
of an appendage equally ufeful and ornamental—I mean a TAIL ; for with an
eminently learned philofopher of North
Britain,

Britain, I am moſt firmly perſuaded, that
it was originally a part of our conſtitution;
and that, in the eye of ſuperior beings,
man, when he loſt that, loſt much of his
dignity. If a conjecture might be indulged
upon the ſubject (and, alas! what but
conjectures can we indulge?) I ſhould be
inclined to ſuppoſe, that the defalcation,
now under conſideration, was coæval with
the change of poſture, difcuſſed above.
No ſooner had man unadviſedly mounted
on two, but his tail dropped off; or rather,
perhaps, in the confuſion occaſioned by the
change, it hitched in a wrong place, and
became ſufpended from his *head*. But how
very eaſy would it be, when *the books are
open*, to make a *transfer*, and reſtore it to
its proper ſituation? That very reſpectable
perſon, whom Swift humourouſly deſcribes,
as " lately come to town, and never ſeen
" *before* by any body," has been known,
upon ſome occaſions, to have appeared in a
*tye-wig*; which, doubtleſs, was his full-
dreſs, for balls, and other public aſſemblies.
But by way of light and airy morning
diſhabille,

difhabille, no one can doubt of his looking admirably well in a *queue*.

I am fenfible this is a topic which requires to be treated with the utmoft caution and delicacy ; and, therefore, feeling the ground to tremble under me, I fhall not venture to advance farther upon it ; but from the difpofition prevalent among us to copy the manners of creatures fo much our inferiors, I fhall conclude by encouraging my readers to hope, the time cannot be very far diftant, when we fhall all have our *tails* again, and once more go upon *all four*. **Z**.

NUMBER

# NUMBER XXIV.

***

## SATURDAY, *August* 25, 1787.

***

*To the* AUTHOR *of the*
## OLLA PODRIDA.

*Roscia, dic sodes, melior lex, an puerorum*
*Nænia.*                     HOR.

IF all the qualities of the mind, or habits of life, which are found to be moſt adverſe to Religion, to Chriſtian Virtue, and Spiritual Hope, were to be enumerated, a ſelfiſh ſordid temper would not appear the laſt upon the liſt. It is not intended by theſe expreſſions to point out in groſs terms a baſe avarice, an hardened churliſh nature,

nature, or the difingenuous craft of men
devoted to the world ; but to expofe a difpofition better covered from contempt, recommended by careful inftruction, and un-
defervedly refpected among men.

We are in hafte to withdraw the minds
of the young from wild and vifionary notions of pleafure and of life : it is better indeed to remove fuch notions prudently and
feafonably, than to wait till difappointment
fnatches them away.  Such gay romantic
fcenes as entertain them in the books they
read, fuch pleafing views of manners, and
of perfons, elevated above the wants of life,
its coarfer inconveniences, its fullen irkfome hours, its attendant troubles and dif-
eafes, give but a falfe draught of the ftate
of man.  Thefe broken rays, perhaps of
loft perfection, cannot, we know, penetrate
far into the fhades of life ; they are the
emanations of minds whofe early purity is
yet untainted by the common ordinary objects and purfuits, the paffions and engagements of real life, disfigured as it is.
It is true fuch views will foon be contra-
dicted by experience, by real images, by
                              dail

daily documents, by repeated and inevitable
truth: but reafon fhould not affume too
much applaufe in fhaking off thefe vain
and empty notions; though fhe feem to
rife fuperior to them, fhe finks in fact too
often much below them. The felfifh rea-
foner and worldly monitor, in banifhing
thefe phantoms, do not always fubftitute
more noble emulations; they pluck away
the weeds and the wild flowers, but they
fow tares at laft. Thefe are the men who
faften impudence by precept upon honeft
natures; who rear and educate the bafer
paffions of the heart, endear them by familiar and popular names, point out their
advantage, their expedience and neceffity:
they chill the warmth of untrammelled and
difinterefted minds: they plunge themfelves
and others into felfifh fordid habits and opinions, in order to avoid the folly or the
inconvenience of thofe which are childifh
or imaginary: they put away airy pleafures
and fpeculations, to addict themfelves to
actual grofsnefs. But can we continue the
dreams of fancy to the ends of our lives?
no more than we can the games and amufe-

R                              ments

ments of children. The hand of experience will pluck away our foft and glitter-
ing robes; the fun will vanifh from our
landfcape; the leaves drop from our fhrubs;
and we muft learn to harden ourfelves
againft the true climate in which we are to
live.

Some traces of delight from thofe fantaftic images of youth remain for recollection; we acknowledge them as true fources
of pleafure, but we cannot recur to them.
Reafon compounds her judgements of different materials: whatever is unnatural
cannot pleafe or edify: it cannot pleafe,
becaufe the fober mind can only be interefted by truth; it cannot edify, becaufe fo
little of it can apply to ourfelves or others.
But the knowledge of thefe truths, as it is
applied by felfifh and worldly men, does
not improve the mind; it rather injures
and contracts it. The ridicule, thrown upon
falfe pleafures and ideal amufements, leads
the way to real fenfuality: the fear of
being deluded, and impofed upon, firft
abates the warmth of true benevolence, and
at laft excufes churlifhnefs and avarice.
What

What then do they gain too often by their boafted experience, by their fagacity and emancipation; but fufpicious hearts, narrow minds, grofs ideas inftead of fanciful ones, real errors, genuine arrogance, and fubftantial ambition? There are men indeed who, under cover of a kind of wifdom, fecretly and indirectly deride all eminent degrees of virtue as romantic and impracticable: if you talk to them of pleafures, or of hopes, that do not meet the fenfes, they will turn them into ridicule: if you fpeak to them of tendernefs, of charity, and zeal, they will demonftrate to you how unfit they are for the purpofes of life. But whether the juvenile and filly inexperience of a warm imagination be well fupplanted by the fubfequent inveterate attachments, may be determined by a clofer eftimate: and if it fhall be found that the real, the fubftantial, and immediate fruition, fo preferred, involves a paradox, is more a notion than the other; deceives us more by univerfal teftimony; hurts us more; is more a fhadow; more a dream; and has an iffue infinitely worfe, a fum of

covenanted

covenanted ills, of woes legitimate and permanent ; there will be little fcope remaining for complacency, and ftill lefs expectation of better habits to fucceed.

If we fhift only from the pleafures and
chimeras of imagination, to the purfuits of
appetite ; if keen defires, or real nakednefs,
fucceed the fports and mafquerade of fancy ;
the change will not be flattering. It is
matter rather of difgrace than gratulation
that we are fubject, in our chofen pleafures,
to the rule and the caprice of prefent things ;
the fund and objects of the fenfes.

But to draw nearer to the mark and end
of thefe reflections—it is clear that fuch
imaginary purfuits, fuch wild and empty
notions, as were firft reprefented, fuch a
temper of mind, occupied in fanciful notions, will be found lefs abhorrent from
what is truly excellent, will be more eafily
converted into right and lively impreffions
of what is really defirable and eminent,
than that well-compacted, that proud and
fenfual difpofition, which is confirmed by
folid enjoyment, fuch as it is, by the real
fruits of worldly prudence, of temporal

acqui-

acquifitions, temporal gratifications, or temporal diftinction. The wild conceits and
fpeculations of the young difclofe 'a tafte
for fome fuperior kinds of pleafure, which
is fupported by the fancy before it finds a
truer foundation—to point out that foundation, is the ultimate defign of thefe remarks; that when the mind outgrows the
thoughtlefs fports of childhood, or the ideal
pageantries of youth, neceffity or appetite
may neither bend the neck to earth, nor furnifh objects to keep up through life an
eafier chace, which leaves us weary when
the day declines, ill-repaid by exercife
alone, or by a dead and worthlefs prize.

To kindle in the foul a purer flame,
whofe radiance may difpel the glooms of
life; to give the mind an object adequate to
its fublimeft fcope and comprehenfion ; to
cherifh regular and reafonable actions, calculated to an end confiftent, abfolute, and
unequivocal; to preclude thofe blank and
cheerlefs hours which harraffed appetite and
overworn invention, which difappointment
or fatiety, which uniformity or fullennefs

of

of temper, which the calms or clouds of life, muſt leave in thoſe who terminate their views upon the preſent ſcene, who take new colours from the ſhifting hues of all things round them, and fluctuate on all their changes; to lift the heart, and raiſe the front of man; ſhould be the care of tender relatives and ſkilful guides; of ſuch as cannot but deſire, that they, on whom they have entailed their weakneſs and their ſorrows, ſhould be partners alſo in their hopes or earth, and in their future glories.

To furniſh ſcenes analogous to thoſe which fancy trod before, but opened to the ſtedfaſt eyes of reaſon and of hope, revealed to calm and ſalutary ſpeculation, and enſured in their reverſion; to trace out proſpects far more raviſhing than all the pages of romance could feign, yet neither inacceſſible nor viſionary, but properly and truly ſuch as may concern and intereſt us, and may be our inheritance and our portion; to keep the pureſt faculties, the nobleſt energies of intellect, the powers and compaſs of the ſoul, exalted, and aſcendant, afcendant, elevated high above the tranfient and embarraffed fcene of temporal viciffitudes and exigencies; fhould be the proper aim of the Philofopher, and is the great prerogative of the

CHRISTIAN.

NUM-

## N U M B E R  XXV.

---

SATURDAY, *September* 1, 1787,

---

*Decipimur ſpecie.*

THERE are, I believe, no paths of literature ſo beſet with difficulties as definition and biography. Of difficulties unſurmounted in biography we have lamentable inſtances in thoſe adventurers who have attempted to write the life of Johnſon; and the errors of definition are ſufficiently apparent in thoſe, who have laboured to inſtruct the world wherein conſiſts true politeneſs.

From

From the writings of Lord Chefterfield
we collect, that politenefs confifts in the
namelefs trifles of an eafy carriage, an un-
embarraffed air, and a due portion of fu-
percilious effrontery, The Attainment of
thefe perfections is the grand object to
which the Son of many a fond and foolifh
parent is directed, from whofe conduct one
might reafonably fuppofe they thought
every accomplifhment, neceffary or ornamental to man, attainable through the
medium of the Taylor, the Hair-dreffer,
and the Dancing-mafter; referving only
for the mind fuch falutary precepts as may
tend to infpire pertnefs and infolent confidence.

In the Galateo of the *Archbifhop of
Benevento are contained all the rules which
are neceffary to introduce a perfon into
company, and to regulate his behaviour
when introduced. Yet I cannot but think
the plan of this, and every other treatife,
too much confined, which would inform
us, that it is the principal end of this qualification to fix the minutiæ of drefs, and

* Monfign. Giovanni de la Cafa.

reduce

reduce manners to a fyftem. He is fuppofed to have attained the fummit of politenefs, who can take an apparent intereft
in the concern of people for whom he
has no regard; be earneft in enquiries after
perfons for whofe welfare he is not folicitous; and difcipline his bow, his fmile,
and his tongue, to all rules of ftudied gri-
mace, and agreeable infipidity. Thus,
that politenefs of which we hear fo much,
the race which every toothlefs dotard has
run, and the goal to which every beardlefs
fool is haftening, is only an hypocritical
fhew of feelings we do not poffefs; an art
by which we conciliate the favour of
others to our own intereft.—The two characters which are generally contrafted
with each other, in order to fhew the perfection of politenefs, and the extreme of its
oppofite, are the Soldier and the Scholar:
The former is exhibited to us with all the
ornament of graceful manners and bodily
accomplifhments, with the advantages of
early intercourfe with the world, and the
profit of obfervation from foreign travel.
The advantages here enumerated will, I
fear,

fear, upon a nearer furvey of them, appear
vifionary and unfubftantial, and not fuch
as are likely in the end to juftify the hopes
of thofe who, in the great love for their
country, remove their fons from fchool
before they can have anfwered any end for
which they were fent thither; and produce them to the world before they can
have any fixed principle to be the guide of
their conduct. They make obfervations,
of which ignorance and wonder are the
fource; they form opinions in which
judgment has no fhare; they travel, and
he who fets out a Mummius is foolifhly
expected to return home a Cæfar. In
enumerating the difadvantages under which
the Scholar labours, we are reminded, that
a ftudious and fedentary life are too apt to
generate peevifh and morofe habits, the
bane of fociety, and the torment of their
own poffeffor. We are told, that the
Student, receiving no inpreffions but fuch
as books are likely to make, cannot apply
his obfervations to the ufage of common
life; that he forms Utopian opinions, and
is furprized to find they cannot be realized;

that

that he becomes jealous of the dignity of
literature, for which the world feems to
have too little refpect ; and that the life,
which was begun with the hopes of excel-
ling in thofe purfuits wherein he finds few
competitors, is at length concluded in the
difappointment of expected reputation ; or
the fcarce more fenfible gratification of
triumphs thinly attended, and applaufes
partially given. In fuch colours is the ftudious man painted to us, by our arbiters
of elegance, who, in their obliging zeal for
the regulation of our manners, confound
learning with pedantry ; and, under pretence of removing from us a trifling evil,
would rob us of a fubftantial good.

"Learning, fays Shenftone, like money,
" may be of fo bafe a coin, as to be utterly
" void of ufe ; or, if fterling, may require
" good management to make it ferve the
" purpofes of fenfe and happinefs." What
Shenftone has here with truth affirmed *may*
be, there are others who have ventured
with fome confidence to declare *muft* be.

True as it is, it would no doubt appear
a paradox to many, fhould any one affirm,

that

that the fureft method of attaining politenefs is to feek it through the medium of literature. We fhould have thought lefs of the politenefs of Cæfar, but for the author of his Commentaries. Chrichton would not have been, called the mirror of politenefs, merely for his fkill in the tournament, nor would " Granville the polite" have been the theme of Mr. Pope's fong, for his addrefs in entering a room. The truth is, we miftake a mental qualification for a bodily one. We expect politenefs to be conveyed to us with our coat from the taylor, or that we may extract it from the heel of a dancing-mafter, when in fact it is only to be obtained by cultivating the underftanding, and imbibing that fenfe of propriety in behaviour, with which the deportment of the body has but at beft a fecondary concern. I know not why it is, but from our mifinterpretation of the word, that politenefs, when applied to a virtuous action, immediately becomes ridiculous. Who would not fuppofe, the chaftity of the Roman General ironically commended, who fhould call that the politenefs of Scipio,

7

254 OLLA PODRIDA. N° 25.

pio, which others have called his conti-
nence?—Or would not the congregation of
a grave Divine be fomewhat furprized to
hear their preacher celebrating the politenefs of the good Samaritan? Yet thefe
acts are the fubftance of that virtue, to
whofe fhadow we compliment away our
rights and opinions, frequently our honefty, and fometimes our interefts.

" Politenefs," fays a good author of our
own time, " is nothing more than an ele-
" gant and concealed fpecies of flattery,
" tending to put the perfon to whom it is
" addreffed in good humour and refpect
" with himfelf."

It is rather, in my opinion, the badge of
an enlightened mind, and, if not a pofitive
virtue in itfelf, it is at leaft a teftimony
that its poffeffor has many qualifications
which are really fuch.—It lives in every
article of his conduct, and regulates his behaviour on every occafion, not according
to the whimfical and capricious rules of
fafhion, but according to fome fixed principles of judgement and propriety.—It prevents the impertinence of unfeafonable joking,

ing, it reftrains wit which might wound the feelings of another, and conciliates favour, not by " an elegant and concealed " flattery," but by a vifible inclination to oblige, which is dignified and undiffembled. To the acquifition of this rare quality fo much of enlightened underftanding is neceffary, that I cannot but confider every book in every good fcience, which tends to make us wifer, and of courfe better men, as a treatife on a more enlarged fyftem of politenefs, not excluding the experiments of Archimedes, or the elements of Euclid.—It is a juft obfervation of Shenftone, that a fool can neither eat, nor drink, nor ftand, nor walk, nor in fhort laugh, nor cry, nor take fnuff, like a man of fenfe.

NUMBER

# NUMBER XXVI.

---

SATURDAY, *September* 8, 1787.

---

WHEN I have had the good fortune to light upon any subject which has been relished by the nice discerning palate of the publick, it is my custom to try whether something more cannot be made of it : for having entered upon business with a moderate stock only in trade, it is expedient for me to husband it well, and to throw nothing away that can be used again. Being born with an antipathy to plagiarism, *I will be free to confess* (as gentlemen express it in the House of Commons)

mons) that I took the hint from my landlord of the Red Lion at Brentford; who,
when fome punch was called for, and there
was no more fruit in the houfe, was over-
heard to fay, in a gentle voice, to Mrs.
Bonnyface, " Betty, Ca'fn't give the old
" lemons t'other fqueeze?"

I have demonftrated, upon a former occafion—I fhould hope, to the fatisfaction of
every impartial perfon in Great Britain—
the manifold advantages accruing to the
community from the multiplication of
newfpapers among us. It has fince occurred to me, that fome directions might be
given, as to the beft method of reading a
newfpaper with profit and advantage. I
mean not, whether it fhould be read lon-
gitudinally, latitudinally, or tranfverfely;
though very great additions have been made
to fcience by experiments of this kind; but
how it may be rendered productive of reflections in different ways, which will prove
of real fervice in life.

I was not a little pleafed, the other day,
upon paying a vifit at the houfe of a perfon
of diftinction in the country, to find the

S                         family

family affembled round a large table, covered with maps, and globes, and books,
at the upper end of which fat a young lady
like a profeffor reading from the chair. In
her hand fhe held a newfpaper. Her father
told me, he had long accuftomed her, while
reading one of thofe vehicles of intelligence, to acquaint herfelf with the feveral
towns and countries mentioned, by turning
to the names in Salmon's *Gazetteer*, and
then finding them out upon the globe, or a
map; in which fhe was become fo great a
proficient, as to be at that time in truth
giving a lecture in geography to her younger
brothers and fifters. It was his farther intention, he faid, that from Campbell's
*Prefent State of Europe*, fhe fhould acquire
a fufficient knowledge of the hiftory of the
kingdoms around us, as well as our own,
to form an idea of their importance and interefts refpectively, and the relation each
bears to the reft. Verily, thought I to
myfelf, this is reading a newfpaper to fome
purpofe!

Children,

Children, very early in life, are eager for a fight of the newfpaper. By being called upon, in a free and eafy way, for fome little account of what is in it, they may be gradually brought to read with attention, and* to fix upon thofe articles which are moft worthy of attention; as alfo to remember what they have read, from one day to another, and put things together.

While we are in the world, we muft converfe with the world; and the converfation, in part, will turn on the news of the day. It is the firft fubject we begin upon; a general introduction to every thing elfe. All mankind, indeed, are our brethren, and we are interefted, or ought to be interefted, in their pleafures and their pains, their fufferings, or their deliverances, throughout the world. Accounts of thefe fhould produce in us fuitable emotions, which would tend to the exercife of different virtues, and the improvement of our tempers. We fhould accuftom ourfelves hereby to rejoice with thofe who do rejoice, and fympathife with thofe who mourn.

When

When any country is likely to become the theatre of remarkable events and revolutions (as, for inftance, Holland, at this prefent moment), it is worth one's while to refrefh one's memory with the hiftory of that country, its conftitution, and the changes it has heretofore undergone, the nature and difpofition of the people, &c.— a fort of knowledge which is fure to be called for. The man who makes himfelf perfect and correct in it, will gain credit, and give pleafure, in every company, into which it may happen to fall.

Whatever inftruction is reaped from hiftory, may be reaped from a newfpaper, which is the hiftory of the world for one day: It is the hiftory of that world in which we now live, and with which we are, confequently, more concerned than with thofe which have paffed away, and exift only in remembrance: though, to check us in our too fond love of it, we may confider, that the prefent likewife will foon be paft, and take its place in the repofitories of the dead.

There

There is a paſſage in the *Night Thoughts*, which I cannot reſiſt the temptation of tranſcribing, as it contains one of the moſt aſtoniſhing flights of the human imagination, upon this awful and important ſubject, the tranſient nature of all ſublunary things :

Nor man alone; his breathing buſt expires;
_His tomb is mortal; empires die; where, now,
The Roman, Greek? They ſtalk, an empty name!
Yet few regard them in this uſeful light,
Tho' half our learning is their epitaph.
When down thy vale, unlock'd by midnight thought,
That loves to wander in thy ſunleſs realms,
O *Death!* I ſtretch my view; what viſions riſe!
What triumphs! Toils imperial! Arts divine!
In wither'd laurels glide before my ſight!
What lengths of far-fam'd ages, billow'd high
With human agitation roll along
In unſubſtantial images of air !
The melancholy ghoſts of dead renown,
Whiſp'ring faint echoes of the world's applauſe,
With penitential aſpect, as they paſs,

All point at earth, and hifs at human pride,
The wifdom of the wife, and prancings of
the great.          ·    ·         NIGHT IX.

Accounts of the moft extraordinary events
in old time are now perufed by us with the
utmoft indifference.    With equal indifference will the hiftory of our own times be
perufed by our defcendants ; and a day is
coming, when all paft tranfactions will
appear in the fame light, thofe only ex-
cepted, by a confideration of which we
have been made wifer and better.

There are few, perhaps, by which we
may not become fo.

What nobler employment for the human
mind, than to trace the defigns of Providence in the rife and fall of empires ;   the
overthrow of one, and the eftablifhment of
another upon its ruins ! to watch diligently
the different fteps by which thefe changes
are effected ! to obferve the proceedings of
the great Ruler of the univerfe, always in
ftrict conformity to the rules with which
he himfelf has furnifhed us ! to behold
generals with their armies, and princes
with their people, executing *his* counfels
                                 while

while purfuing their own ! to view upon
the ftage of the world, thofe fcenes which
are continually fhifting, the different actors
appearing in fucceffion, and the gradual
progrefs of the drama, each incident tending to develope the plot, and bring on the
final cataftrophe !

In the midft of thefe fecular commotions,
thefe conflicts of contending nations, it is
ufeful to obferve the effects produced by
them on the ftate of religion upon the
earth ; while, among the powers of the
world, fome protect, and others perfecute ;
fome endeavour to maintain it in its old
forms, and others wifh to introduce new ;
all perhaps, more or lefs, aim at convert-
ing it into an engine of ftate, to ferve their
own purpofes, and to avail themfelves of
that influence which it muft always have
on the minds of men. Above and beyond
thefe human machinations, a difcerning
eye fees the controuling power of Heaven ;
Religion preferved amidft the tumultuous
fluctuations of politics ; and the Ark failing in fafety and fecurity on the waters
which threatened to overwhelm it.

When

When we read of the events taking place in our own country, the subjects become more interesting, and we are in danger of having our passions rouzed and fomented. Let us therefore be upon our guard, judging of nothing by first reports; but awaiting the calmer hour of reason preparing to decide on full information. For the prosperity of our country let us be thankful and grateful; in its adversity, sorrowful and penitental; ever careful to correct our own faults, before we censure those of others.

With respect to individuals and their concerns, examples (and they are not wanting among us) of piety, charity, generosity, and other virtues, should effectually stir us up to copy, to emulate, to surpass them; to join, so far as ability and opportunity will permit, in designs set on foot for the promotion of what is good, the discouragement and suppression of what is otherwise. And here, there is great choice: many such designs are on foot; and let those, who have talents for it, bring forward more. All are wanted.

The

The follies, vices, and confequent mi-
feries of multitudes, difplayed in a newfpaper, are fo many admonitions and warn-
ings, fo many beacons, continually burn-
ing, to turn others from the rocks on
which *they* have been fhipwrecked. What
more powerful diffuafive from fufpicion,
jealoufy, and anger, than the flory of one
friend murdered by another in a duel ?
What caution likely to be more effectual
againft gambling and profligacy, than the
mournful relation of an execution, or the
fate of a defpairing fuicide ? What finer
lecture on the neceffity of œconomy, than
an auction of eftates, houfes, and furniture,
at Skinner's, or Chriftie's ?—" Talk they
" of morals" ? There is no need of
Hutchenfon, Smith, or Paley. Only take
a newfpaper, and confider it well ; read it,
and it will inftruct thee, *Plenius et melius
Chryfippo et Crantore.*

A newfpaper is, among other things, a
regifter of mortality. Articles of this kind
fhould excite in our minds reflections fimilar to thofe made by one of my predecef-
fors,

fors, on a furvey of the tombs in Weftminfter Abbey. They are fo juft, beautiful,
and affecting, that my reader, I am fure,
will efteem himfelf under an obligation ·to
me for bringing them again into his remembrance, by clofing this paper with a
citation of them :

    " When I look upon the tombs of the
" great, every emotion of envy dies in
" me; when I read the epitaphs of the
" beautiful, every inordinate defire goes
" out ; when I meet with the grief of pa-
" rents upon a tomb-ftone, my heart melts
" with compaffion ; when I fee the tomb
" of the parents themfelves, I confider the
" vanity of grieving for thofe whom we
" muft quickly follow ; when I fee kings
" lying by thofe who depofed them, when
" I confider rival wits placed fide by fide,
" or the holy men that divide the world
" with their contefts and difputes, I reflect
" with forrow and aftonifhment on the lit-
" tle competitions, factions, and debates of
" mankind. When I read the feveral dates
" of the tombs, of fome that died yefter-
                               " day,

" day, and fome fix hundred years ago, I
" confider that great day when we fhall all
" of us'be contemporaries, and make our
" appearance together *.".

* Spectator, Vol I. No. 26.

Z.

NUM-

# NUMBER XXVII.

SATURDAY, *September* 15, 1787.

*Mores hominum multorum videt & urbes.*

HORACE.

The grown Boy, too tall for School,
With Travel finishes the Fool.

*Gay's Fables.*

WE are informed by Plutarch, that Lycurgus forbad the Spartans from visiting other countries, from an apprehension that they would contract foreign manners, relax their rigid discipline, and grow fond of a form of government different from their own. This law was the result

4                                                    of

of the moſt judicious policy, as the com-
pariſon made by a Spartan in the courſe of
his travels would neceſſarily have produced
diſaffečtion to his country, and averſion to
its eſtabliſhments. It was therefore the
deſign of the rigid legiſlator to confirm the
prejudices of his ſubjeċts, and to cheriſh
that intenſe flame of patriotiſm which afterwards blazed out in the moſt renowned exploits.

So propitious is the Britiſh government
to the rights of the people, ſo free is its
conſtitution, and ſo mild are its laws, that
the more intimate our acquaintance with
foreign ſtates is, the more reaſon we find
to confirm our predileċtion for the place of
our birth. Our legiſlature has no neceſſity,
like that of the Spartan Republick, to ſecure
the obedience of its ſubjeċts by making ignorance an engine of ſtate. But although
England may riſe ſuperior in the compari-
ſon with foreign countries, it is much to
be wiſhed, that its pre-eminence was more
frequently aſcertained by cool heads and
mature underſtanding; and that ſome check
was given to the general cuſtom of ſending
youths

youths abroad at too early an age. Innumerable inftances could be adduced to prove,
that, fo far from any folid advantages being
derived from the practice, it is generally pregnant with great and incurable
evils. As foon as boys are emancipated
from School, or have kept a few terms at
the Univerfity, they are fent to ramble
about the Continent. The critical and
highly improper age of nineteen or twenty
is ufually deftined for this purpofe. Their
curiofity is eager and indifcriminate; their
paffions warm and impetuous; their judgement merely beginning to dawn, and of
courfe inadequate to the juft comparifon
between what they have left at home, and
what they obferve abroad. It is vainly expected by their parents, that the authority
of their tutors will reftrain the fallies of
their fons, and confine their attention to
proper objects of improvement. But grant-
ing every tutor to be a Mentor, every pupil
is not a Telemachus. The gaiety, the follies, and the voluptuoufnefs of the Continent addrefs themfelves in fuch captivating
forms to the inclinations of youth, that
they

they foon become deaf to the calls of admonition. No longer confined by the fhackles of fcholaftick or parental reftraint, they launch out at once into the wide ocean of fafhionable indulgence. The only check which curbs the young gentleman with any force, is the father's threat, to withhold the neceffary remittances. The fon, however, expoftulates with fome plaufibility, and reprefents that his ftyle of living introduces him into the brilliant circles of the gay and great, among whom alone can be obtained the graces of polifhed behaviour, and the elegant attainments of genteel life. How much he has improved by fuch refined intercourfe is evident on his return home. He can boaft of having employed the moft fafhionable Taylor at Paris, of intriguing with fome celebrated Madame, and appearing before the Lieutenant de Police for a drunken fray. He may, perhaps, more than once have loft his money at the Ambaffador's card parties, fupped in the ftables at Chantilli, and been introduced to the Grand Monarque at Verfailles. The acquifitions he has made are fuch as muft

eftablifh

eftablifh his character, among thofe who
have never travelled, as a *virtuofo* and a *bon
vivant*. By great good fortune he may
have brought over a Paris watch, a coun-
terfeit Corregio, and a hogfhead of genuine
Champagne. But it is well if his mind be
not furnifhed with things more ufelefs than
thofe which he has collected for his pocket,
his drawing-room, and his cellar. He has,
perhaps, eftablifhed a kind of commercial
treaty with our polite Neighbours, and has
exchanged fimplicity for artifice, candour
for affectation, fteadinefs for frivolity, and
principle for libertinifm. If he has continued long among the votaries of fafhion,
gallantry, and wit, he muft be a perfect
Grandifon if he return not to his native
country in manners a monkey, in attainments a fciolift, and in religion a fceptic.

From the expedition of fome travellers,
we are not to conclude, that knowledge of
the world may be caught with a glance;
or, in other words, that they are geniufes
who " grafp a fyftem by intuition." They
might gain as much information if they
fkimmed over the Continent with a balloon.

The

The various places they fly through appear like the fhifting fcenes of a pantomime, which juft catch the eye, and obliterate the faint impreffions of each other. We are told of a noble Roman, who could re-collect all the articles that had been pur-chafed at an auction, and the names of the feveral buyers. The memory of our tra-vellers ought to be of equal capacity and retentivenefs, confidering the fhort time they allow themfelves for the infpection of curiofities.

The fact is, thefe birds of paffage con-fult more for their fame than their im-provement. To ride poft through Eu-rope is, in their opinion, an atchievement of no fmall glory. Like Powel, the cele-brated walker, their object is to go and re-turn in the fhorteft time poffible. It is not eafy to determine how they can more pro-fitably employ their whiffling activity than by commencing jockies, expreffes, or mail-coachmen.

Ignorance of the modern languages, and particularly the French, is a material ob-ftacle againft an Englifhman's reaping

the defired advantages from his travels. It
is a common cuftom to poftpone any application to them until a few months before
the grand tour is commenced. The fcholar vainly fuppofes that his own moderate
diligence, and his mafter's compendious
mode of teaching, will work wonders, by
making him a complete linguift. From a
flight knowledge of the cuftomary forms of
addrefs, and a few detached words, the
Fench language is fuppofed to be very
eafy. No allowance is made for the variety of the irregular verbs, the nice combi-
nation of particles, the peculiar turn of
fafhionable phrafes, and the propriety of
pronunciation. The great deficiencies in
all thefe particulars are abundantly apparent as foon as *Milord Anglois* lands on the
other fide of the channel. After venturing
to tell his friends, to whom he has letters
of recommendation, that he is *ravifhed* to
fee them, his converfation is at an end.
His contracted brow, faltering tongue, and
embarraffed air, difcover that he labours
with ideas which he wants words to exprefs.
Even the moft juft remarks, the moft bril-

liant

liant conceptions of wit, are fmothered ·in their birth. To fuch a diftreffing cafe, the obfervation of Horace will not apply—

" *Verbaque provifam rem non invita fequentur.*"

If he can arrive after much ftammering and hefitation at the arrangement of a fentence, it abounds with fuch blunders and anglicifms as require all the politenefs even of a Frenchman to excufe. Frequent attempts will without doubt produce fluency, and conftant care will fecure correctnefs; but the misfortune is, that the young traveller is employed by words, when his mind ought to be engaged with things. It is not lefs unfeafonable than ridiculous, that he fhould be perplexing himfelf with the diftinction between *femme fage* and *fage femme*, when he ought to be examining the amphitheatre at Nîmes, or the canal at Languedoc.

Ignorance of the languages is a great inducement to the Englifh to affociate together when abroad. The misfortune of this practice is, that they fpend their time in poifoning each other's minds with prejudices againft Foreigners of whom they

know little from perfonal experience, and
of whom they have not the laudable ambition of knowing more. Their more active
employments confift in fuch diverfion as
they have tranfplanted from home. They
game, play at cricket, and ride races. The
Frenchman grins a contemptuous fmile at
thefe exhibitions; and fhrewdly remarks,
that Monfieur John Bull travels more to
divert him than to improve himfelf. Rather than give occafion for this ridicule,
our young gentlemen had better remain at
home, upon their paternal eftates, and collect their knowledge of other countries
from Brydone's Tour, Moore's Travels, or
Kearfley's Guides.                    Q.

# NUMBER XXVIII.

---

SATURDAY, *September* 22, 1787.

---

*To the* AUTHOR *of the ·*
OLLA PODRIDA.

—— *When I did hear*
*The motley fool thus moral on the time,*
*My lungs began to crow like Chanticleer,*
*That fools ſhould be ſo deep contemplative ;*
*And I did laugh, ſans intermiſſion,*
*An hour by his dial.*                        SHAKSPEARE.

S I R,

MANY people indulge themſelves in
the too frequent introduction of
what they are pleaſed to call moral ſenti-
ment into their converſation. Whilſt they
are thus endeavouring, by the trite precepts

T 3                                          of

of dull and fententious gravity, to inculcate the leffons of virtue, they oftentimes put common fenfe to the blufh, and generally make that ridiculous which they wifh fhould appear amiable.——I fhall endeavour to illuftrate my obfervation, by prefenting you with a fhort fketch of a relation, with whom as a boy of fixteen, in the intervals of fchool vacation, I have occafionally fpent a week or two.

Mr. Solomon Hatchpenny is an uncle of mine, who being moft part of the week a Tobacconift in the Borough, is on Saturday and Sunday a Country Gentleman, dwelling four miles from London. He is a very good fort of man, goes to Church every Sunday, where he fhuts his eyes, but declares he never fleeps ; has three wigs, pays every one his own, and keeps a four-wheel chaife. His Country-houfe, which has been greatly improved fince he bought it, by the addition of a bow-window and a bench, ftands within three yards of the road ; and, as he is unwilling to difplay lefs grandeur than his neighbours, he has laid out his ground, confifting of a garden of forty-four fquare feet,

feet, with that tafte by which the family
of the Hatchpennys has ever been diftinguifhed. It contains a bafon with the ufual
compliment of two artificial fwans (which
my Uncle affures me when he bought them
were as white as alabafter) and a gravel
walk, each end of which is guarded by a
pafteboard Grenadier. In the middle of his
walk is a dial, from which the morning
fun is excluded by the Grenadier's Cap, and
upon his houfe are three weathercocks, each
pointing a different way. He generally
takes an opportunity to prove to his guefts,
that his Sentinels are as exact reprefentations of live Soldiers as can come from the
hands of a Painter and Glazier, by informing them, that a Sparrow having fettled
on the fhoulder of one of them, he heard
a child, who on paffing exclaimed, " *Look,*
" *Mama, the Corporal has caught a Bird.*"
This circumftance is to Mr. Hatchpenny a
fource of heart-felt fatisfaction : He attri-
butes the miftake of the child to his own
fkill in furnifhing the deceit. He is pleafed with the idea that he has given proof
of his underftanding in the very inftance

T 4 which

which declares his want of it.—He is an
example of happinefs arifing from ignorance, which, contrary to the lot of every
other fpecies of happinefs, no man envies
in another, and no man wifhes for himfelf.
Excufe my obfervations, and permit me to
proceed. I am informed, that my uncle
Solomon is a politician at the club, and
amongft his neighbours a wit; that he has
been known to utter fhrewd jokes upon
the miniftry, to quote profane rhymes from
Poor Robin's Almanack, and to indulge
himfelf in all thofe fanciful relaxations of
the mind to which every good citizen is
entitled, not inconfiftent with his trade,
his underftanding, or his tafte. It is,
however, his peculiar ftudy to hide every
little fally of his wit from my obfervation,
and confine all converfation uttered within
my hearing to morality; the eflence of
which, according to his opinion, confifts
in gravity and a long face. This gravity
I never knew my uncle relax but once, and
then it was in order to tell me, that a
gentleman, who came to folicit his vote for
a lecturefhip in the Borough, had abfolutely won him over from an oppofite party by
paying a pretty compliment to his country-
box,

box, which he was pleafed to denominate
*Tully's Tufculum*.  I took that opportunity
of making an attempt (an aukward one,  I
fuppofe, becaufe it was not underftood) to
pay the fame kind of pretty compliment
to his Tobacco warehoufes, which I begged leave to chriften *Tully's Offices*.  My
uncle and I fometimes traverfe what he
calls his *premiffes*, which without much
bodily exertion may be accomplifhed in
fomething lefs than four minutes and a
half, but, according to our plan of proceeding, it generally confumes near an hour.
The leaden fwans (which by a very claffical metamorphofis are now become black)
are the innocent caufes of much impatience to me ; they delay us in our journey
round the premiffes, while they furnifh
my uncle with an opportunity to difplay
his difcoveries in morality, and to defcant
upon the rapid flight of time :—" *Not*
" *feven years ago* (fays he) *till next twenty*
" *fourth of July, did I buy thofe birds of*
" *Mr. William Dreadnought, Plumber, in*
" *Fenchurch ftreet:—They were then as*
" *pretty bits of fowl as ever were turned out*

" *of*

" *of a fhop.*——*Learn from this, Nephew,*
" *that the ftrongeft things will decay; and*
" *confider the rate at which time paffes.*"——
" *Yes, Sir*—*Sixty minutes to the hour, twelve*
" *hours to the day, and twelve months to the*
" *year.*" — " *Right, Nephew, calendar*
".*months.*" It was fettled calendar months,
and we proceeded.—The weathercocks
only delayed us while we obferved, that
they were happily emblematical of the
mutability of human events ; that one of
them wanted greafing, and that a high
ftation was no exemption from the inconveniencies and wants of life.   We now
reached the gravel-walk, where I ventured, with all the gravity of fpeech and
countenance I could fummon, to hint my
doubts as to the propriety of his having
fixed up in his garden two objects
which might poffibly deceive fome people into an opinion that they were men,
when in fact they were not fo.   But, to
qualify my obfervation, I thought it prudent to throw in fomething which he
might underftand as a compliment, and
induce him to open his whole mind upon

fo momentous a fubject. I told him that a petty tradefman might pleafe himfelf in deceptions of that kind, without the danger of mifleading any one; but that I thought it rather improper in him, to whofe motions the world turned the eye of obfervation, who had been known never to refufe the payment of a bill at fight, who had never indulged himfelf beyond a Chelfea bun, and a glafs of Herefordfhire cyder on a Sunday, and who was undoubtedly the firft tobacconift in the whole ftreet.— I faw my uncle was pleafed with my argument—He attempted rather to excufe than defend what he had done. He confeffed it was a deceit, yet he hoped a harmlefs one, that, when he was younger than he now is, he had facrificed fomething to tafte; he remembered, to fay the truth, when he firft put them up, that his confcience rather mifgave him, but, to quiet his apprehenfions, he had written upon each of their gun-locks, " *To prevent miftakes, Thefe are not real men, but only fham ones.*

"W. D. FECIT."

I was

I was fully fatisfied with a fubject on which whatever arguments I might have conceived, my countenance would not fuffer me to declare.

I left the houfe of this moral Philpfopher a few days ago with many good injunctions, which he who remembers may at leaft be entertained, if not edified. In the laft conference which I enjoyed with him, he delivered himfelf to me in fomething like the following words:—" *My* " *dear Nephew, I have your intereft very* " *much at heart, and fhould be glad to fee you* " *as well in the world as myfelf. You are* " *certainly much improved, and can now, I* " *dare fay, have a juft value for a few max-* "*ims, which I fhall lay down for the regula-* " *tion of your conduct. Truft me, I know a* " *little of thefe matters, Old heads, and Old* " *fhoulders ; and though I fay it that fhoud'nt* " *fay it, I can tell a fix from a nine, as* " *well as thofe that make fuch a flourifh with* " *their wife pates, and empty pockets.—With* " *regard to your ftudies, your mafter can pro-* " *bably direct you as well as I can ; I only* " *advife you, above all things, don't puzzle*

I                                            " *your*

" your brains, and waſte your labour in writ-
" ing verſes. I never knew a fellow that
" had a ſhilling in his pocket write verſes.
" You may as well expect to pick up gold under
" the pump at Aldgate as to get any thing by
" it. I caution you againſt reading novels
" and elegies, and all bad books. There is
" a book I have heard, which pretends to
" prove, that there is no ſuch thing as time :
" But this is all a ſham, and I tell you there is,
" and very precious it is. He who loſes it had
" better loſe his dinner; and to him who makes
" the moſt of it 'tis as money in the ſtocks.
" There's a little money for you, go, and
" mind your book, and don't ride jackaſſes on
" Sundays; for the poor beaſts ſhould have a
" day's reſt, and you'll only tear your beſt
" breeches, and incur the diſpleaſure of your
" maſter."

I ſhall here finiſh my account of Mr.
Hatchpenny, only informing you, that he
is a married man ; and, ſhould the patience
of your readers not be quite exhauſted, I
ſhall take ſome opportunity of giving you a
little inſight into the character of my Aunt.
She is not a moraliſt of the ſame kind
exactly

exactly as her hufband, and will not therefore afford an example of the fame fpecies
of folly. They fhine in different fpheres,
and are upon moſt confiderations better
afunder.——Tell your readers, if you pleafe,
leſt they fhould not have obſerved it, that
the dull folemnity of proverbial wifdom,
which confifts in "fhreds of fentences,"
and remnants of moral fayings, being applicable to all occafions, and acceffible to
all underſtandings, is no proof of wifdom
or honefty. And let thofe, who are fatif-
fied with fuch kind of knowledge, improve
their fyſtem, by adding to it fome excellent treatiſes from the repofitory of Mr.
Newbery, *adapted to the meaneſt capacities,*
" price twopence halfpenny, adorned with
" cuts."

I am, Sir, yours, &c.

SOCRATES IN EMBRIO.

NUMBER

NUMBER XXIX.

SATURDAY, *September* 29, 1787.

*— Ridiculum acri*
*Fortius et melius plerumque fecat res.* HOR.

IT is wifely ordained by the laws of England, that *the perfon of the Monarch is facred*; as alfo, that *the King can do no wrong.* The meaning of this laft maxim I take to be, that, if wrong fhould happen at any time to be done, the blame is to be laid upon the adminiftration, and not upon the King.

A friend,

A friend, fome years ago, took me into
the Houfe of Commons, to attend the debates upon the opening of a Seffion ; when
an honourable gentleman made fo free with
the Speech, which I had but juft before
heard moft gracefully pronounced by his
Majefty from the throne, that my hair
ftood an end, and I was all over in a cold
fweat; till, towards the clofe of his ora-
tion, he relieved and reftored me, by mentioning, in a parenthefis, that the fpeech
was always confidered, in that affembly, as
the fpeech of the *Minifter*.

Sheltering myfelf, therefore, under this
diftinction, I cannot refrain from offering a
few remaks on a late production, pregnant, as many are of opinion, with much
mifchief to the community. The reader
fees that I mean, *A Proclamation for the
encouragement of piety and virtue, and for
preventing and punifhing of vice, profanenefs,
and immorality.*

That the fcheme propofed fhould be carried into execution, does not indeed feem
probable. When we confider how long
vice, profanenefs, and immorality, have
been

been increafing among us, what a powerful party they have formed, how much
fafhion is on their fide, and how very,
ftrong the tide runs, the attempt may be
thought to refemble that of the man, who
endeavoured to ftop the Thames at London
bridge, with his *hat*; unlefs the rich and
the great would fet the example.

I have always been an enemy to *pains
and penalties.* The word *punifhment* is a bad
word; and the thing itfelf is much worfe.
When once it begins, the wifeft man living cannot tell where it will end, or what
will become of our liberties. For as the
fheep-ftealer faid, " If a gentleman cannot
" kill his own mutton, without being
" hanged for it, I fhould be glad to know
" what we have got by the Revolution."
In fhort, one muft be without a nefe, not
to fmell fomething here of arbitrary power.

The idea of a Sunday, unenlivened by a
little innocent *play*, is a very dull and
dreary one. I know a family in town, that
has made the experiment. The confequence was, that before nine in the evening, the members of it found themfelves fo

U                              crofs,

crofs, peevifh, and out of temper, that
had it not been for an early fupper, and a
glafs of good wine, they could not have
gone to bed in chriftian charity with each
other.

But much more diftrefsful ftill was the
cafe of a lady, whofe hufband, being in the
commiffion, had lent his affiftance to fupprefs gaming on a Sunday, in a neighbouring public houfe. It ftruck him that
cards on that day, in a private houfe,
might not, juft then, be quite fo proper;
and he ventured to hint as much to his
lady. She had always apprehended the
Gofpel to have been defigned for the *poor*;
and was aftonifhed to find that any thing
in the Proclamation could apply to perfons
of her rank in life. " The party was
" made, and what could be done?"—A
thought, however, luckily occurred; and
when the company was affembled, after an
apology fuitable to the occafion, inftead
of the card tables, fhe introduced the entertainment of *Catches and Glees.* The thing
took mightily, and was judged a pretty
variety. Otherwife, a difappointment of
such

fuch a nature, fpreading, as it muſt have done, like an electrical fhock, through all the polite circles, might have bred bad blood, and produced a general infurrection. It fares with religion as with a fhuttlecock, which is ſtricken from one to another, and refts with none. The rich apprehend it to have been defigned for the poor; and the poor, in their turn, think it calculated chiefly for the rich. An old acquaintance of mine, who omitted no opportunity of doing good, difcourfed with the barber who fhaved him on his manner of fpending the Sabbath (which was not quite as it fhould be), and the neceffity of his having more religion than at prefent he feemed to be poffeffed of. The barber proceeding in his work of lathering, replied, that he thought he had *tolerably well for a barber*; as, in his apprehenfion, one third of the religion, neceffary to fave a gentleman, would do to fave a barber.

I mention this, becaufe I have received a letter of confiderable length, praying redrefs of grievances, from a perfon who lets lodgings in Broad St. Giles's. He

fpeaks

fpeaks of a very fnug and comfortable neighbourhood there, which is likely to be broken up, and difperfed, by the Proclamation, and nobody can well tell why.

He himfelf holds twenty houfes by leafe, which are let out, ready-furnifhed. Matters are conducted in a manner fo perfectly œconomical, that though there is no more than one bed in each room, there are ufually two or three, and fometimes even four occupiers of that one room and bed. That the furniture is of an expenfive and luxurious kind, no one can fay; as it confifts only of a ftump bedftead, a flock bed, a pair of fheets (frequently only one fheet), a blanket or two, a chair or two (generally without backs), and a grate, but moftly without fhovel, tongs, and poker. The fheets are ufually marked with the name of the owner; and the words, *ftop thief!* are added, for private reafons.

In two adjoining allies are forty more houfes, let out in like fort to inhabitants, in number 400, confifting of whores, pickpockets, footpads, houfebreakers, and thieves of every defcription, from all quarters

ters of the town. But what then ? *They* muſt have lodgings, as well as other people ; and, if they were to be in the ſtreet all night, it would be dangerous for the reſt of his Majeſty's ſubjects to paſs. To avoid ſuſpicion, the houſes are continually lighted, and kept open all night ; and to ſhew that hypocriſy has no place there, what uſed to be practiſed only in private at *midnight*, is now practiſed in public at *midday*.

To accommodate the *poor*, there are twopenny lodging-houſes. One man, in particular, makes up, every night, thirty-five beds, and takes in men and women, at twopence or threepence a night ; but if a man and woman come in together, he receives one ſhilling a night for the two.

No ſociety can be under better regulations than this is. Thus, for inſtance, when a poſtitute has decoyed a man, and robbed him, the miſtreſs of the houſe has half the pay and the plunder : and if one of theſe ladies intrude upon that beat and walk, which another regards as her *exclu-*

U 3                                 *five*

*five right*, the matter is determined, as much greater matters are, by a *battle*.

Nor can there be reaſon to fear, that this ſociety ſhould ever become ſo numerous, as to be any annoyance to the publick; ſince care is taken, that a ſufficient number is hanged, every ſeſſion, to maintain a balance; and ſome rooms are always reſerved for the reception of the dead bodies, which are brought back after execution, to their old lodgings, till they can be otherwiſe diſpoſed of.

Such is the ſubſtance of my friend's letter, which he deſires may be communicated, through the channel of my paper, to his countrymen, that they may know what they have to expect from the preſent ſyſtem of deſpotiſm; when a few neighbours cannot live peaceably together, without being diſturbed, and hunted out, by *Proclamations*. He hopes all honeſt men will join with him in a petition for *the removal of evil counſellors*; and concludes with the old Britiſh axiom, *My houſe is my caſtle*; under no dread, as it ſhould ſeem, of the retort courteous once made to ſuch a declaration

ration by a magiſtrate in Oxford, of arbitrary principles ; " Then, Sir, the *caſtle*
ſhall be your *houſe*."

It is not eaſy to eſtimate the loſs which
the community at large will ſuſtain by the
diſſolution of this worthy neighbourhood.
For if a gentleman be robbed of his watch,
it muſt be replaced by another : if his
portmanteau be ſtolen, he muſt buy new
cloaths and linen : if his houſe be broken
open, and ſtripped of its furniture, he
muſt apply to the upholſterer : if he be
beaten and wounded, to the ſurgeon : nay,
ſhould he be even killed, the undertaker and
the ſexton will be the better for it : and if
the uſual quantity of gin be not conſumed,
ruin muſt ſeize on thoſe who vend it.
Trade muſt ſtagnate. Thus incontroverti-
bly doth it appear, that *private vices* (if indeed they may be called vices) *are public
benefits.*

I ſay, " if they may be called vices ;"
becauſe I do not ſee why, ſhould we ſo
pleaſe, they may not be called virtues.
The nature of things in themſelves is nothing ; our *opinion* of them is all : and if

our

our opinion alters, the names of things
fhould alter with it. Indeed, they do, and
muft do fo. Thus, when two gentlemen
go out with piftols, and fhoot each other
through the head, or the heart, it is no
more than *an affair of honour*: when one
feduces the wife or the daughter of another,
it is merely an *attachment*: and to cheat a
man out of his eftate, is only to *pluck a
pigeon*. In the neighbourhood above de-
fcribed, the *nomenclature* is much farther
advanced, and has nearly attained perfection. They have a language peculiar to
themfelves, in which when they relate
their tranfactions, they may have been
doing what is perfectly juft and right, for
any thing we can tell to the contrary, fince
the words are not to be found in any dic-
tionary but their own.

Here then, as fome will think, is a
more expeditious way of preventing vice,
than by proclamation ; and, what is much
to be defired, of doing it without infliction
of punifhment, by the fole and fimple expedient of voting *vice* to be *virtue*.

The

The fcheme is plaufible; but, I muft confefs, I have my doubts. If we once vote vice to be virtue, I am afraid, that, by a neceffity of nature, *virtue*, per contra, muft become *vice*; and fo we fhall but be where we were: there will ftill be vice in the world.

When the welfare of his country is con- cerned, every man loves to be a little bit of a projector. On going deeper into the fubjeᴄt, I think I have hit upon a plan, which will make root and branch work of it, and do the bufinefs effectually.

That the effect may ceafe, the caufe muft be removed. Now, what is the caufe of vice? Moft undoubtedly, the *law:* for, were there no law, there could be no tranf- greffion. Abolifh then, at once, the ufe of all law, human and divine. I grant the ftep a bold one, requiring a minifter of firmnefs and refolution to take it; but when once taken, the advantages will be many and great.

In the firft place, vice will, at one ftroke, be extirpated from the face of the earth;

for

for when a man has no law but his own will, we may defy him to do any thing illegal. Never truft to *moral* impoffibility, where *phyfical* is to be had.

- Secondly, it will put an end to the expence and trouble of law fuits; and (as equity would fall with law) to all tedious and everlafting fuits in Chancery, fo much and fo long complained of.

Thirdly, it will be a faving to the nation of one tenth of the produce of all the lands in England and Ireland; and confequently put a ftop to the ravages of the *White-boys* and *Right-boys*, in this latter kingdom, as well as all difputes between minifters and their parifhioners, in the former; fince, as there would be no more occafion for reading prayers and preaching, the payment of tithes muft, of courfe, be at an end.

Fourthly, it will procure a perpetual holiday for the gentlemen of either robe, who, in future, will have nothing to do, but to hunt, fhoot, and play at cards. The fame may be faid, refpecting the members of both houfes of parliament.

Fifthly,

Fifthly, it will make Sunday as cheerful a day, as any day of the week.

Laftly, it will remove all odium from the magiftrates who have granted a Licence to the *Dog and Duck*.

Such are the conveniences that would attend the execution of my plan ; and after confidering the fubject on all fides, for fix hours, in my elbow-chair, I proteft, I cannot think of any one inconvenience, to fet againft them ; nor can I devife any method likely to be fo effectual in redreffing the grievances occafioned by the Proclamation to the *fubject*.

It remains only, that I mention one, which may poffibly be occafioned by it to the *Crown*; and which, indeed, I might not have thought of, but for the vifit paid me, as I was clofing this paper, by an honeft Farmer—" So, Robin (faid I to "him), rare news from London ! The " King is to be ferved *now* only by good " and virtuous courtiers !"—" Ah, Lord " have mercy upon me, Sir (replied Robin),

" God

" God blefs his Majefty, and grant him
" long to reign ! But I am afraid as how
" he will be fometimes obliged to HELP
" HIMSELF."

Z.

NUMBER

# NUMBER XXX.

SATURDAY, *October* 6, 1787.

*Difficilis, querulus.* Hor.

MY good Sir—What's your name?
Your Englifh name, I mean; for
neither I, nor the Parfon of our parifh, know
what to make of your *Olla Podrida.* If it
were Latin, Greek, or Hebrew, the Doctor fays he could give a good account of it:
but you Oxford and Cambridge wits (efpecially the latter) have lately got a habit
of introducing half a page of Italian, French,
or Spanifh (untranflated) into your works,
though it is five hundred to one, not one

I                                                    iii

in five hundred underſtands thoſe languages. Well; but this *Olla Podrida*—my wife thinks it means a powdering-tub, in which tongues or hams, beef and pork, are ſalted and preſerved againſt Chriſtmas; as letters and eſſays, wife ſayings and apophthegms, ſprinkled with your attic ſalt, are preſerved in your miſcellany for our winter evenings' amuſement. This, however, is my firſt complaint; " That I don't know what to make of the title of your work."

My ſecond ſubjeɛt of complaint is this : my Grandſon, who is at the Univerſity, and is your acquaintance, ſent me word that there was a new *Paper*, lately come out, which every body read ; and, as a *Paper*, now-a-days, means a News-paper, I deſired him to ſend it me down : but, what was my diſappointment, when I found not a word of News in it ! Not a robbery or a murder ; not a forgery, a rape, or an elope-ment; nor, what I more wiſhed for, not a letter or even a paragraph to abuſe the Mi-niſtry ; to reprobate the Commutation-tax or the Commercial Treaty ; nor any pro-phetic calculation to ſooth my fancy ; to

demon-

demonftrate the defperate ftate of this devoted Nation, and prove that we are tottering on the verge of annihilation—This,
I fay, is the object of my *fecond* complaint.

But, *thirdly,* as your paper reaches us on
a Monday morning, I comforted myfelf, at
beft, with the hopes of entertaining my
wife and daughter with fomething cheerful
and facetious, after a rigid and gloomy obfervance of the Sabbath, in confequence of
his Majefty's Proclamation (for we have
now no card-affembly at our houfe, only
half a dozen old Ladies who join us at tea;
and take a folemn retrofpect of every fin
and tranfgreffion, which their neighbours,
not themfelves, have been guilty of, the
preceding week)—But even in this hope I
was fruftrated; for I had juft put on my
fpectacles, and read a few lines in your
paper, when the exceffive poignancy of
your wit—[*Here my modefty obliges me to
omit a few words of compliment.*]

This then is my *third,* but not my *laft,*
complaint; for complaining and grumbling
is the only comfort I have in this world;
and this, Sir, though a very old and trite
topic,

topic, is the fubject of this letter. My reafons for troubling you I will beg leave to
explain.

My Grandfon, whom I mentioned, fpent
a good part of his puerile years under my
roof; and has taken it into his head that I
am a very learned man (though I never had
a learned education) from a cuftom I have
got of retiring from my family, many
hours in the day, to my ftudy, where I
was always found, when called to dinner,
with a great folio before me ; and at the
inftant any one came to the door, I was
juft then turning over my leaf ; and, as if I
were in the midft of my fubject, told them
I would come immediately, and ordered
them to fit down to dinner. This had the
air of a profound ftudent and deep meditation ; when perhaps I was only weighing
my guineas, calculating my intereft money,
or my next half year's rent ; or, at beft,
conning over fome of the oppofition papers
(every one of which I take in) as food for
my querulous difpofition.

As

As I am unwilling however to difcover to my family that I made no ufe of my pompous library, and read nothing but Newfpapers; and to oblige my Grandfon aforefaid, I have fent you a paragraph from an old author, in folio, well known in his day, which graphically defcribes the *Dif-eafe* (for I am confcious it is a difeafe) under which I myfelf and many of my neighbours labour—that of grumbling and complaining, from morning till night, from mere habit and indulgence, or for want of fomething elfe to fay.

The moft important fubject of our Complaint, is the ftate of publick affairs; for which, perhaps, there *may* be fome reafon: But, though I have lived threefcore years in the world (from the days of Sir Robert Walpole to Mr. Pitt's Adminiftration), I never knew it otherwife.

I have been fettled thefe thirty years on my eftate in the country: But neither I nor my tenant, in all that fpace of time, have experienced one fruitful feafon; or hardly one feafonable day—We have been plagued with too much rain or too much

X                        dry

dry weather : fometimes the froft has been too fevere ; fometimes the winter too mild, and the corn too rank—In a bad harveft we dreaded a famine—In a plentiful year we expected to be ruined by the *low* price of grain.

I go to the coffee-houfe at our next mar-ket town—I hear the fame grumbling and complaints. In the winter, " Blefs me, " Sir, how could you ride over the Down " this cold wind ? In fummer, are not " you melted with heat, or choked with " duft ? In autumn, I am told it is a *nafty* " fog—In the fpring the north-eaft winds " will be the death of us."—Thus that beautiful variety, which Nature has fo wifely contrived for the benefit of the whole creation, is made the conftant fub-ject of murmuring and difcontent.

I have a very good neighbour, who is an invalid ; he has a fmall pudding made for himfelf, by a particular receipt, every day of his life ; I frequently dine with him ; he grumbles the whole dinner-time about his pudding, but he eats it all ; and his wife tells me he has done the fame

thefe

thefe feven-years; but fhe never knew him leave a morfel of his pudding for the children.

If you were to fee us with one or two more of our fociable neighbours, over a bowl of punch, or a tankard of ale, you would conpare us to the children of Ifrael, weeping by the waters of Babylon, in their captivity—fuch a fhaking of the head, and lifting-up of hands; fuch gloomy prefages and difmal inuendos! " Well, I fay no- " thing; but if this weather continues, God " fend we may be all alive this day three " months !"

But every one muft fee daily inftances of fuch people, who complain from a mere habit of complaining; and make their friends uneafy, and ftrangers merry, by murmuring at evils that do not exift, and repining at grievances which they do not really feel.

But this is fufficient to introduce the character, which I mentioned, drawn by Bifhop Hall; and which proves, that the fame evil has exifted from the days of So-lomon king of Ifrael, to thofe of one who

X 2  fancied

fancied himfelf as wife as Solomon, James
the firft, King of England—" It is naught,
" it is naught, faith the buyer; but when
" he is gone away then he boafteth."
Thus it was in the days of Solomon: In
James's reign, Dr. Jofeph Hall gives this
account of

## The MALCONTENT.

" He is neither well, full nor fafting;
" and though he abound with Complaints,
" yet nothing diflikes him but the prefent;
" for what he condems while it *was*, once
" paft, he magnifies and ftrives to recall it
" out of the jaws of time. What he hath
" he feeth not, his eyes are fo taken up
" with what he wants; and what he fees,
" he careth not for, becaufe he cares fo
" much for that which is not.

" When his friend carves him the beft
" morfel, he murmurs, ' That it is an
" happy feaft wherein each one may cut
" for himfelf.' When a prefent is fent
" him, he afks, ' Is *this* all? And what no
" *better!*' and fo accepts it, as if he would
" have

3

" have his friend know how much *he* is
" bound to him for vouchfafing to receive
" it.

" It is hard to entertain him with a pro-
" portionable gift. If nothing, he cries
" out of thankfulnefs; if little, that he is
" bafely regarded; if much, he exclaims
" of flattery, and expectation of a large
" requital. Every blefling hath fomething
" to difparage and diftafte it: children
" bring cares; fingle life is wild and foli-
" tary: Eminence is envious; retirednefs
" obfcure, wealth burthenfome, mediocrity
" contemptible. He never is tied to efteem
" or pronounce according to reafon. Some
" things he *muſt* diflike, he knows not
" *wherefore*, but he likes them not; and
" fometimes rather than not cenfure, he
" will accufe a man of virtue—Every thing
" he meddleth with he either *findeth* im-
" perfect, or *maketh* fo."

I am, Sir, yours, &c.

B.

X 3

# NUMBER XXXI.

---

SATURDAY, *October* 13, 1787.

---

*Ubi per focordiam, vires, tempus, ingenium,*
*defluxere, naturæ infirmitas accufatur.*

SALLUST.

IT is the common topick of complaint amongſt Moraliſts, that Mankind is a vain and idle Race; that we aim at attainments for the enjoyment of which our nature has not qualified us; and that we ſuffer thoſe abilities which are entruſted to us, to be frittered away in mean employments, or to be eaten up by the ruſt of idleneſs.

2

nefs.—It is thus that, in general denuncia-
tions againft human depravity, all perfons
at times indulge themfelves ; fome gratify
their pride by noticing the frequency of
thofe failings, from which they confider
themfelves as exempt ; and others find an
opportunity of excufing their favourite follies, by placing thofe frailties to the account
of human weaknefs, which are due to their
wilful negleƈt of right, or their headftrong
perfeverance in error. They make little
hafte to repent of thofe crimes, in the par-
ticipation of which they fee mankind fo
univerfally engaged, and fondly imagine
that, in the general defeƈtion from virtue,
the frailties of an individual are of fmall
account. While we are thus willing to
impofe upon ourfelves, apologifing for our
vices by arguments which only prove the
general tendency to be vicious, every man
contributes fomething to the increafe of
that evil, of whofe bulk and growth every
man continues to complain.

Succefsfully have the labours of thofe
wife men been expended, who, by their
zeal for the welfare of mankind, and their

accurate knowledge of human nature, have
been able to furnish the world with precepts
of morality, which from their brevity are
eafily committed to memory; and from
their good fenfe and propriety convey their
meaning to the minds of the moft unen-
lightened. The leffons they have left are
intended to inftruct us in the duties we owe
to Religion and Society; to excite us to virtue, by ftigmatizing vice; and to check the
pride of man, by reminding him of his limited capacity. Yet the benefits thus con-
ferred upon us are too frequently abufed
by cunning and defigning men. The arguments which were intended to reftrain
extravagance, are wielded for the defence
of covetoufnefs, and each extreme of vice
excufes itfelf by attacking its oppofite.
The fon of avarice, thriving in his mifery,
has abundance of maxims, which he pours
forth without relenting upon the votaries of
heedlefs gaiety and unfruitful diffipation,
who are content in return with urging the
infufficiency of wealth, and the folly of
thofe who feek it. Various are the apophthegms by which Philofophy is enabled to
                                    condemn

condemn ignorance; and ignorance is quite fatisfied with itfelf in ridiculing the vanity of human wifdom.

An attempt has lately been made to ref-cue the lower orders of people from their extreme of ignorance, by the appropriating one day in the week to the inftilling of re-ligious knowledge into the minds of the young, and exciting in them a defire of in-tellectual improvement. For the profecu-tion of this plan, fermons have been preach-ed, fubfcriptions opened, and every mode of perfuafion and encouragement been adopted, that wealth, learning, and bene-volence could fuggeft. Yet to thefe lauda-ble defigns there have been found many enemies. Armed with the fallacies of logic, they have with fufficient ingenuity demon-ftrated to us, that the ignorance of the multitude is a public good; that to the " hewers of wood, and drawers of water," learning is injurious, or unprofitable; and that the hufbandman and the mechanick have other objects on which their attention is more properly engaged than wifdom and fcience. All the arguments which were

firft

firſt produced to reſtrain the arrogance of
the *overwiſe*, are made uſe of to reconcile
ignorance to its darkneſs, and to hide the
light from thoſe who, having never enjoyed
it, are little ſolicitous to acquire what they
have ſo long been able to live without.
'Many of theſe reaſoners have anſwered
ſome private end.  Some have diſcovered
the ſkill with which they can argue in a
bad cauſe ; and others, under the ſanction
of ſuch reaſoning, have indulged their avarice, by ſparing their money.  But let him
who would prove, that ignorance is either
a bleſſing or a virtue, remember, that he
advances the poſition of a wicked man,
which he muſt ſupport with the arguments
of a fool.  The ſame reaſon which informs
us, that to make ſuch an attempt is unjuſt,
adds the comfortable aſſurance, that to ſuc-
ceed in it is impoſſible.

There is, perhaps, ſome cauſe of complaint againſt the people themſelves,  who
appear too little anxious for their own
welfare, who neglect to catch the opportunity which preſents itſelf of emerging
from their darkneſs, and by their inattention

tion thwart the defigns of thofe who intereft themfelves in their behalf, or render
the fuccefs of them partial and limited.
There is, I believe, in the minds of the
lower clafs, an almoft univerfal prevalence
of inclination to receive inftruction from
one of their own order. They choofe rather to deal with the fame perfon for their
cabbage-nets and their chriftianity, their
pickled pork and their prayers, than receive
their religious information from the hands
of him whom learning has made more able
to inform them, and who is more likely to
be honeft, if it be only that he has lefs
temptation to be otherwife. They have no
value for what they do not underftand, and
no inclination to underftand what thofe
have taught them is unprofitable, whofe
intereft it is to flatter their ignorance, and
indulge their prejudices.

There are many perfons whom betrayed
confidence, or difappointed expectation,
have driven from the world, to indulge in
private their ill-founded refentment againft
the Sons of Men. They leave the haunts
and " the bufy hum of Men," to brood in
folitude

folitude over their difcontents ; they continue to live in the ftudious and conftant
neglect of the duties they owe to fociety,
and endeavour, by perferverance, to per-
fuade themfelves they can defpife Mankind.
Not unfrequently to this compound of
wickednefs and folly do they give the title
of Philofophy. It is the peculiar tendency
of fuch Philofophers to take upon themfelves the office of fcrutinizing the fprings
of human action, with no other intent than
to difcover their imperfections. They
employ their penetration with invidious
accuracy and malicious eagernefs, to detect
vices which were hidden from the world ;
they exhibit them with the oftentation of a
difcovery ; they exaggerate them with every
art and expedient their invention can fuggeft, or their fagacity approve.—This is
the philofophical fyftem of many a hermit.
But be the fuccefs of fuch men's labours
what it may, they will be fo unfortunate as
to find Virtue enough in the world to defeat their hopes, and Happinefs fufficient
to enfure their mifery.

Upon

Upon the whole, perhaps, the Philofophy of a Reclufe has little claim to our encouragement. That which is fometimes unfriendly, and generally ufelefs, is feldom commendable. The knowledge which is cultivated, and not called into ufe for the publick good, confers little benefit upon man ; and the Religion which is exercifed in fecret, with whatever fervour of devotion, lofes much of its efficacy when it hides fuch an example from the world.

It is too often that thefe reclufe and fplenetic Philofophers, whom I have mentioned, denounce their comprehenfive anathemas againft the Sons of Men, and condemn the whole fpecies for the crime of an individual.

It is, perhaps, a dangerous indulgence, by which we ever allow ourfelves to declaim in general terms againft the depravity of human nature, and to give way to the too frequent tendency of our hearts, when we are irritated by particular offences to fay in our hafte, " All Men are Liars."

It

It might not be amifs for thofe who are folicitous to fupply their neighbours on every occafion with the appofite precepts of proverbial wifdom, to be cautious left they become more defirous of indulging their fpleen than their benevolence ; more fond of correcting vice, than reforming it ; and left they find more pleafure in the detection of evil, than in the bringing good to light.

# NUMBER XXXII.

SATURDAY, *October* 20, 1787.

*The short and simple annals of the poor.*   GRAY.

## To the AUTHOR of the OLLA PODRIDA.

SIR,

If you should esteem this little tale worth a place in your amusing publication, you will probably hear more from him, who is yours,          A WANDERER.

BEING on a tour to the North, I was one evening arrested in my progress at the entrance of a small Hamlet, by breaking the fore-wheel of my phaeton. This

320 OLLA PODRIDA. N° 32.

This accident rendering it impracticable for me to proceed to the next town, from which I was now sixteen miles distant, I directed my steps to a small cottage, at the door of which, in a woodbine arbor, sat a man of about sixty, who was solacing himself with a pipe. In the front of his house was affixed a small board, which I conceived to contain an intimation, that travellers might there be accommodated. Addressing myself therefore to the old man, I requested his assistance, which he readily granted.; but on my mentioning an intention of remaining at his house all night, he regretted that it was not in his power to receive me, and the more so, as there was no inn in the village.—It was not till now that I discovered my error concerning the board over the door, which contained a notification, that there was taught that useful art, of which, if we credit Mrs. Baddeley's Memoirs, a certain noble Lord was so grossly ignorant. In short, my friend proved to be the Schoolmaster, and probably Secretary, to the Hamlet. Affairs were in this situation when the Vicar made his appearance.

ance. He was one of the moſt venerable figures I had ever ſeen; his time-ſilvered locks ſhaded his temple, whilſt the lines of misfortune were, alas! but too viſible in his countenance. Time had ſoftened, but could not efface them.—On ſeeing my broken equipage, he addreſſed me; and when he began to ſpeak, his countenance was illumined by a ſmile.—" I preſume, " Sir, ſaid he, that the accident you have " juſt experienced will render it impoſſible " for you to proceed. Should that be the " caſe, you will be much diſtreſſed for " lodgings, the place affording no accom- " modations for travellers, as my pariſhion- " ers are neither *willing* nor *able* to ſupport " an alehouſe; and as we have few tra- " vellers, we have little need of one : But " if you will accept the beſt accommoda- " tion my cottage affords, it is much at " your ſervice."—After expreſſing the ſenſe I entertained of his goodneſs, I joyfully ac- cepted ſo deſirable an offer.—As we entered the hamlet, the ſun was gilding with his departing beams the village ſpire, whilſt a gentle breeze refreſhed the weary hinds,

Y who,

who, feated beneath the venerable oaks that
overfhadowed their cottages, were repofing
themfelves after the labours of the day, and
liftening attentively to the tale of an old
Soldier, who, like myfelf, had wandered
thus far, and was now diftreffed for a lodging. He had been in feveral actions, in
one of which he had loft a leg; and was
now, like many other brave fellows,

——"Doom'd to beg
 " His bitter bread thro' realms his valor fav'd."

My kind hoft invited me to join the
crowd, and liften to his tale. With this
requeft I readily complied. No fooner did
we make our appearance, than I attracted
the attention of every one. The appearance of a ftranger in a hamlet, two hundred miles from the capital, is generally
productive of furprife; and every one ex-
amines the new comer with the moft attentive obfervation.——So wholly did my arrival engrofs the villagers, that the Veteran
was obliged to defer the continuation of his
narrative, till their curiofity fhould be gratified.——Every one there took an opportunity

nity of teftifying the good will they bore
my venerable hoft, by offering him a feat
on the grafs. The good man and myfelf
were foon feated, and the brave Veteran
refumed his narrative, in the following
words :—" After," continued he, " I had
" been intoxicated, I was carried before a
" juftice, who was intimate with the cap-
" tain, at whofe requeft he attefted me
" before I had fufficiently recovered my
" fenfes to fee the danger I was encoun-
" tering. In the morning, when I came
" to myfelf, I found I was in cuftody of
" three or four foldiers, who, after telling
" me what had happened, in fpite of all I
" could fay, carried me to the next town,
" without permitting me to take leave
" of one of my neighbours. When they
" reached the town it was market-day, and
" I faw feveral of the people from our vil-
" lage, who were all forry to hear what
" had happened, and endeavoured to pro-
" cure my releafe, but in vain. After
" taking an affecting leave of my neigh-
" bours, I was marched to Portfmouth,
" and there, together with an hundred

" more,

" more, embarked for the coaft of Africa.
" During the voyage, moft of our number
" died, or became fo enfeebled by ficknefs
" as to make them unfit for fervice. This
" was owing partly to the climate, partly
" to the want of water, and to confinement
" in the fhip. When we reached the coaft
" of Africa, we were landed, and experienc-
" ed every poffible cruelty from our offi-
" cers. At length, however, a man of
" war arrived, who had loft feveral mari-
" ners in a late action; and I, with fome
" others, was fent on board to ferve in
" that ftation. Soon after we put to fea,
" we fell in with a French man of war.
" In the action I loft my leg, and was near
" being thrown overboard; but the hu-
" manity of the chaplain preferved my life,
" and on my return to England procured
" my difcharge. I applied for the Chelfea
" bounty; but it was refufed me, becaufe
" I loft my limb when acting as a marine:
" and, as I was not a regular marine, I was
" not entitled to any protection from the
" Admiralty. Therefore I am reduced to
" live on the good will of thofe who pity
                                    " my

" my misfortunes. To be fure, mine is a
" hard lot ; but the King does not know it,
" or (God blefs his Majefty !) he is too good
" to let thofe ftarve who have fought his
" battles."

The village clock now ftriking eight,
the worthy Vicar rofe, and, flipping fomething into the old man's hand, defired me
to follow him. At our departure, the
Villagers promifed to take care of the old
man. We returned the farewell civilities
of the ruftics, and directed our fteps to the
vicarage. It was fmall, with a thatched
roof. The front was entirely covered with
woodbine and honeyfuckle, which ftrongly
fcented the circumambient air. A grove
of ancient oaks, that furrounded the houfe,
caft a folemn fhade over, and preferved the
verdure of the adjacent lawn, through the
midft of which ran a fmall brook, that
gently murmured as it flowed. This, together with the bleating of the fheep, the
lowing of the herds, the village murmurs,
and the diftant barkings of the trufty curs,
who were now entering on their office as
guardians of the hamlet, formed a concert,

Y 3

at leaft equal to that in Tottenham-court-
road.   On entering the wicket, we were
met by a little girl of fix years old.   Her
drefs was fimple, but elegant ; and her appearance fuch as fpoke her deftined for a
higher fphere.   As foon as fhe had informed her grandfather that fupper was ready,
fhe dropped a courtefy, and retired.   I delayed not a moment to congratulate the
good old man on poffefling fo great a trea-
fure,   He replied, but with a figh ; and we
entered the houfe, where every thing was
diftinguifhed by an air of elegant fimplicity
that furprifed me.   On our entrance, he
introduced me to his wife ; a woman turned
of forty, who ftill poffeffed great remains
of beauty, and had much the appearance
of a woman of fafhion.   She received me
with eafy politenefs, and regretted that fhe
had it not in her power to entertain me
better.   I requefted her not to diftrefs me
with unneceffary apologies, and we fat down
to fupper.   The little angel, who welcomed
us at the door, now feating herfelf oppofite
to me, offered me an opportunity of contemplating one of the fineft faces I had ever
beheld,

beheld. My worthy hoft, obferving how much I was ftruck with her appearance, directed my attention to a picture which hung over the mantle. It was a ftriking likenefs of my little neighbour, only on a larger fcale.—That, Sir, faid he, is Harriet's mother. Do you not think there is a vaft refemblance? To this I affented; when the old man put up a prayer to Heaven, that fhe might refemble her mother in every thing but her unhappy fate. He then ftarted another topick of converfation, without gratifying the curiofity he had excited concerning the fate of Harriet's mother; for whom I already felt myfelf much interefted.—Her tale, however, fhall be the fubject of a future paper. X·

NUMBER

------

SATURDAY, *October* 27, 1787.

------

*To the* AUTHOR *of the*
OLLA PODRIDA.

SIR,

I HAVE often beheld with concern the fhameful condition of many churches in England; and I may venture to fay, that the ruinous ftate in which they are fuffered to continue, is one caufe of the want of real piety in thofe who attend them. *They* muft have a large ftock of religion in their hearts, who can preferve

any

any fpirit of devotion in fome of thefe fa-
bricks, where there is frequently nothing
to be feen, or heard, which can fix the attention, or raife the mind to heaven. The
Romanifts adorn their churches with every
thing which can make them to appear
grand, folemn, and like what is called the
Houfe of God. Their mufic and finging
are fine; and all things in their fervices and
ceremonies confpire to raife their devotion.

I was led to this fubject by a late excur-
fion into the country, to a village not
twenty-five miles from London. The
houfes were much fcattered about, and
appeared beggarly ; but within fight of the
church there flood a gentleman's feat,
which was laid out with all the elegance
that could be beftowed upon the houfe and
grounds. The church-yard joined to the
park. Having furveyed every thing there,
it being Sunday, I went into the church ; to
which one miferable bell, much like a fmall
porridge-pot, called half a dozen people,
which number comprehended the congregation. The church-yard itfelf was low
and wet; a broken gate the entrance ; a
few

few fmall wooden tombs and an old yew-
tree the only ornaments. The infide of the
church anfwered the outfide ; the walls
green with damp ; a few broken benches ;
with pieces of mats, dirty and very ragged ;
the ftairs to the pulpit half worn away ;
the communion-table ftood upon three legs ;
the rails worm-eaten, and half gone. The
*Minifter* of this noble edifice was anfwera-
ble to it, in drefs and manners. Having
entered the church, he made the beft of
his way to the chancel, where he changed
his wig ; put on a dirty, iron-moulded,
ragged furplice ; and, after a fhort angry
dialogue with the clerk, entered his defk,
and began immediately without looking
into the book. He read as if he had ten
other churches to ferve that day, at as
many miles diftance from each other. The
clerk fang a melancholy folo ; neither tune
nor words of which I ever heard before.
Then followed a fhort, confufed, hurried
difcourfe ; after this the fmall congregation
departed ; which had confifted of a gentleman and his family from the diftance of
about a mile and half, and two old men,
who

who conftantly attended for fixpence a piece, given by that family. The door was then fhut, till the next Sunday came round.

Thefe are literally and truly facts : and that many other country churches are no better, either within or without, nor better ferved or attended, every body who has gone through the fmaller villages in England muft know. In fome of the moft admired parts of our admired country, in the neighbourhood of the capital, in parifhes frequented by people of fortune, and where perhaps three or four noble families attend divine fervice every Sunday in the fummer feafon, the churches are fuffered, year after year, to be in a condition, in which not one of thofe families would fuffer the worft room in their houfe to continue for a week.

This deplorable ftate of our churches fhews, I think, the ftate of piety amongft us more than any fingle circumftance, and has an effect upon the minds of young perfons which is very difcouraging. A wretched, cold, damp building, far removed

moved often from' all habitable dwellings; within fight of which few people of confequence care to live ; made the receptacle of the dead ; vifited by the living only once a week ; and then endangering the health of thofe who vifit it,—do we wonder that people are glad to be difmiffed from fuch a place, where nothing but horror and melancholy ftrike their eyes and their thoughts ? Nor can the fineft difcourfe from the pulpit difpel the gloom : and the pfalm-finging in moft country churches is far from contributing towards this falutary end.

Who can expect, that the young and gay will prefer this fcene to the pleafures of the world ? It is not in general to be expected. Would but the rich and great in every village, who lavifh fums of money on their own perfons, furniture, houfes, grounds, &c. &c.—would they but beftow a little of it towards making the Houfe of God, if not equal with their own habitations, at leaft decent and chearful, and fuch as may be entered fafely and without fear; very great indeed would be the effect on multi-

multitudes ! It is difficult to conceive how a fmall portion of a large income can be expended more to the credit of the donor, or to the benefit of his neighbours.

We naturally call to mind, upon this occafion, the uneafinefs felt and expreffed by the royal prophet, on confidering the magnificence of his own houfe, and the little or no care taken of the Ark of God. And if we refleĉt ferioufly on the *neceffity* of having places confecrated to facred pur-pofes, and the *importance* of their being kept up with due reverence, two other remarkable paffages in Holy Writ will occur to every thinking perfon. When the fecond temple was built, and adorned by order of king Artaxerxes, we find Ezra addreffing himfelf to heaven in thefe words; " Bleffed be the Lord God of our " fathers, who has put fuch a thing as this " into the king's heart, to beautify the " Houfe of the Lord." And we cannot but admire the wifdom of the Jews ; who when afking of our Lord a favour for the Centurion, fay, " He loveth our nation,

" and

" and hath built us a fynagogue."    Then
the Saviour went with them.

I am, Sir,

Your obedient humble fervant,

*A Friend to Decency in Religious Worſhip.*

THE obfervations made by my correfpondent are, I fear, but too juft; and I
moſt readily embrace the opportunity of
recommending them to the confideration of
all whom they may concern.

The inhabitants of moſt country pariſhes
are prevented by their poverty from doing
much in matters of this kind.  The neceffary repairs are often a fufficient burden.
Opulent families ſhould therefore ſtep forward, and take upon them the articles of
ornament and beauty, or at leaſt convenience and comfort.  They themfelves
would be the firſt to enjoy the advantages ;
of which it may not, furely, be accounted
the leaſt, to be faved from the neceffity of
bluſhing, when foreigners, or perfons of a
different perfuafion, behold the wretched
condition of the church by them frequented.  A few good examples could not fail of
being

being followed; and fafhion, in this particular, might foon be put on the fide of re-ligion.

Indeed, unlefs the nobility and gentry fhall be pleafed to lend their affiftance, from having bad churches, we fhall come to have none at all. Many of them were built about the fame time ; and about the fame time, if not well looked to, will be falling : and it is eafier to fupport, than to build.

It may be queftioned, whether the Go-thick form, though fo venerable for its an-tiquity, do not itfelf occafion fome of the inconveniences above lamented. A fmaller and more compact room would often con-tain the congregation; and the fervice might be performed in it with more eafe and bene-fit both to the fpeaker and the hearer. It would be lefs fubject to damp and cold, and .at the fame time more light and cheerful. For notwithftanding the celebrated line of Milton, there is no natural connection be-tween darknefs and religion, which is the fource of joy and comfort, of light and

4                                          life,

life, to the human heart, and fhould difpel gloom and melancholy, wherever it comes.

Towards the promotion of this defirable end, a due performance of pfalmody could not fail greatly to contribute, as it was moft undoubtedly intended to do. At prefent, in many country churches, it is either difmal, or ridiculous; and our people are frequently induced to fall off to other religious affemblies, by the fuperior melody to be heard in them. There is hope, however, of fome reformation among us in this part of divine worfhip; as many worthy clergymen have turned their thoughts this way, and felected proper tunes and proper words for the purpofe. But whoever wifhes to fee this matter thoroughly difcuffed, and a proper plan propofed, muft confult the fenfible and excellent pamphlet lately publifhed by Dr. Vincent on the fubject.

Z,

# NUMBER XXXIV.

---

SATURDAY, *November* 3, 1787.

---

*To the* A U T H O R *of the*
OLLA PODRIDA.

*Fungar vice Cotis.*      HOR.

S I R,

WHEN you commenced your career, as a periodical editor, you enumerated with a minutenefs of detail the various ingredients of which your Farrago was to be compofed. Having ever efteemed a difcuffion of the merits of literary compofitions a very pleafing and profitable exercife

Z          of

of the judgment, with great fatisfaction I perceived that criticifm formed no inconfiderable part of your defign. In your earlier numbers, my wifhes were gratified by feveral judicious ftrictures on particular works of fome ancient and modern writers. But lately, whether deeming fuch fpeculations unworthy of your attention, or catching the momentary but virtuous phrenzy of reformation, you have devoted your Lucubrations to objects, to which his Majefty's moft gracious Proclamation, and the exertions of thofe intelligent magiftrates, the juftices, might be directed, with equal propriety, and perhaps with as great a probability of fuccefs.

I mean not to reprehend your co-operative induftry, but am defirous only of recalling to the recollection of your readers, that criticifm was included in your original plan ; and that the fubject of this Letter, though of a different complexion from fome of your recent numbers, is not contradictory to the general tenor of your defign.

It

It is not my intention to trouble either you or your readers with remarks on any voluminous compofition of eminent writers, or fcrupuloufly to balance the nice difcriminations of varying commentators: No, Sir, mine is a virgin-theme, as yet untouched by the rude hand of criticifm ; and unreftrained by the galling fhackles of prefcriptive method. And, perhaps, my efforts may not be unattended with fome advantage immediately to yourfelf, as the compofitions to which I allude have commonly been diffufed through periodical channels. Thefe compofitions are thofe narrations of blended fiction and fentiment, which, too inconfiderable from their fize to fwell into circulatory duodecimos, affume the general humble denomination of TALES, and are diftinguifhed by the epithets *tender, pathetic, fentimental, founded on fact,* &c. &c.

As Ariftotle deduced his Rules from the great Originals who preceded him, it fhall be my province to follow fo illuftrious an example, and in this primary effay to inculcate fome general precepts, and not

to

to point out in detail or extract individual excellences which are profusely scattered though the ample labours of writers of this description.

It is essential to a Tale that it should be tender, for who is there that would not desire for his Works the precious balm of a sigh or a tear, rather than that they should excite the applause of a smile or the boisterous acclamation of laughter?

It should not abound too much in incident, lest the curiosity be excited as much as the finer feelings.

The opening of a Tale should be abrupt, and the author should commonly profess that his knowledge of it had arisen from some unforeseen accident. This saves the trouble of a long introduction, and brings the author and reader fairly at once into the subject. A piece of butter on a torn leaf, the being benighted on a long journey, the traveller's horse losing a shoe, have been such hacknied expedients that I cannot possibly approve their repetition. The introduction of the mail-coach is however a new and fortunate epoch; and I

doubt

doubt not of its being fpeedily adopted by feveral writers in every variation of fracture, until the whole ftock of cafualties be exhaufted.

The principal incident fhould not be extravagant, but be fome common occurrence, that it may come home to the bofoms of a great number. A tender fair-one feduced by her lover—a dutiful fon turned out of doors by an unnatural father—a marriage of love and inclination thwarted by unfeeling parents—and all common events of a fimilar nature, are admirable topics.

So much for the plot or ground-work, in which at intervals fhould be interfperfed inferior circumftances, pathetic if poffible; but the more minute they are, the greater will be their effect. A dog—a cow lowing for its calf—a weeping willow—a withered oak—an old woman—thin grey hairs on a human head—and the like, may certainly be introduced with great fuccefs.

The diction may be allowed to be generally unequal, but fhould unqueftionably be florid and elevated at thofe intervals of

Z 3                    the

the narration where such embellishments may be requisite. Horace's prohibition of the "*purpurei panni*" must be totally disregarded.

Exclamations should never be used without the most absolute necessity. They are a species of affront on the feelings of a reader, who throws down the book with indignation when he is *informed* at what passages he is to be affected. *Alas!* has had its day, and must now submit in its turn to the common chance of worldly revolutions. Indeed, it would be scarcely noticed, were not the mark of interjection *!* commonly annexed to it.—Dashes are more striking and pathetic—and are besides a very neat addition of typographical ornament.

In respect to Epithets, great caution is indispensable. The sun is ever *golden*, the moon ever *silver:* the sea is *azure*, and the meadow *verdant:* the foliage of the trees is commonly *green*, except in the sombre or dark-pathetic, when the autumnal tinge greatly enhances the pathos.

Mythology and Allegory must be introduced with circumspection. The *darts* of *Cupid,*

*Cupid*, the *fires* of *ambition*, the *warmth* of *love*, the *coldnefs* of *difdain*, from their general acceptation, may be ufed without danger.

Allufions derived from Natural Philofophy are more novel and brilliant—the *electrical fhock* of *paffion*, the *vibration* of *reciprocal feelings*, and all phrafes of the fame caft, if the reader be a young lady at a boarding-fchool, or a young gentleman behind a counter, tend at once to dazzle and furprize.

To infinuate or even to directly advance a coincidence between the Hero or Heroine, and any relative accompanying circumftance, is wonderfully efficacious, but is a felicity, though frequently attempted, not always attained by the moft eminent authors. The following inftances may probably exemplify my meaning :—*In one corner of the field was a venerable elm, bare at the bottom, with its top fcantily crowned with leaves, which formed no inappofite fimilitude of the venerable owner, verging to the grave by a gradual and natural decay*—this is of the latter kind—in the direct fpecies may

be

be claffed fuch paffages, as, *the lovely Maria, cherifhed by the tender care of a parent, delighted to contemplate the fragile and fragrant woodbine twining its flender folds around the fupporting poplar.*

Though at firft fight it may appear inconfiderable, it is really material to affign, appropriate, and characteriftic names and places; *Caffander*, *Cleora*, and all the lift of Romantic or Hiftoric appellations, have been long exploded, and invention is now freely permitted to create and to apply. The name of the Hero fhould therefore excite refpect by a due arrangement of harmonious and fonorous letters; and that of the Heroine fhould melt into liquid foftnefs. Titles of amiable perfonages fhould gently flow: fuch as are intended to create difguft, fhould hoarfely rumble.

Place is far from being an unimportant confideration in the texture of tales.—To introduce the reader to an amiable pair, fitting by a good coal-fire, is a minute but unfentimental circumftance. I would always therefore recommend a bower, which, though not common in real, is very convenient

venient in fictitious gardens—but left it might be miftaken for one of the lath edifices fo frequent under this denomination in the vicinity of London, it fhould likewife be covered with honeyfuckle or jafmin, *whofe truant fprigs the Heroine's gentle hand may be fuppofed to have conducted along the convex trellis.*

The Denouement of a Tale muft be fimple if the principal incident be fo. Yet it will admit endlefs variations, and in all cafes, where the author is in the leaft degree embarraffed, a Fragment is a never-failing expedient—and here I cannot but commend the great convenience of thofe intervals which occur in periodical publications; for by them an author is enabled to drop his narrative all at once, and to leave his reader for a week in an agreeable ftate of fufpence and expectation.

Morality, though not effential, is a pretty ornament to a Tale; yet it fhould be fparingly adopted. I have ever greatly admired the infinuation which authors of this defcription fo delicately convey refpecting the conjugal fidelity of their married heroines;

for

for we are univerfally informed, that the boys are the very pictures of their fathers, and that the girls have all the graces of their mothers.

Such, Sir, are fome of the opinions I have formed on this fubject, which I have thrown together without order or connection; and if from them the rifing generation of tale-writers may cull any ufeful or improving hints, my ambition will be gratified : If *you* imagine that they may contribute to the amufement of the publick, they are very much at your fervice. A. M.

NUMBER

# NUMBER XXXV.

SATURDAY, *November* 10, 1787.

*Ille ego qui quondam——*

SIR,

A Correfpondent, who may or may not have engaged the attention of your readers, once more addreffes you. My laft letter to you, which contained an account of Mr. Hatchpenny, contained likewife my promife to give you fome infight into the character of his wife. I fhall therefore proceed in my plan without farther ceremony, notwithftanding that my correfpondence with you has procured me, among my fchoolfellows, the title of " *The Sucking So-* " *crates.*"

Mrs.

Mrs. Hatchpenny is that fort of woman, which the kindnefs, or the farcafm of the world (I am at a lofs to fay which) calls a managing Houfewife. Being rather limited in her ideas of human capacity, fhe confiders it as the fum total of every virtue *to make things go as far as they can*, and the perfection of accomplifhments to keep her houfe clean. Her refinements in œconomy are the general topics of her converfation, and fhe triumphs in defying her neighbours to fay they ever faw a fpeck of dirt upon her hearth, or a chair out of its proper place.

Nor long ago I heard her informing a company, that fhe never hired a man-fervant unlefs he could whiftle. When her audience were ftaring at each other with looks of eager enquiry, fhe added, " when he goes to draw the beer, I conftantly attend him to the top of the cellar-ftairs, and infift upon his whiftling all the time he remains below :" concluding naturally enough, that the fame mouth cannot whiftle and drink at the fame time.

My

My Aunt makes her Solomon and me
fcrape our feet twenty times a day; and
every Saturday night we are compelled to
go up ftairs without our fhoes, becaufe the
houfe has been wafhed, and Molly has
fomething elfe to do, befides *fcrubbing after
us for ever.*

Notwithftanding her attention to œconomy, fhe is fond of fine clothes, or, as fhe
calls it, " *looking like other people* ;" to ac-
complifh which, being now about eleven
years paft her meridian, and weighing
about twenty-three ftone avoirdupoife, fhe
dreffes herfelf in white, with a pink fafh,
and a proper affortment of pink ribbons. If
you have ever been fo fortunate, gentle
reader, as to catch an *Aurora borealis* in
the *via lactea*, you cannot be at a lofs for a
fimile to which you may liken the Heroine
of my hiftory.

The converfation of my Aunt, particularly when fhe *looks like other people*, has
fomething in it not perhaps very peculiar,
yet not altogether unworthy of notice.
She is what I have heard in the Borough
called, *a fine-fpoken Gentlewoman.* By
which

which I am led to conceive their fine fpeaking confifts in volubility of utterance, and
a readinefs in the vulgar tongue. Her
fpeeches, however, are full of animated
matter, and rhetorical figure, and delivered in a tone of voice much like that of
Caius Gracchus without his pitch-pipe.—
She talks of " *giving the hydra-head of*
" *fafhion a rap on the knuckles* ;" and, when
fhe wants a fimile, generally has recourfe
to a fugar-loaf, a roll of pig-tail, or the
Monument; fometimes however obferving,
that the coaches rattle by her door like *any
thing.*

Thus her ftyle is ornamented with the
beft flowers of rhetoric, fimiles, and metaphors; fimiles which, by a peculiar felicity, convey no ideas of fimilitude; and
metaphors which illuftrate nothing but
their own confufion.

- My Aunt has many amiable qualities.
Her fidelity to Solomon is unimpeached,
and invincible. She is conftant in her attendance at Church, unlefs perchance fhe
has received a card of information, that
Mrs. Deputy Peppercorn will wait on Mrs.

2                                    Hatch-

Hatchpenny to dinner on Monday. In this cafe fhe prudently ftays at home, whips up five fyllabubs when there will be only four at dinner, returns her card of compliments, and waits with impatience to fee Mrs. Peppercorn. The good lady has a juft claim to the title of compaffionate. She cannot bear thofe vile people who drive oxen through the ftreets of London, and *cut the poor creters about the legs till they look enough to make one fick.* But compaffion, which confifts only in words, does not content her. She gives in charity to a poor boy every week a penny, contriving within the feven days to fend him at leaft on fourteen errands. My Aunt contents herfelf with the idea that no one can fay fhe is uncharitable. I have fomewhere heard of an ingenious Philofopher, who turned his fhirt, and obferved with the fame fpirit of contentment and fatisfaction, " *What a comfort there is in clean linen !*"

Mrs. Hatchpenny was fo kind as to take me with her, on Saturday laft, to a tea-drinking party, at Brompton, to which my uncle Solomon was invited; but the

wind

wind being in the eaſt, and ſtocks low, he fancied he had a cold, and ſtayed at home. As we went by appointment *early*, we had diſcuſſed ſome weighty points before the tea entered. We had already learnt, that Miſs Primroſe gave fifteen ſhillings a yard for her apron, and that ſhe bought it from the ſhop at the corner of Juniper-ſtreet. Captain Makeweight had bruiſed his ſide by a fall in the Artillery ground, his ſword getting between his legs, and thereby laying him ſprawling. Mr. Titus Oats, a country couſin, had loſt his turnips by the fly—Miſs Tallboy had ſprained her ancle, by climbing an apple-tree—Mrs. Poſſet had been at the Hackney aſſembly ; and to be ſure Miſs Cardanium was the belle of the place, till ſhe began dancing, and then ſhe moved for all the world like a raw militia-man to the quick march—Or, ſaid the lady of the houſe, with a good-humoured ſmile, like an elephant upon hot bricks— Or (added my Aunt) like St. Paul's upon four wheels. The tea now arrived, and between the rattling of the cups, we had only time to fling in an obſervation or two

like

like the chorus of a Greek play, when the perfons of the dialogue are taking breath. We paffed a few ftrictures upon the widow Scramble's (fourth) marriage; and after the removal of the tea-table, and a fhort review of our abfent neighbour's conduct, a general converfation took place, each addreffing the perfon who fat upon the neareft chair. My Aunt in the mean time could not help glancing firft at the apron which had created a former converfation, and then at her own, being confcious that fhe had given two and twenty fhillings a yard for *every inch* of her's—Unfortunately, no one afked the price of it, and fhe found herfelf under the difagreeable neceffity of informing the company, unfolicited, that fhe bought it at the fame time when Mr. Hatchpenny fined for fheriff;—which is now feven years, come next Lord Mayor. My Aunt then took occafion to defcant upon the convenient fituation of their fhop in the Borough; to do the bufinefs of which, fhe obferved with fome emphafis, " *they were obliged to keep four journeymen, peck and perch all the*

A a *year*

*year round, one day with another.*—Happily I was at hand to explain to the company, which I did with great pleafure, that the words *peck* and *perch* (a favourite mataphor with my Aunt) were an allufion to the inhabitant of a bird-cage, and meant nothing more than board and lodging.

"How do you like your neighbours the Hatchpennys?" faid Mifs Primrofe, in a whifper to the lady of the houfe.—"They are monftroufly entertaining," faid the other.—A dialogue of a curious nature then commenced, in which it was remarkable, that the one regularly began a fentence, and the other as regularly finifhed it. "As for him (faid the firft) he's a churlifh old fool, with all the qualities of a bear"—"except his dancing," returned the other.—"She's a great œconomift, I hear"—"Yes, in every thing but her fpeech."—"She's the envy of her neighbourhood, for her great prudence,"—"and her green pickles."—"Her reputation, and her gown, are ever without fpot"—"The one becaufe fhe's fo unreafonably ugly, and the other becaufe

fhe

ſhe takes ſuch excellent care of it." "She's
very nimble at cards"—"and, never having
been detected in cheating, may be ſaid to
have had a perpetual run of good luck."—
How far this dialogue proceeded, I know
not, for our candle and lanthern now called
us to the peaceful abode of my Uncle,
whom, upon our return, we found, contrary
to all the rules of domeſtick felicity, ſitting
with one foot upon the hearth, and a bottle
by his ſide, which I ſtrongly ſuſpect to have
contained ſome of the right Herefordſhire.
Upon our entrance, the poſition of the foot
was quickly altered, and the bottle placed
in the cup-board. My Aunt withdrew, in
order to diveſt herſelf of her ſplendour,
before the ſupper came, remarking point-
edly enough, that the *wear* and *tear* of
clothes in carving was amazing and pro-
digious.—The incidents of the next two
hours were few, and may be eaſily told—
Stocks had, from the accounts of that evening, riſen one and a half, and my Uncle's
cold was better.—At length, after a ſhort
diſſertation upon the folly of mankind,

and

and the extravagant demands of the Chelfea
bun-makers, we recollected that it was Saturday night, pulled off our fhoes, and retired to reft.

        I am, &c.
           SOCRATES IN EMBRYO.

NUM-

# NUMBER XXXVI.

SATURDAY, *November* 17, 1787.

*Cum Græciam univerſam itinere rapido per-*
*agraverit, nihil fore de Græciâ, nihil vere At-*
*ticum aut quovis modo memorabile domum repor-*
*tabit; cum ſcilicet ſatis habuerit peregrinantium*
*plurimorum ritu, locorum nomina forſan & ſitus*
*in tranſcurſu notâſſe; interea vero civium mo-*
*res & inſtituta, præclara & Virtutum & Inge-*
*nii monumenta, oculo diligenti & curioſo neuti-*
*quam exploraverit.*

Burtoni in Πειαλογιαν Dedicatio.

THE various advantages which a Traveller may derive from an acquaintance with the modern languages, are too

A a 3          obvious

obvious to require a minute detail. There is one, however, which deferves particularly to be pointed out, for, inconfiderable as it may appear in the eftimation of young men of fortune, it will have no fmall weight with their Parents and Guardians. I allude to the confiderable expence which may be prevented by thofe who are able to converfe with the natives of other countries in their own language. He who is a tolerable Linguift may be fuppofed to underftand manners and cuftoms; and few men, however knavifh, will attempt to cheat him who feems as wife as themfelves. Ready and plaufible converfation will difconcert the attacks of impofition, and elude the ftratagems of chicane. The French imagine that England produces as much gold as the coaft of Africa; and that Monfieur John Bull leaves his native country merely to fcatter his money with thoughtlefs profufion about the Continent. In confequence of this extravagant opinion, he rarely efcapes without paying five times the real value for every commodity. His pocket is fuppofed to be a rich bank, upon
which

which every rapacious Frenchman may draw at pleafure; and of courfe demands are made upon it with inceffant avidity, and unrelenting extortion. Thefe remarks are indebted for no fmall degree of confirmation to the following authentic anecdote. An officer of the regiment d'Artois, who was on a journey from London to Paris, fpent the night at the *Hotel d'Angleterre*, at Calais. On examining his bill the next morning, he found that he was charged a guinea for his fupper, which had confifted only of cold meat and a bottle of *vin de pais*. Enraged at fo grofs an impofition, he fummoned the mafter of the Inn, and infifted upon an abatement. *Milord*, faid the landlord, *I cannot difgrace an Englifhman of your rank by charging him a lefs price. Sirrah*, replied the Officer, *I am not a man of quality, but a poor Lieutenant in the fervice of the Grand Monarque. Morbleu!* rejoined the Landlord, *I confefs I have made an egregious blunder.—I hope your honour will forgive me if I reduce my demand to half a crown.*

It

It is not less necessary for a traveller to set out with these qualifications, which will enable him to repel the incroachments of imposition, than it is desirable for him to have stored his mind with domestick information.   The author of the *Tableau de Paris* remarks, with great justness, that we are not best acquainted with those things which every day affords us an opportunity of seeing.   Curiosity is a languid principle where access is easy, and gratification is immediate.   Remoteness and difficulty are powerful incentives to its vigorous and lasting operations.   By many who live within the sound of Bow Bell, the internal wonders of St. Paul's, or the Tower, may not be thought in the least degree interesting.   Yet how justly would such persons be classed with the *incurious* of Æsop if on visiting their country friends it should appear, that they had never been in the Whispering Gallery, or seen the Lions !  Equally ridiculous is that Englishman who roams in search of curiosities abroad, without having previously inspected the great beauties of nature and art at home.   Sir

*Solomon*

*Solomon Simple*, before he was informed at Venice that the *Pantheon*, and *St. Stephen's*, *Walbrook*, in London, were two of the firſt pieces of architecture in Europe, had never heard that ſuch buildings exiſted.

When a man ſays he is going to viſit foreign countries, it is neceſſary to be acquainted with his diſpoſition and turn of mind to underſtand what he deſigns by the declaration. The Scholar, the Connoiſſeur, the Man of Faſhion, the Merchant, intend to convey very different ideas by the ſame phraſe. They may all be carried to the Continent in the ſame Ship, but, as their ſchemes are of the moſt diſſimilar kinds, they ſeparate never to meet again. Like the diverging rays of Light, they all iſſue from the ſame point, but go off in various directions. Their reſpective purſuits eſtabliſh the analogy which is obſerved between Travelling and the Study of Hiſtory. Characters, Manners, Cuſtoms, Laws, Government, Antiquities, Arts, Sciences, and Commerce, form the materials for obſervation to the Traveller as well as the Reader. Theſe offer to both the higheſt, as well as the loweſt, intellectual gratifications. The Philoſopher
improves

improves his Theories by an intimate acquaintance with the characters of mankind; and the Trifler kills his time in a manner entertaining to himfelf and inoffenfive to the publick.

It is the fashion of the prefent times to fkim over the furface of things, and to dive to the bottom for nothing. General knowledge is moft unqueftionably moft defireable, becaufe it is beft calculated for general intercourfe with mankind. He, however, who dares to make falfe pretenfions to it, meets with Ridicule whilft he lays fnares for Applaufe. Such likewife is the reward of thofe who talk familiarly of Perfons whom they never knew, and defcribe Places which they never faw. When fertility of invention deferts the ftandard of truth to aid the boafts of vanity, it becomes not only a dangerous but a defpicable talent. *Captain Lemuel Sinbad* (who never extended his travels beyond Flanders) will tell you he fhook hands with old Frederick the laft time he reviewed his troops at Potfdam. Mention the Emperor of Germany, he will pofitively affert, that he

had

had a private converfation with him upon
the improvement of Gun Barrels. As for
the Earthquakes in Calabria, he accompanied Sir William Hamilton to afcertain the
extent of their effects. He went frequently
to fhoot with the King of Naples, and was
informed at Conftantinople, by a Bafhaw of
three Tails, that the Grand Signior would
certainly declare war againft the Emprefs.
The Captain relates his incredible adventures in different companies with fuch material variations of circumftances, as repel
belief, and deftroy probability. He is generally as much at war with himfelf, as with
the accounts given by others. But neither
the incredulous laugh, nor fhrewd cavils
of his friends, can cure him of his darling
paffion for fiction, becaufe he can fupport
the tottering frabrick of romance with the
props of fubtle and prompt argument.
Nothing pleafes him more than to find that
the eel of fophiftry will often elude the
ftrongeft grafp of objection. The Captain
bears a clofe refemblance to the noted
Pfalmanazar, to whom when it was objected, that, as the fun was vertical at Formofa,

all

all the fires muft be extinguifhed, readily, replied, *that to prevent fuch inconveniencies the chimnies were built obliquely.*

By way of conclufion to this paper, fuch a fketch of chara&er and detail of circum-ftances fhall be exhibited as may probably be thought UTOPIAN. Whether they be matters of fa& or not, is by no means a fubje& of importance. If the plan laid down be pra&icable, the falutary effe&s refulting from its execution cannot be de-nied ; becaufe it will remove various incon-veniencies, and fupply obvious defe&s in the inftru&ions which have been frequent-ly given to Young Travellers.

*Frederick Manly,* after having paffed through a publick fchool with applaufe, was fent to the Univerfity at the age of eighteen, under the immediate care of a private Tutor. He applied with great dili-gence to claffical and mathematical ftudies until he reached his twentieth year, when his father thought it was neceffary for him to lay a folid foundation of domeftick knowledge, before the fuperftru&ure of foreign travel was ere&ed. This domeftick

Knowledge

Knowledge confifted in an inveftigation of
the Principles of the Conftitution, the fyftem of Laws, and the adminiftration of
Juftice : it comprized a general inquiry into the fevcral branches of Commerce and
Manufactures, the ftate of Agriculture,
Learning, and the Arts ; and concluded
with an examination of the Reafonablenefs
of National Religion. The defects or errors
of books on thefe interefting topicks were
remedied by converfations with intelligent
perfons ; and the vague fyftems of theory
were rectified by obfervations on the actual
ftate of things. To diverfify thefe purfuits,
*Manly* made the regular Tour of Great Britain with the double intention of furveying
natural and artificial curiofities, and of converfing with thofe who were eminent for
Manners, Attainments, or Genius. On
vifiting the Continent, a more extenfive and
interefting profpect was difplayed to his
view; but he did not diffipate his curiofity
amidft a frivolous and perplexing variety
of objects. As he had been long habi-
tuated to the acquirement of ufeful knowledge,

5

ledge, his refearches were directed to that
alone. He poffeffed the beft means of
procuring fatisfactory and genuine information, as he converfed in the French,
Italian, and German languages, with elegance and fluency. Such was the fuccefs
with which he facrificed to the Graces,
that the Ladies were charmed with the politenefs of his manners; and fuch was the
highly cultivated ftate of his mind, that
foreigners in general gained confiderably
by the interchange of ideas. His heart
was happily fecured againft the feductions
of illicit amours, by an early attachment
to a Lady, whofe temper and turn of mind
were congenial with his own. Their abfence was alleviated by a regular Correfpondence. His defire to contribute to her
entertainment and information, made every
object doubly interefting, and gave the
keeneft edge to his curiofity. He furveyed
the beft fpecimens of antient and modern
Art with a degree of Rapture which bor-
dered on Enthufiafm. His Tafte was not
the offspring of Affectation, but the gift of
Nature,

Nature, improved by Experience. Harmony of colours, Symmetry of parts, and the Name of a great Mafter, were, in his eftimation, merely excellencies of the fecond clafs. Sculpture and Painting had no charms for him, exclufive of the Force and Beauty of their effect. Rome and Florence were the principal places of his refidence, becaufe in them the fine Arts had depofited their moft valuable treafures. At the expiration of three years he returned to his native country, and was united to the Miftrefs of his affections. His manners were refined, but not formal: his drefs was fafhionable, but not foppifh; his deportment eafy, but not finical. His conftitution was invigorated by exercife, and his fortune unimpaired by extravagance. Scepticifm had not undermined, nor Bigotry contracted, his religious principles. He gave a proof how high a polifh the Britifh Diamond will take; his example fully evinced, that it cannot be excelled either in folidity or luftre. His prejudices were worn away by enlarged intercourfe with Mankind. His philanthropy was ardent,

2 and

and his patriotifm not lefs fpirited than
rational. *Manly*, in fhort, was a citizen
of the world, who had carefully weighed
the merits of *all* cultivated nations, and
made England the place of his refidence,
becaufe her excellencies preponderated in
the fcale.                            Q.

NUM-

# NUMBER XXXVII.

---

SATURDAY, *November* 24, 1787.

---

## CONTINUATION *of the* VICAR'S TALE.

SUPPER being removed, after chatting fome time, my worthy hoft conducted me to my bed-chamber, which was on the ground floor, and lined with jaf-mine, that was conducted in at the windows. After wifhing me good night, he retired, leaving me to reft.—The beauty of the fcenery, however, and my ufual propenfity to walk by moon-light, induced me to

leave my fragrant cell. When I fallied
forth, the moon was darting her temperated
rays through the fhade that furrounded the
cottage, tipping the tops of the venerable
oaks with filver. After taking a turn or
two on the lawn, I wandered to the fpot,——
" where the rude forefathers of the
" hamlet fleep." It was fmall, and for
the moft part furrounded with yew-trees of
an antient date, beneath whofe folemn
fhade many generations had mouldered into
duft. No fooner did I enter, than my attention *was caught* by a pillar of white
marble, placed on the fummit of a fmall
eminence, the bafe of which was furrounded
with honeyfuckles and woodbines, whilft
a large willow overfhadowed the pillar.
As I was with attention perufing the epitaph, I was not a little alarmed by the
approach of a figure, cloathed in a long
robe.——The apparition continued advancing
towards me with a flow ftep, and its eyes
fixed on the ground, which prevented it
obferving me till we were within reach of
each other.——Great was my wonder at re-
cognizing my worthy hoft in this fituation ;

7

nor

nor was his aftonifhment lefs at finding
his gueft thus courting the appearance of
goblins and fairies.—After each had expreffed the furprize he felt, I proceeded
to enquire whofe duft was there enfhrined.
To my queftion he returned anfwer:—
"There, Sir, fleeps Harriet's mother, an innocent, but unfortunate woman. Pardon,
me, Sir, faid he, if for a moment I indulge
my forrow, and bedew my Harriet's grave
with tears,—a tribute that I often pay her
much-loved memory, when the reft of the
world are loft in fleep."—Here he paufed,
and feemed much agitated. At length he
requefted my permiffion to defer the recital
of Harriet's woes till the next day, as he
found himfelf unequal to the tafk of proceeding in the painful detail. To this propofal I readily acceded, and we returned
home. I retired to my room, but every
attempt to procure fleep proved ineffectual.
Harriet had fo wholly occupied my thoughts,
that no moment of the night was fuffered
to pafs unnoticed. At length, " when
" foared the warbling lark on high," I left
my couch, and rejoined my worthy land-

lord,

lord, who was bufily employed in the arrangement of his garden. Though I declined mentioning the fubject of our laft night's adventure,—yet he faw the marks of anxious expectation in my countenance, and proceeded to gratify the curiofity he had infpired.—"It will be neceffary," faid he, " before I proceed to relate the woes that befel my daughter, to give a fhort fketch of my own life.—Six and twenty years ago, Mrs. ——— came hither for the benefit of her health, the air being recommended as highly falubrious. On her arrival, fhe gave out that fhe was the daughter of a clergyman, who was lately dead, and had left her in narrow circumftances.—I thought it my duty to vifit her, and offer her any little attention in my power. She received me with politenefs, and expreffed a wifh to cultivate my acquaintance. I continued to repeat my vifits for fome time without fufpecting that there was any thing partilar in her hiftory,—till one morning I found her in tears reading a letter fhe had juft received. On my entrance fhe gave

it

it to me: it contained a notification from
Lord B——'s agent, that her ufual remittances would no longer be continued. On
opening this letter, I was led to fuppofe
that her connection with Lord B—— was
not of the moft honourable nature. But
all my fufpicion vanifhed on her producing
feveral letters from Lord B—— to her
mother, with whom he had been long connected.—From thefe letters I learnt, that
Mrs. —— was the daughter of Lord
B—— by Mifs M——, fifter to a
Scotch baronet, whom he had feduced and
fupported during the remainder of her life.
But he had, it feems, determined to withdraw his protection from the fruit of their
connection. Mrs. —— declared fhe knew
not what ftep to take, as her finances were
nearly exhaufted. I endeavoured. to comfort her, affuring her that fhe fhould command every affiftance in my power:—On
hearing this, fhe feemed a little fatisfied,
and became more compofed. After fitting
with her fome time, I returned home, to
confider in what manner I might moft

eafily afford protection to the young orphan, whofe whole dependance was on my fupport.—If I took her home to live with me, as I was unmarried, it would give offence to my parifhioners. My income was too confined to admit of my affording her a feparate eftablifhment. Thus cir-cumftanced, I determined to offer her my hand. You will, no doubt, fay it was ra-ther an imprudent ftep for a man who had feen his fortieth year to connect himfelf with youth and beauty : but as my brother was then living, it was impoffible for me to render her the leaft affiftance on any other plan. She received my propofal with grateful furprife, and accepted it without hefitation.—In a few days we were married, and have now lived together fix and twenty years in a ftate, the felicity of which has never been interrupted by thofe difcordant jars which are fo frequently the concomi-tants of matrimony : though, alas! our peace has received a mortal wound from one, the bare mention of whofe name fills me with horror!—But not to digrefs : Be-

fore

fore the return of that day which faw me
bleffed with the hand of Emily, my happinefs received an important addition, by the
birth of a daughter, who inherited all her
mother's charms.  It is fuperfluous to add,
that fhe was equally the idol of both her
parents ; and as fhe was the only fruit of our
marriage, fhe became every day a greater
favourite.  My wife had received fuch an
education as rendered her fully capable of
accomplifhing her daughter in a manner
far fuperior to any thing her fituation required, or perhaps could juftify.  To this
agreeable employment, however, fhe devoted her whole time; and when Harriet
had reached her eighteenth year, fhe was
in every refpect a highly accomplifhed woman.  She was become what that picture
reprefents her.  With an amiable temper
and gentle manners, fhe was the idol of
the village.  Hitherto fhe had experienced
a ftate of felicity unknown in the more
exalted ftations of life—unconfcious, alas !
of the ills that awaited her future years.

It

It is with reluctance I proceed in the melancholy narrative.—One evening, as a young man, attended by a fervant, was paffing through the village, his horfe ftartled, and threw him. Happening to be on the fpot at the time, I offered every affiftance in my power, and conveying him to my cottage, difpatched his fervant in queft of a furgeon, who declared our patient was not in any danger, but recommended it to him to delay his departure for a day or two. His health, however, or rather his love, did not admit of his travelling for near a fortnight; during which time he eftablifhed his intereft with Harriet by the moft pleafing and unremitting attention to her flighteft wifhes.— When about to depart, he requefted leave to repeat his vifit on his return from his intended tour, dropping, at the fame time, fome diftant hints of his affection for Harriet, to whom he was by no means indifferent.

Mr. H—— (for fo our gueft was named) informed us, previous to his departure, that

that he had a fmall independent fortune;
but that from a diftant relation he had
confiderable expectation. After bidding an
affectionate adieu to Harriet, he fet out
on his intended tour, which lafted for a
month :"—the effects produced by his abfence muft however be referved for another
paper. X.

NUMBER XXXVIII.

---

SATURDAY, *December* 1, 1787.

---

CONCLUSION *of the* VICAR'S TALE.

" DURING the time of Mr. H——'s absence, Harriet appeared penfive, and I obferved with pain that he had made no flight impreffion on her heart. At length Mr. H—— returned, and Harriet's reception of him left us no room to doubt her attachment. During his fecond vifit he was very affiduous to fecure the favour of all the family : with Harriet he eafily fucceeded ; nor were Mrs. T—— or myfelf difpofed to diflike him. His manners were elegant, and his wit lively.

At

At length he obtained from Harriet the promife of her hand, provided her parents fhould not object. Hitherto I had never been induced to make any enquiries concerning his circumftances and character. Now, however, by his direction, I applied to a Mr. E———ns, a clergyman of his acquaintance. This gentleman, now in an exalted ftation in the church, then Chaplain to Lord C———, informed me, that Mr. H——— was in every refpect a defirable match for my daughter; and that whenever his Coufin fhould die, he would be enabled to maintain her in affluence and fplendor :—he added that his character was unexceptionable. Little fufpecting the villainous part Mr. E———ns was acting, I readily confented to the propofed union, and performed the ceremony myfelf. Mr. H——— requefted that their marriage might be kept a fecret, till the birth of a fon and heir. This propofal rather alarmed me, but it was too late to retreat ; and knowing no one in the great world, it was impoffible for me, previous to the marriage, to procure any account of Mr. H———,

but

but fuch as his friend communicated to me. Thus circumftanced, I could only confent; and as Harriet readily adopted every pro-pofal that came from one fhe fo tenderly loved, the matter was finally agreed on. After ftaying a few days, he fet off for London, but foon returned, and paffed the whole winter with us; and in the fpring Harriet was delivered of that little girl you fo much admire. I now preffed him to acknowledge my daughter as his wife. To this he anfwered, that, had fhe brought him a fon, he would readily have complied with my requeft; but that his coufin was fo great an oddity, that he could not bear the idea (to ufe his own expreffion) " of having " his fortune lavifhed in a milliner's fhop :" ‘ But,’ added he, ‘ if you infift upon it, I will now rifk the lofs of all his fortune, and introduce my Harriet to his prefence.’ Harriet, however, again interfered, and defired that Mr. H——— might not be forced into meafures that might in the end prove deftructive of his future profpect, and induce him to regret the day he ever faw her. Thefe arguments prevailed, and

Mr.

Mr. H——— was fuffered to continue as a member of the family without any farther notice being taken of the fubject. In this manner had three years elapfed undiftinguifhed by any remarkable event,— Mr. H——— generally paffing half the year with us, and the remainder in London, attending, as he faid, on his coufin; when one day, as he was fitting with us at dinner, a chaife and four drove up to the houfe. The fervants enquired for Mr. H———, and on hearing he was there, opened the carriage door. A gentleman, dreffed like an officer, jumped out, followed by a lady in a travelling drefs; — they rufhed immediately into the room. Their appearance amazed us; but Mr. H——— betrayed the moft vifible marks of confter-nation. The lady appeared to be about thirty. She was a woman by no means deftitute of perfonal charms. The moment fhe entered the room, fhe feized upon Harriet, and, loading her with every horrible epithet, proceeded to indulge her paffion by ftriking her innocent rival. On feeing this, an old fervant of mine feized the

lady,

lady, and forcibly turned her out of the house, then faſtened the door. It was not till now that we perceived the abſence of Mr. H———, who had, it ſeems, retired with the lady's companion. Whilſt we were ſtill loſt in amazement at the tranſ-action we had juſt witneſſed, we were alarm-ed to the higheſt pitch by the report of a piſtol. Harriet inſtantly fainted. Whilſt Mrs. T——— was recovering her, I flew to the ſpot from whence the ſound proceeded, and there found Mr. H——— weltering in his blood, with a piſtol lying by him. I approached, and found him ſtill ſenſible. He informed me, that the lady's brother and he had fought, and that ſeeing him fall, they had both eſcaped as faſt as poſſi-ble. I inſtantly procured aſſiſtance, and conveyed him to the houſe, where he was put to bed, and a ſurgeon was ſent for. In the mean time Harriet had ſeveral fits, and we were very apprehenſive that the hour of her fate was approaching. On the arrival of the ſurgeon, he declared the wound Mr. H——— had received would probably prove mortal, and recommended

the

the arrangement of his affairs. Mr. H——
recieved the news with great agony, and
defired that I might be left alone with him.
No fooner was this requeft granted, than
he addreffed me in the following terms.
' In me, Sir, behold the moft unfortunate,
and, alas ! the moft guilty of men. The
lady, whofe ill-timed vifit has loft me my
life, is,—I tremble to pronounce the word,
—my wife.' Seeing me pale with horror,
he proceeded. 'No wonder, Sir, that you
fhould behold with horror one who has
repaid *unbounded hofpitality by unequalled
villainy.* The bare remembrance of my
own guilt diftracts me. The awful hour
is now faft approaching, when I muft receive my final doom from that heaven
whofe laws I have fo daringly violated. To
redrefs the injuries I have committed, is,
alas ! impoffible. My death will be an
atonement by no means fufficient. I cannot, however, leave this world till you
fhall be informed, that ten thoufand pounds,
the whole of my property that is at my difpofal, has long ago been transferred by me
into the hands of truftees for the benefit of

my

my much injured Harriet, and her unhappy infant. In my own defence, I have nothing to urge. Suffer me only to remark, that my misfortune arose from the avarice of my father, who forced me into a marriage with the woman you lately saw, and whose brother has been the instrument in the hand of Providence to inflict on me the doom I so much merited. If possible, conceal from Harriet that I was married. Picture, for her sake, 'an innocent deception, and tell her that I was only engaged to that lady. This will contibute to promote her repose, and the deception may possibly plead the merit of prolonging a life, so dear to you: for the elevated mind of my Harriet would never survive the fatal discovery of my villainy. But, oh! when my unhappy child shall ask the fate of him who gave her being, in pity draw a veil over that guilt which can scarcely hope to obtain the pardon of heaven.'—There he ceased, and uttering a short prayer, expired.—Happily for Harriet, she continued in a state of insensibility for three days, during which time I had the body removed to a neighbouring
house,

houfe, there to wait for interment. Having addreffed a letter to Mr. H——'s agent in town, he fent orders for the body to be removed to the family burying place, where it was accordingly interred. Harriet recovered by flow degrees from the ftate of happy infenfibility, into which the death of Mr. H—— had plunged her. Her grief became filent and fettled. Groans and exclamations now gave way to fighs and the bitter tears of defponding grief. She feldom or never fpoke—but would cry for hours together over her haplefs infant; then call on the fhadow of her departed Henry, little fufpecting the irreparable injury he had done her. It was with infinite anxiety I beheld the decline of Harriet's health. Prone as we ever are to hope what we ardently defire, I now defpaired of her recovery. Whilft in a ftate of hopelefs inactivity, I was doomed to witnefs the lingering death of my lamented Harriet, I received a vifit from an old friend. On his arrival I allotted him the apartment formerly inhabited by Mr. H—— and Harriet. About midnight he was awakened by fome

C c one

one entering the apartment. On removing the curtain, he difcovered, by the light of the moon, my adored Harriet in a white drefs. Her eyes were open, but had a vacant look that plainly proved fhe was not awake. She advanced with a flow ftep; then feating herfelf at the foot of the bed, remained there an hour, weeping bitterly the whole time, but without uttering a word. My friend, fearful of the confe-quences, forbore to awake her, and fhe re-tired with the fame deliberate ftep fhe had entered. This intelligence alarmed me ex-ceffively. On the next night fhe was watch-ed, and the fame fcene was repeated, with this difference, that, after quitting the fatal apartment, fhe went to the room where her daughter ufually flept; and laying herfelf down on the bed, wept over the child for fome time; then returned to her apart-ment. The next morning we waited with anxiety for her appearance at breakfaft; but, alas!"—Here a flood of tears afforded to my friend that relief which he fo much needed; and we returned to the houfe. After paffing fome days with this worthy couple,

couple, I proceeded on my tour, quitting, with reluctance, the abode of forrow and refignation:—Thofe whom the perufal of this tale may intereft, will, if ever they vifit the banks of the Alna, find that the author has copied his charaĉters from nature.

X.

NUM-

## N U M B E R  XXXIX.

---

SATURDAY, *December* 8, 1787.

---

Τυμβῶ⸃ε ςηλῄ⸃ε; τὸ γαρ γερας εςι ϑανόν⸃ων.

Iliad 16. v. 457.

*What Honours Mortals after Death receive,*
*Thofe unavailing Honours we may give.*

POPE.

THAT Fame is the univerfal Paffion is by nothing more confpicuoufly difcovered than by Epitaphs. The generality of Mankind are not content to fink inglorioufly into the grave, but wifh to be paid that Tribute of Panegyrick after their Deaths, which in many cafes may not be due to the Virtues of their Lives. If the

5                                    Vanity

Vanity of the departed has not been provident of monumental Honours, the Partiality of Friends is eager to fupply them. Death may be faid with almoft equal propriety to confer as well as to level all diftinctions. In confequence of that event, a kind of chemical operation takes place; for thofe characters which were mixed with the grofs particles of Vice, by being thrown into the alembic of flattery, are fublimated into the effence of Virtue. He who during the performance of his part upon the ftage of the world was weakly applauded, after the clofe of the drama, is pourtrayed as the favourite of " *every Virtue under Heaven.*" To fave the opulent from oblivion, the fculptor unites his labours with the fcholar or the poet, whilft the ruftick is indebted for his mite of pofthumous renown to the carpenter, the painter, or the mafon. The ftructures of fame are in both cafes built with materials whofe duration is fhort. It may check the fallies of pride to reflect on the mortality of man; but for its compleat humiliation let it be remembered, that epitaphs and monuments decay. Had not

C c 3                              Cicero

Cicero been affifted by his memory, he
could never have decyphered the mutilated
verfes on the tomb of Archimedes. The
Antiquarian fearches in vain for the original infcriptions on Chaucer and Sidney.

The obfervations of the illuftrious Johnfon on epitaphs are marked with acutenefs
as well as extent of judgement. In his
Criticifms, however, on thofe of Pope, he
has fhewn a petulance of temper and fafti-
dioufnefs of tafte, at the fame time that he
acknowledged the barrennefs of Pope's topicks, and the difficulty of diftributing to
numbers that praife which is particular and
characteriftic. He who is a critic fhould
confider, that, according to the natural progrefs of human opinions, he may become
the fubject of criticifm. If Johnfon had
ever conjectured that he muft one day be
tried by his own laws, more lenity would
probably have been fhown to Pope. The
Doctor remarks, " that an epitaph ought
" not to be longer than common beholders
" have leifure and patience to perufe." Of
the few he has left behind him, that on
Hanmer is furely objectionable for its prolixity.

lixity. He reprobates with juft feverity any
allufions to claffical cuftoms, and the fituation of Roman tombs. The lines of Paf-
feratius on Henry of France are quoted, to
fhow the impropriety of addreffing the Reader as a traveller. Yet the Doctor forgot
his ftrictures and his quotation when he
concluded his character of Thrale with
" *Abi, Viator.*"

The preceding Remarks are intended as
an Introduction to a plan which I take this
opportunity of laying before the publick.
It is my Defign to publifh a Collection of
the moft remarkable Epitaphs with critical
Obfervations. Particular attention will be
paid to their Arrangement, of which it
fhall be the object of the remaining part of
this Paper to exhibit an exact Specimen.
Without fpinning too many Threads of
Claffification, a few ftriking and general
diftinctions only fhall be adopted. The
LEARNED—the SUBLIME—the CHARAC-
TERISTIC—the COMPLIMENTARY.—The
firft Clafs is intended to allure the Scholars
of our famous Univerfities to fubfcribe
liberally to the Work. To let the Reader

into a fecret, it was originally my defign to
have publifhed this part in a Folio by itfelf, with a pompous Dedication. Happening to fee a Goofe finged with a leaf of
the *Pietas Oxonienfis*, I was frightened from
the profecution of my plan by fo unlucky
an omen. My intended Work will notwithftanding comprize Learning enough to
fatisfy the appetite of a reafonable Linguift.
There will be no room for complaint if I
begin with *Perfian*, and end with *Latin*.
The firft Epitaph fhall be that on *Hadgi
Shaughfware*, in Saint Botolph's, Bifhop-
gate ; and the laft fhall be the laconic *Fui
Caius*, at Cambridge.

Under this head many ingenious and
novel opinions will be advanced relative to
the *Language* as well as the *Sentiments* of
thofe Compofitions. It will be proved to a
demonftration, that the *learned* Languages
are abfurdly ufed except for *learned* Men.
Some one has well obferved, that, if the
Dead could hear their own fepulchral
Praife, they would be put to the blufh. Some,
without doubt, would with amiable diffi-
denceadopt the elegant fentiments of Fron-
tinus,

tinus, " Impenfa Monumenti fupervacua " eft ; Memoria noftri durabit, fi Vitâ me- " ruimus." " Superfluous is the Expence of " the Tomb, fince our Memory will flou- " rifh, if our Conduct has merited that " Honour."—But multitudes muft be in- fenfible to the emotions of Shame, unlefs they were endued with the Gift of Tongues. The moral Defign of an Epitaph is to infpire an emulation of the virtues of the deceafed. This cannot be effected, unlefs the Language which records thofe Virtues be intelligible to Perfons who are in a fituation to emulate them. The Ta- lents and Munificence of *Bufby* and *South* are tranfmitted to Scholars by a Vehicle which is familiar to them ; but how can the Ladies improve by the Example of the beautiful. *Mrs. Arundel*, who is cele- brated in a Latin Infcription in Saint Mary's, Oxford ? or how is the Courage of our Sailors likely to be increafed by the Cice- ronian Periods on *Rooke* at Canterbury ?

The SUBLIME.—This Species is con- fined to thofe who occupy the moft diftin- guifhed Niches in the Temple of Fame. Sim-

Simplicity and Brevity are its Characteri-
fticks. Such Names as Bacon, Locke, and
Newton, want not the Flowers of Eloquence, or the Parade of Periods, to deco-
rate their Monuments. The tomb of Sir
Chriftopher Wren has a local propriety
from his being buried in St. Paul's, which
gave birth to an Infcription worthy of that
illuftrious Reftorer of Attic Architecture.

" Subtus conditur hujus Ecclefiæ & Ur-
" bis Conditor, qui vixit Annos ultra
" nonaginta, non fibi fed bono publico.
" *Lector, fi Monumentum requiris, circum-*
" *fpice.*"

The CHARACTERISTICK. — A Clafs
which far excels all the reft, as it contains
Examples of fplendid Talents and eminent
Virtues marked with peculiar and appropriate Praife. Not only thofe Epitaphs
wherein their due meafure of Applaufe is
diftributed with nice difcrimination to Philofophers, Poets, Warriors, and Statefmen,
will be introduced under this head, but
fuch likewife as have preferved the Memory of the lowly and the ignoble. Thefe
Compofitions are as difficult to be met with

as

as accurate Miniatures. Dr. Johnſon would
have ſaid that Pope's Verſes on Mrs. Corbet
was a very proper Exemplification of this
Species. Perhaps the following by
Hawkeſworth, in Bromley Church-yard, is
by no means inferior to it :

" Near this place lies the body of Eliza-
" beth Monk, aged 101, the Wife of John
" Monk, Blackſmith, by whom ſhe had
" no Children. But Virtue would not
" ſuffer her to be childleſs. An Infant, to
" whom and to whoſe Father and Uncles
" ſhe had been Nurſe, became dependent
" upon Strangers for the Neceſſaries of
" Life ; to him ſhe afforded the protection
" of a Mother. This parental Charity was
" returned with filial Affection, and ſhe
" was ſupported in the feebleneſs of Age by
" him whom ſhe had cheriſhed in the
" Helpleſſneſs of Infancy. Let it be remem-
" bered, that there is no ſtation in which
" Induſtry will not obtain Power to be li-
" beral, nor any Character on which
" Liberality will not confer Honour. She
" had long been prepared by a ſimple and
" unaffected Piety for her End. To pre-
" ſerve

" ferve the Memory of this Perfon, but
" yet more to perpetuate the Leffon of her
" Life, this Stone was erected by volun-
" tary Contribution."

The COMPLIMENTARY.—This article comprifes Infcriptions in which the dead are more indebted for their praife to invention than to merit. The writers of epitaphs ought to be hiftorians, and not poets.

Their panegyrick often fatigues with prolixity, and difgufts with fulfomenefs. Take away the dates from complimentary epitaphs, and they have all the appearance of dedications. They exhibit the demigods of the golden age, or the immaculate heroes of romance. Like Addifon's Cato, they feem to have been out of the reach of human paffions or infirmities—of a nature too much exalted to excite pity, and famed for excellencies too tranfcendent for imitation. Sometimes, however, it happens, that common topicks of encomium are touched with fo mafterly a hand, that they charm with an irrefiftible grace, and have all the force of novelty. For a panegyrift to declare, *That a Lady is deferving of the higheft highest praife—that fhe is as beautiful as an angel*—and *that fhe is remarkable for uniform piety*—feems as if he could not ftrike out of the beaten track.—But furely it is out of the power of a vulgar bard to pourtray fuch ideas in the following manner.

On Lady CATHERINE PASTON,
Pafton Church, Norfolk, 1628.

Can Man be filent and not Praifes find,
For her who lived the Praife of Woman-kind?
Whofe outward frame was lent the world to gueſs,
What fhapes our fouls fhall wear in happinefs.
Whofe Virtue did all ill fo overfwaye,
That her whole life was a communion-daye.

As my publication will be extended only to thofe Epitaphs which are really infcribed on tomb-ftones, the *ludicrous* and the *gay* will of courfe be omitted. Let him whofe inclination may lead him to perufe fuch, be referred to Magazines and Jeft-books. He will there find that Epigram, Pun, Satire, and Burlefque, have attempted to throw a gleam of levity upon a fubject which is too awful to be made ridiculous. Wit and Humour

Humour never more miſtake their object,
than when they aim their Shafts at Man in
a State of Diſſolution. But, however wan-
ton and injudicious their ſallies have been,
they have never prophaned the ſanctity of
Chriſtian Temples by affixing their Productions to them. Such an Indecorum
militates too ſtrongly againſt Piety and
Senſibility, to be tolerated with Patience.
To ſport with the Characters of the departed is a ſufficient Triumph for Gaiety,
without being permitted to erect a Tro-
phy over their Graves.

The Peruſal of Epitaphs is not to be
conſidered as a frivolous and light amuſement. If ſuch only be the Objects of Attention as have been noticed with our Applauſe, it is unqueſtionably an Introduction
to pleaſing Knowledge, and an Incentive to
moral Improvement. What Biography is
to Hiſtory, an Epitaph is to Biography.
It is a ſketch which marks the great Out-
lines of Character, and excites curioſity to
view the Portraits as painted on the Pages
of Hiſtory. It is likewiſe an Epitome of a
Sermon, which teaches the moſt uſeful
Truths

Truths in the moſt comprehenſive Form. Monumental Inſcriptions remind us, that Time is on the Wing,—that every Rank and Age muſt fall a prey to his Depredations,—that the Moments of Life are too precious to be ſquandered away on trifles — that Religion is the only Support againſt the Horrors of Death, and the only Guide to the Joys of Eternity.

Q.

N U M-

# NUMBER XL.

---

SATURDAY, *December* 15, 178y.

---

*Carpimus indecores joculari carmine mores.*

FOR the fubftance of this paper, I
have ventured to make an extract
from a very pleafant and witty Latin author,
who wrote about two hundred and thirty
years ago. To which I have fubjoined
what may be more properly called a Para-
phrafe than a Tranflation.

The book I allude to is entitled, " *De*
" *Morum Simplicitate, Auctore Frederico*
" *Dedekindo,*" a Poem in three books. The
author was a German, and his work, I
believe,

believe, gave rife to that fpecies of humour,
of which Swift fhewed himfelf completely
mafter, in his " Advice to Servants;" and
which has been fince imitated in puulica-
tions of very modern date.;——particularly
in " Advice to Officers," and the " facetious hints of Geoffrey Gambado, Efq."—I
know not that Swift has any where mentioned this Author, though his works contain
many paffages which incline me to believe he
had perufed him with confiderable attention.
I have extracted the firft chapter of his firft
book, in order to give fome fpecimen of
that ftyle, whofe origin has been attributed
to various Writers, in various times and
countries, fome giving it to Rabelais, and
others to Cervantes. Dedekindus appears
from his preface and conclufion to have
been a man of great Senfe, and refined
Manners. That he has fallen into obfcu-
rity, is, perhaps, to be attributed to the
few copies of his works, of which the
World is in poffeffion. His verfification
has the eafe and elegance of Ovid. Every
Critic will difcover that he has not the purity of the Auguftan Age; yet every one

D d                          will

will read him with pleafure, who is not too faftidious to be eafily pleafed.

Since I read his book, and rendered the fentiments as near as I could, of the firft chapter, into Englifh, I have difcovered, that the work has been tranflated by a Mr. Bull, in 1739, and dedicated, very properly, to Dean Swift, who firft (as the tranflator fays) introduced into thefe kingdoms of Great Britain and Ireland an ironical manner of writing, to the difcouragement of vice, ill-manners, and folly, and the promotion of virtue, good-manners, and good fenfe.

The Original contains an apology at the beginning, and another at the end, for the Indelicacy into which the Author is unavoidably led.—The "*fidus interpres*" lived at a time when fuch a kind of wit met with a patron in almoft every reader. He feems rather to have laboured in expreffing fully every grofs idea which ought to have been foftened, or might have been omitted without injuring the work.

The Preface and Conclufion are improperly paffed over without any notice by
the

the tranflator. Upon the whole, the fate
of the tranflation (which is at prefent almoft
totally unknown) is not to be lamented.
The Author of the following Verfion will be
amply rewarded for his pains, if he can be
in the fmalleft degree inftrumental in bringing forward the Original into that Notice
which it manifeftly merits.

———————

*Quæ modeflia fervanda fit manè in veflitu,
capillis, facie & dentibus mundandis.*

Quifquis habes odio rigidi præcepta magiftri,
   Qui nifi de morum nil gravitate docet,
Huc propera, & placidis utentem vocibus audi;
   Non tonat hic aliquis triftia verba Cato.
Da mihi te docilem craffo fermone loquentem;
   Nec dubita, parvo tempore doctus eris.
Difcipulus facili fuperare labore magiftrum
   Crede mihi antiquâ fimplicitate potes.
Et licet hæc aliquis rigidâ de gente Sophorum
   Vituperet, morum, quæ documenta damus;
Non tamen illa tibi quicquam nocuiffe videbis;
   Sedula fi mufæ juffa fequêre meæ.

           I. Fulcra

## I.

Fulcra foporiferi cum liqueris alta cubilis,
    (Quod fieri medium non decet ante diem)
Egregiè civilis eris, fi nulla parentes
    Manè falutandi fit tibi cura tuos.
Non homini cuiquam felicia fata preceris,
    Sæpe tibi grates dicere ne fit opus.
Profpera quamtumvis optes, quid proderit illis?
    Optima non damnum eft perdere verba leve.
Gens fine manè fuos Hebræa falutet amicos
    Quam tenet implicitam multa fuperftitio.
Cur tibi tam levium fit cùra fuperflua rerum ?
    Canitiem juftos cura dat ante dies.

## II.

Non habet exiguas quaque pandiculatio vires,
    Si medicos par eft credere vera loqui.
Accidit ex longo nervos torpere fopore,
    Atque malè officii munus obire fui.
Excitat hos certo tibi pandiculatio motu
    Utere : nec mores dedecet illa tuos.

## III.

Nec reliquis furgens te veftibus indue, nudæ
    Indufium fatis eft impofuiffe cuti.
Sed reliquas geminis veftes complectitor ulnis,
    Afpera fi duro frigore fævit hyems ;

                          Scilicet

Scilicet in calido jucundius eſt hypocauſto,
 Induere, a ſævo ne violere gelu. ·
Nec moveat virgo vel fœmina ſi ſit ibidem,
 Tu tamen uteris moribus uſque tuis.
Sique tuis quiſquam faƈtis offenditur, illum
 Cernere ſi talem nolit, abire jube.
Quiſque tibi cedat, nec tu conceſſeris ulli,
 Conditione tua es liber, & eſſe velis.

### IV.

Tandem ubi veſtitus fueris, pendere ſolutas
 In genibus caligas (res decet illa) ſines.
Namque ita virginibus tacitâ ratione placebis,
 Teque ſibi obtabit quæque puella virum.
Non ſat eris ſimplex ſi corpus, vane, ligare
 Cæperis; et ventri vincula dura nocent.

### V.

Ne nimis evadas moratus, peƈtere crines
 Neglige, negleƈta eſt forma decora viro.
Fœmineæ crines ornare relinquito turbæ;
 Comantur juvenes quos levis urit amor.
Crede mihi, dominum te nulla puella vocabit,
 Si te compoſito viderit eſſe pilo.
Sint procul a nobis juvenes ut fœmina compti,
 Scribit Amazonio Creſſa puella viro.
Eximio tibi erit decori, ſi pluma capillis
 Mixta erit, & laudem providus inde feres.
Scilicet hoc homines poteris convincere ſigno,
 Non in ſtramineo te cubuiſſe toro.

D d 3                    VI.

## VI.

Sint capitis crines longi, nec forcipe tonfi,
  Cæfaries humeros tangat ut alta tuos,
Tutus ut a trifti rigidæ fis frigora brumæ,
  Vertice prolixus crinis alendus erit.
Cuncti homines quondam longos habucre
      capillos,
  Quas modo virgineus curat habere chorus.
Regna pater quando Saturnus prifca tenebat,
  Tunc fuit in longis gloria magna comis.
Simplicitas veterum laudatur ubique virorum,
  Qua potes hos femper fit tibi cura fequi.

## VII.

Dedecus effe puta faciemve manufve lavare,
  Commodius craffo fordet utrunque luto.
Qui volet his vefci, per me licet, ipfe lavabit,
  Dicito : res curæ non erit illa mihi.

## VIII.

Forfan erit dentes qui te mundare monebit,
  Sed monitis parens inveniêre cave.
Recta valetudo corrumpi dicitur oris,
  Sæpe novâ fi quis proluat illud aquâ.
Quid noceat, dentes quod fint fuligine flavi ?
  Ifte color rubei cernitur effe croci.
Ifte color fulvo quoque non culpatur in auro,
  Auro quod nunquam non amat omnis homo.
Dentibus ergo tuis cur fit color ille pudendus ?
  Si fapis, hanc a te fac procul ire fidem.

                                        Forc'd

Forc'd to be grave, though wifhing much to
    fmile,
Who hears, impatient of the humdrum ftyle,
Grave Preachers, on grave fubjects, gravely
    profe,
So dull they tempt, fo loud·they mock repofe;
Let him to me in gayer mood attend,
Nor dread fome thund'ring Cato in a friend.
If aught my fong avail, 'tis plain, not nice,
He'll prove a finifh'd fcholar in a trice.
To vent their fpleen, elate with learned pride,
My theme let fchoolmen, if they will, deride;
With willing ear who liftens to my rules,
Shall hear unmov'd the clamours of the fchools.

## I.

Quit, quit thy bed, what time the bufy fun
('Twere vulgar fooner) half his courfe hath run.
No kind return maternal care demands,
And fcorn the blelfing from a father's hands.
Let others hail the day with praife and prayer,
Eternal gratitude's eternal care.
For common welfare let the fond fool pray,
(With many a godly fentence thrown away)
To whom Religion in her zeal hath given
Dire fuperftition and a fear of heaven.
Far, far from thee, be fuch ignoble aims,
Life with dull care all fellowfhip difclaims.

II.

## II.

To ſtretch and yawn is great relief to ſome,
Bracing the ſlacken'd nerve with ſleep o'ercome.
This Doctor Filgrane ſtoutly will maintain,
And ſhall Apothecaries talk in vain?
Beſides, how pleaſing 'tis ſome youth to ſee,
Gape, ſtretch, and yawn, and all that, gracefully!

## III.

Be ſure, with half your clothes thrown on, to
  ſtand,
(Coat, ſtockings, garters, dangling in your hand,)
Cloſe o'er the parlour fire, for thee 'twas
  made,
Nor let the cold thy gentle limbs invade.
O'er the ſame fire tho' nymph or matron glow,
'Twere but falſe modeſty ſhould bid you go.
If friends too nice your plan to cenſure move,
Bid them be gone to ſcenes they more approve;
To thee, no doubt, all things, all men, ſhall
  bend;
Thy right is liberty, thy right defend.

## IV.

At length you're dreſt, take care, below the
  knees,
Let the looſe boot hang down with graceful
  caſe,

In

In this, fome namelefs grace, fome charm un-
    known,
Wins the whole fex, and every girl's your own.
Loofe let your waiftcoat fly, while fnug your
    chin
Lies couch'd behind a well-fpread chitterlin.

## V.

To tend with anxious touch the plaited hair,
Leave to the love-fick fchool-boy and his fair.
Do thou ftep forth in eafy difhabille,
Your uncomb'd ringlets floating as they will;
For beaux fo finical in drefs and air
Scarce get a fcrawl from Chloe once a year.
Thus to her lover writes the Cretan lafs,
" I hate thefe coxcombs that before their glafs,
" For ever fix'd, are nothing till they're dreft,
" And then but bearded women at the beft."
All from the downy bed you'll haply bear,
('Tis no fmall grace) a feather in your hair.
From which mankind this inference may draw,
" Ne'er fleeps the gentle youth on bed of ftraw."
And praife fo eafily, fo nobly won,
What beau, what prudent beau, would ever
    fhun ?

## VI.

To crop thy flowing hair, lo ! ready ftands
The ruthlefs barber with unhallow'd hands,

Fly,

Fly, fly his touch, you'll wifh, amid the fno:v,
Beneath your wonted perriwig to glo:v.
In times of old, by ribbon unconfin'd,
Their long lank locks were glory of mankind.
Such locks the nymphs now wear (in filks
    who ruftle),
In rich luxuriance reaching to the buftle.
Fie on our bob-tail'd race, thefe days are o'er,
And time fhall fee ftrait heads of hair no more.

### VII.

Some foufe in water every morn their face,
And think clean hands give fomething of a
    grace.
Who on their fingers feed, for lack of meat,
Such men fhould wafh their food before they
    eat.

### VIII.

Some are fuch fools, they clean their teeth, and
    cry,
An unclean tooth is loathfome to the eye.
Take heed, Dame Nature fays, obey her laws,
Cold water is the Devil in your jaws.
What tho' your grinders, odious to the view,
Vie with the crocus in her yellow hue?
Or golden guinea to exceed afpire.
The crocus and the guinea all admire.
Take my advice, remain in perfect eafe,
Be your teeth black, blue, green, or what you
    pleafe!

NUM-

# NUMBER XLI.

---

SATURDAY, *December* 22, 1787.

---

" *He that prefers the boaſted excellence of*
" *antient times to the endearments and the*
" *embelliſhments of modern life, may be*
" *charged with the depraved taſte of the*
" *Hottentot, who, on his return to his*
" *native country, ſhook off the European*
" *dreſs, nauſeated European food, and in-*
" *dulged in all the exceſſes of his country-*
" *men.*"

PARR'sSermons.—[Quotation by memory.]

THE Declaimers on Morals have frequently poured forth their Invec-
tives againſt the Living, in favour of the
Dead.

Dead.  The virtues of paſt ages have been
conſidered by them as purer than the preſent, more worthy of imitation, and more
conducive to happineſs.  It will neither be
a uſeleſs ſpeculation, nor a matter of in-
ſuperable difficulty, to explode this vulgar
error, and to prove to thoſe who have had
the misfortune, as ſome think it, to be born
in the eighteenth century, that it is as free
from groſs violations of Rectitude and Decorum as any that have preceded it.

It will be readily admitted by every Perſon of an enlightened Underſtanding, that
the number of our public Executions can
be  no criterion of the depravity  of  our
manners, or our progreſs in vitious refinement.  When laws are multiplied to ſuch
an immenſe degree, there muſt infallibly
be more victims to their neglect, as the
more cobwebs the ſpider ſpins, the more
heedleſs flies are likely to be caught.  We
leave, therefore, the comparative number of
names, which have lately filled the annals
of Newgate, to the conſideration of the officers of the police, who are moſt benefited
by their augmentation, and who would be
moſt

moft injured, if every ftatutable offence were not profecuted to conviction ; and proceeding to a review of the Religion, the Manners, and the Amufements of the Age, fhall draw fuch conciufions as will abundantly prove our pofition.

That there is fome fhare of Profligacy, Infidelity, and Irreligion, confpicuoufly in the prefent age, few will be hardy enough to deny; but that real Virtue, Piety, and Truth, are both practifed and countenanced, muft be equally evident, to all whofe minds are not tinctured with the gloom of Fanaticifm, or foured with the leaven of Mifanthropy. In the Church, in the State, in the Senate, and at the Bar, we have Men, eminent for the difcharge of duty : Men who adorn elevated rank by corresponding manners; and are unfafhionable enough to think Religion has charms, and Virtue an inherent luftre.

The prefent times afford many eminent examples of religion and piety among the higheft orders of the State ; of the Nobility, paying a due refpect to the doctrines of

Chrif-

Chriſtianity in general, and ſhewing a promptitude to vindicate the national Church in particular; and yet treating Diſſenters of every denomination with candour and affeƈtion. A conduƈt like this exalts true religion, and points out the Alliance of Chriſtianity to Heaven. The prejudices of illiberal minds are always as hoſtile to its progreſs, as they are diſgraceful to the breaſt that indulges them. In former days, religion was ſtained with violence and blood; it now begins to aſſume its native luſtre, and to be marked with its genuine charaƈteriſtics; it breathes " peace " and good-will to men."

To form a due Eſtimate of the Morals of the preſent age will be an eaſy matter. They are influenced by Religion; and if the latter be pure and generally praƈtiſed, the former will of neceſſity receive a poliſh from its conneƈtion. That Charity triumphs over Avarice; that the ſocial obligations are fulfilled with a more exaƈt obſervance; that the Virtues of Humanity have gained an Aſcendancy over Cruelty and Revenge ; are pofitions that need only be named to be allowed.

It is not to be denied, that former Ages were replete·with examples of heroifm, magnanimity, and a contempt of death : I give them full credit for fuperior abfte-mioufnefs, and more refigned humility : they produce men who were zealous for religion, who were lovers of their country, and foes to tyrants ; men, who were valiant in war, and amiable in peace,—but where was to be found that polifh which is uni-verfally diffufed over modern·manners? that civilization, that mildnefs, and grace, which reprefs the burfts of furious paffions, and foften the ferocity of Rudnefs and Barbarity?

War, the peft of the human race, and the difgrace of reafon, was once carried on with horrors now unknown.   The public enemy, when difarmed, is now treated with the indulgence of a private friend ; and, inftead of dragging the vanquifhed at our chariot-wheels, Humanity and Gentle-nefs go hand in hand to foften the feverity of defeat, and to reconcile the conquered

to

to himfelf. The fame amiablenefs of manners is vifible in humbler circumftances,
and difplayed on lefs important occafions.
The fnarling Cynic may call all this effe-
minacy, and dignify favage qualities with
the appellation of virtues : he may denominate piety a weaknefs, and ftigmatize
the humane with want of fpirit. But let
it be obferved, in anfwer to his cavils, that
whatever renders mankind more amiable,
and more refined, whatever binds one to
another with more endearing ties, is a virtue, and a virtue deferving applaufe.

As Manners are intimately connected
with our Religion, fo our Amufements
have a clofe affinity to our Manners. The
boifterous mirth, the rude joy, the indeli-
cate witticifms, which ufed to delight even
the higheft ranks, are now degraded to the
loweft ; and if refinement progreffively
goes on, we may hope in time to fee even
the lower orders of Society too enlightened
to tafte them. The obftreperous jollity of
the bowl, though fometimes admitted, is
now no longer boafted of. The moft
fplendid triumphs of Bacchus are not confidered

fidered as conferring glory on the moſt zealous of his votaries ; and he, who can vanquiſh his companions over the bottle, is as little valued by thoſe who pretend to refinement, as, a few years hence, he will moſt propably be, who can lay no claims to merit, except his reſolution in riſking his neck over a five-bar gate ; or killing his horſe, that he may boaſt the paltry atchievement of being in at the death.

But of all the amuſements that modern times can exhibit with juſt pretenſions to applauſe, the Stage, in its preſent ſtate, is one of the chief. The lewd alluſion, the profane jeſt, and the imprecatory expletives of language, are now reliſhed only by thoſe whoſe ideas are circumſcribed by the meanneſs of their birth, and the ſcantineſs of their education ; or whoſe minds have never imbibed right ſentiments of genuine humour, and ſterling ſenſe. But it is not the public Stage to which I would confine my commendations; as its managers have the Million to pleaſe, they are too often obliged to do violence to their own Judgement, in order to gratify a vitiated and vulgar

E e                             taſte.

tafte. It is the eftablifhment of private Theatres that I particularly advert to, as a proof of the fuperior tafte and elegance of this age over every preceding one. This may juftly be denominated an æra in the fcenic art, when trick and artifice are banifhed, and their places fuccefsfully fupplied by eafy manners. Whoever has had the pleafure of feeing the performances of our nobility and gentry on their own Stages, where only the moft admired and moft decorous pieces are reprefented, and where the actors appear more ambitious to imitate real life than to fhine in affected fituations, muft confefs, that the dominion of tafte has widely extended itfelf, and that frivolous or vicious paftimes are exchanged for rational and inftructive purfuits. In confequence of this diffufion of dramatic performances, the Stage is more likely than ever to become *the School of Virtue, and the Picture of living Manners.* For in whatever light the furly dogmatift may confider plays in general, it may be afferted, on fafe grounds, that they may be good in particular; they may impart much knowledge

ledge without the langour of ftudy; and warn from error without an approach to the verge of guilt. Iiideed, where Vir-tue obtains thofe rewards which Heaven will beftow, and-poetic juftice fhould never withhold; and where vice fmarts for its crimes, and is not rendered alluring by the attraction of pleafing qualities; then the Stage may be confidered as an auxiliary to the Pulpit,—for Morality and Religion muft ever be united.

M.

## NUMBER XLII.

---

SATURDAY, *December* 29, 1787.

---

*Cavendum eſt, ſi ipſe ædifices, ne extra modum Sumptu et Magnificentiá prodeas.*

CICERO de Officiis.

WHEN Greece and Rome had emer-ged from Barbariſm to an exalted State of Civilization, a diſtinguiſhed place among the Arts was given to Architecture. The accompliſhed Pericles, aſſiſted by the refined genius of Phidias, adorned Athens with thoſe Temples, Theatres, and Porti-cos, which even in Ruins have excited the Admiration of Poſterity. After Auguſtus had eſtabliſhed the peace of the Roman world,

world, a fimilar Difplay of Magnificence was exhibited, and equalled, or rather furpaffed the Glory of Athens. This memorable Era of Architecture is eminently diftinguifhed by the Elegance of the *Palatine Temple of Apollo,* and the Sublimity of the *Pantheon.*

The progrefs of Refinement from publick to private Works muft neceffarily be hafty and immediate, becaufe nothing is more natural to Man than Imitation, particularly of that which is the Object of his Wonder and Applaufe. They who daily furveyed fuch Edifices as were remarkable for Capacioufnefs and Grandeur, projected the Erection of fimilar Structures upon a more confined Plan. Their Defigns were frequently carried to fuch an Excefs in the Execution, as to pafs the Limits of Convenience and Economy, and give a loofe to the Sallies of Oftentation and Extravagance. From this Source was derived the juft Indignation with which Demofthenes inveighed againft the degenerate Athenians, whofe Houfes eclipfed the publick Buildings, and were lafting Monuments of Vanity

nity triumphant over Patriotifm. The
Strictures of Horace flow in a fimilar
Channel, and plainly indicate that the fame
prepofterous Rage for Building prevailed
among the Romans. Even if we make
Allowance for the hyperbolical Flights of
the Lyric Mufe, we muft ftill fuppofe that
vaft and continued Operations of Architects
were carried on by Land and Water, "*fince*
" *a few Acres only were left for the Exer-*
" *cife of the Plough, and the Fifh were fenfible*
" *of the Contraction of their Element.*"

The Tranfition from the Antients to the
Moderns is eafy and obvious. It muft
be confeffed, that, like fervile Copyifts, we
have too clofely followed the Originals of
our great Mafters, and have delineated
their Faults as well as their Beauties. The
Contagion of the Building-Influenza was
not peculiar to the Greeks and Romans,
but has extended its Virulence to this country, where it rages with unabating Violence. Neither the Acutenefs of Pott, nor
the Erudition of Jebb, are neceffary to
afcertain its Symptoms in various Parts of
England. Bath, Briftol, Cheltenham,
Brighton,

Brighton, and Margate, bear evident Marks of its wide Diffufion. The Metropolis is manifeftly the Centre of the Difeafe. In other Places, the Accumulation is made by occafionally adding Houfe to Houfe; but in London, Street is fuddenly added to Street, and Square to Square. The adjacent Villages in a fhort Time undergo a complete Transformation, and bear no more Refemblance to their original State, than Phyllis the Milk-maid does to a Lady Mayorefs. The Citizen who twenty Years ago enjoyed at his Country Seat pure Air, undifturbed Retirement, and an extenfive Profpect, is now furrounded by a populous Neighbourhood. The purity of the Air is fullied with fmoke, and the Profpect is cut off by the oppofite Houfes. The Retirement is interrupted by the London Cries, and the Vociferations of the Watchmen. In the Vicinity of the Capital every Situation is propitious to the Mafon and the Carpenter. Manfions daily arife upon the Marfhes of Lambeth, the Roads of Kenfington, and the Hills of Hampftead. The Chain of Buildings fo

E e 4

clofely

clofely unites the Country with the Town, that the Diftinction is loft between Cheap-fide and Saint George's Fields. This idea ftruck the Mind of a Child, who lives at Clapham, with fo much Force, that he obferved, " *If they go on building at fuch a* " *Rate, London will foon be next Door to* " *us.*"

A ftrong light is often thrown upon the Manners of a People by their proverbial fayings. When the Irifh are highly enrag-ed, they exprefs a Wifh which is not tempered with much of the Milk of kind-nefs, by faying, " *May the Spirit of Build-ing come upon you.*" If an Irifhman be once poffeffed by this Demon, it is difficult to ftop his Progrefs through Brick and Mor-tar, till he exchanges the Superintendance of his Workmen for the Confinement of a Prifon. But this Propenfity is not merely vifible in the Environs of Dublin, or upon the Shores of Cork; it is equally a Charac-tereftic of the *Sifter Kingdom.*

England can furnifh not a few Inftances of Men of Tafte who have fold the beft Oaks of their Eftates for Gilding and Gi-randoles,

randoles,—of Fathers who have beggared
their Families to enjoy the Pleasure of
seeing Green-houses and Pineries arise under their Inspection ;—and of Fox-hunters
who have begun with a Dog-kennel, and
ended with a Dwelling-house. Enough is
every Day done by the Amateurs of Wyat
and Chambers, to palliate the Censure of
Ostentation and Uselessness that is lavishly
thrown upon the King's House at Win-
chester, and the Radcliffe Library at Oxford.

My Cousin, *Obadiah Project, Esq.* formerly a respectable Deputy of Farringdon
Ward Within, retired into the Country,
when he had reached his grand Climacte-
ric, upon a small Estate. While he lived
in Town, his favourite Hobby-horse, which
was Building, had never carried him farther than to change the Situation of a
Door, or erecting a Chimney. On settling
in his new Habitation, as he was no Sports-
man, he found himself inclined to turn
Student. His Genius led him to peruse
Books of Architecture. For two Years
nothing pleased him so much as *The Buil-*
*der's*

*der's Compleat Guide*, *Campbell's Vitruvius*, and *Sandby's Views*. All thefe heated his Imagination with the Beauties of Palaces, and delighted his Eye with the Regularity of the Orders, for which he felt a vague and confufed Fondnefs. He had, perhaps, no more Idea of the Diftinction between a Cornice and a Colonnade, than the monftrous Craws. Unluckily, *Sir Maximilian Barleycorn* was his Neighbour, who had lately erected a Houfe upon the Italian Plan. As my Coufin was laying out his Garden, he found that the Soil was compofed of a fine Vein of Clay. It immediately ftruck him, that Bricks might be procured at a very cheap rate. The Force of Inclination, combined with Rivalfhip, and encouraged by Opportunity, is too powerful for Man to refift. He therefore flew to tell his Wife of the grand Difcovery, and inveighed with much Warmth againft the Smallnefs of their Parlour, the Badnefs of the Kitchen Floor, and the ruinous State of the Garrets. She mildly reprefented that they had no Money to throw away upon a new Houfe, and that the old one might

might cheaply be put into repair. Her Remarks had juft as much Effect, as the Advice of the Barber and the Curate had upon Don Quixote. The next day he played Geoffry Gambado, by taking a ride to confult Mr. *Puff* the Architect. Mr. Puff was confident that the old Houfe muft fall down in a Day or two, and propofed the following Plan for a new one, which exactly reflected my Coufin's Ideas. The Rooms were to be all Cubes. In Front, a Venetian Door, with a Portico fupported by Brick Pillars, with wooden Capitals; and fix Bow-windows. A Balcony was propofed, but afterwards given up becaufe it was *vulgar.* My Coufin retired to a neighbouring Cottage. The old Houfe was pulled down, and the Brick-Makers began their Operations. Unfortunately the Wind happened to blow in fuch a Direction as to create much Annoyance with Clouds of Smoak from the Kilns. Whilft my Coufin was half fuffocated and half buried in Rubbifh, Sir Maximilian Barleycorn and his Lady came to pay a Morning Vifit. They entered the Cottage juft at

the

the Moment when Mrs. Project was fetting the Boiler upon the Fire, and her
Hufband was paring Potatoes. They were
obliged to perform thefe Offices for themfelves, becaufe the only Servant for whom
they could find Room had been turned off
that Morning for abufing Carpenters and
Mafons. Sir Maximilian haftily took his
Leave, and fwore by his Knighthood, *that
Apes were the loweft Animals in the Creation.*
My Coufin had calculated, that as he burnt
his own Bricks for home Confumption,
they would not be fubject to any Tax. An
Excifeman undeceived him before the
Houfe was finifhed, by hinting that he
had incurred a heavy Penalty, which he
was obliged to pay. He contrived, however,
to keep up his Spirits, by marking the
Progrefs of his Houfe, and the Improvements around it. Not far from the Venetian Door was a Horfepond, which the
Genius of Project enlarged into a circular
Piece of Water. He requefted his Friends
to fuggeft the moft tafty Ornaments. One
propofed a Shepherd and Shepherdefs upon
a Pedeftal in the Middle. Another obferved,

ed, that if Farmer Peafcod's Gander could
be placed in it when Company came, they
would give him Credit for keeping a Swan.
A third, whofe Notion of Things was improved by frequent Vifits to Vauxhall, was
fure that a Tin Cafcade would look very
pretty by Moon-light. Projeƈt, not liking
to take up with one good Thing, when
four were to be had, refolved to adorn his
Water with them all. He foon after removed into his New Habitation, long before the Walls were dry. An Ague and
Fever were the Confequence of this rafh
Step. His Fever was probably increafed
by Puff's Bill, to pay which he fold the
greater Part of his Eftate. During his
Illnefs, he gradually awoke to a Senfe of
his late Imprudence, requefted the For-
givenefs of his Wife for not liftening to her
Advice, and begged me to imprefs his
dying Injunƈtions indelibly on my Memory, " *Never build after you are five and*
" *forty; have five Years Income in Hand be-*
" *fore you lay a Brick; and always calculate*
" *the Expence at Double the Eftimate.*"

Q.

NUM-

# NUMBER XLIII.

---

SATURDAY, *January* 5, 1788.

---

*Rerum concordia difcors.*——

S HOULD a Dutchman make his appearance as an Opera-dancer, a Frenchman be prefented to us as a Bruifer, a
German as Wit, or a Hottentot as a Mafter
of the Ceremonies, we fhould be all ready
to exclaim, *They are ftrangely out of Cha-*
*racter.* Frequently will this exclamation
proceed from any one who is attentive to
the Language which flows around him,
as he paffes through the crowded ftreets of
London.

London. He will obferve, not without fome furprize, the bold and venturefome bargains of a mean and fqualid-looking Mifer; he will hear the declamatory dif- cuffions of a political Peruke-maker; and be difgufted with the technical vulgarities of a Jockey Lord. Let him transfer his attention from the converfation to the lives and conduct of mankind, and a fhort feries of events will teach him not to be furprized, fhould he find inconfiftencies as unaccount- able and as motley a mixture of heteroge- neous qualities. Chance may difcover to him fituations wherein the Fop becomes a Sloven, the Rebel a Tyrant, the Syco- phant a Churl, the Patriot a Courtier, and the Libertine a religious Difputant. He who is hackney'd in the ways of Men is gradually familiarized to thefe incongrui- ties. The frequent occurrence of what might at firft amaze him, lofes the power of exciting furprize, when it lofes its no- velty. That which was formerly beheld with aftonifhment and averfion, is at length regarded with fixed unconcern, or calm ac- quiefcence.

The

The ftorms of the Ocean were once terrible to the Boy who, now he is become a Mariner, furveys them without dread, and hears them without complaint.

The incongruities abovementioned do not confine themfelves to particular charaĉters, but are fo univerfally diffufed through all ranks and denominations of men, as to appear not fo much the mark of particular failings, as a general charaĉteriftic of our nature, a common ingredient in the human conftitution, from the flippant levities of the Boy too tall for fchool, to the ferious and folemn trifling of the Philofopher. Who has not obferved the Moralift deal forth his leffons of virtue to the world, while de declares by his conduĉt that he doubts the efficacy of his own doctrine? He extols the value of time, while he fuffers it to pafs in idle complaints or fruitlefs contemplation on the rapidity of its flight. He can afcertain with nice and accurate diftinĉtions the boundaries of Virtue and Vice; he can exhort us to the practice of the former, with the volubility of declamation, or deter us from the latter

by

by expofing it with the poignancy of animated ridicule. But it too frequently happens, that Cicero with the publick is Clo-
dius at home, and that in the armour of
the Chriftian Hero we find Sir Richard
Steele. All the palliations which friendfhip could fuggeft to the biographer of Sa-
vage, have not been able to hide from the
world the imprudence, the folly, and the
vice, for which he might be ftigmatized,
from his own writings.

*Quam temere in nofmet legem fancimus iniquam.*

It is perhaps neceffary, that for the duration of one good difpofition of Mind,
another fhould exift by way of relief to it.
Vivacity is a proper companion for Seriouf-
nefs, Chearfulnefs for Piety, and Conde-
fcenfion for Magnanimity.

— — — — — *Alterius fic*
*Altera pofcit opem res, et conjurat amicè.*

Such a contraft has a fine effect in the
picture of the Soul. It is a virtue in him
who holds the moft elevated fituation occafionally to lay afide the formalities of his
Rank without degrading himfelf. For

F f greatnefs,

greatnefs, even if regal, mult have its relaxations. The bow which is always bent
lofes much of its elafticity. The wifdom
and exalted character of Agefilaus did not
prevent him from engaging in puerile
amufements with his Children. The virtuous Scipio and the fagacious Lælius diverted themfelves with picking up Shells
upon the fea-fhore. To draw an example
from more recent times, the great Newton
not unfrequently left the Caufes of the
Tides, and the Excentricities of Comets,
to play with his Cat.

Such is the motley tablet of man's mind,
that we fee painted upon it not only the
mixed colours of virtue and vice, but of
virtues which affift, and of vices which
increafe by fupporting each other. Generofity difciplined by prudence makes its poffeffor liberal, without profufion, and an
œconomift without parfimony. It preferves
him from the imputation of weaknefs by
mifplaced benevolence, and thereby furnifhes him with the double power of holding out affiftance to thofe who want it.

Although

Although the mifts of prejudice had gathered thick around Johnfon when he became the biographer of Swift, he could not but vindicate his parfimony from the cenfure of meannefs, becaufe it was exercifed only as the auxiliary to his Beneficence. Generofity indeed may be confidered as the projectile Force of the Mind, which would fly off to the moft extravagant length, did not Prudence act as a power of attraction to keep it within its proper orbit.

The fame bofom is oftentimes diftracted by the conflict of contending paffions, totally different in their exertions, but alike baneful in their influence. Prodigality and avarice meet but to try whether the one can fcatter with the wilder extravagance, or the other fave with the more rigorous and unwearied meannefs. Thus are they alternately encouraged by each other. Avarice furnifhes the means for profufion, and profufion makes avarice more necefiary. "To be greedy of the property of others, "and lavifh of his own," were the ftrongeft traits of Catiline's mind. In modern life, among thofe who are curfed with a fimiiar difpofition, no one is more remarkable than the *Gamefter.*

Cruelty' and cowardice, ignorance and prefumption, infolence and fervility, are the general affociates, yet the general opponents. They are united to harrafs each other; they engage, and like Antæus gather ftrength from every defeat. He who can contemplate thefe inconfiftencies and attempt to reconcile fuch abfurdities to reafon, may hunt for beauties in Offian, or unalloy'd purity in a Birmingham coin; or fhould he find fuch toil ineffectual, let him extract candour from a profeffed Critic, ranfack the world for an Attorney of moderate peculation and tolerable honefty, or liften with credulity to the narrative of Captain Lemuel Gulliver.

How frequent are our exclamations, in a fhameful fpirit of ftudied negligence, or liftlefs inactivity, that time is a heavy burthen to us! how loud are our complaints that we have nothing to do! Yet how inconfiftent are thefe exclamations, and thefe complaints, with the declarations which truth and reafon fo often extort from us,

I that

that the flight of time reproaches us with our fupinenefs, and that a day never paffes without our " having left undone thofe " things which we ought to have done !"

While we are thus capricious and con-tradictory in our actions and opinions, ever wifhing that completed which we ever de-lay to begin, lamenting over imaginary wants, neglecting to enjoy bleffings we poffefs, grafping at the fleeting phantom of happinefs, and regardlefs of the fubftan-tial form of it, human life appears like a patchwork of ill-forted colours; like the fantaftic and incongruous phantafms of a dream, or, for aught I know, like the mifcellaneous ingredients of an Olla Po-drida.

NUM.

SATURDAY, *January* 12, 1788.

———————————

*À te principium, tibi definet.*—    V<small>IRG</small>.

Of felf fo dear I fang in number one,
By felf fo dear I'll end as I've begun.

IF there be any of my readers, whether
    inhabiting the retirements of the Ifle
of Muck, frequenters of the religious re-
ceptacles of St. James's or St. Giles's, or
tenants of a bow-window in Shoe-lane, to
whom it fhall be a matter of momentary
concern that they are now reading the laft
Number

Number of the OLLA PODRIDA ; to such I would return thanks for the patience with which they have toiled through my pages, and adminifter fome confolation under their prefent difappointment. I have the fatif-faction to reflect that I take my leave of the world, at a time when it cannot be at a lofs for amufement. The Ifle of Muck has, no doubt, thofe pleafing recreations by which the gloom of a winter's evening is eafily diffipated. The exercife of hot-cockles, and the agreeable diverfion of blindman's-buff, has moft likely found it's way even to the inmoft of the Hebrides, where fimpli-city has fo firmly withftood the inroads of refinement, and where a deviation from Barbarifm feems to have been confidered as a defection from Virtue. Let me remind my friends in Shoe-lane likewife, that the ceflation of this paper's appearance amongft them ought not to be confidered as a ca-lamity, while the feafon furnifhes fuch a variety of entertainment : He, who from reafons which I will not pretend to enquire into has perufed with any degree of plea-

fure

fure the numbers of this work, now finds his mental amufement happily diverfified by " the Bellman's addrefs to his Mafters and Miftreffes all," in which, I muft add, be he Poet, Moralift, Philofopher, or Lounger, he will meet with ample fubject for difcuffion or contemplation.

Amongft other traits of our national character, I know not that our obfervance of religious feftivals has ever been noticed. The hiftories of nations furnifh us with no examples of fuch annual enthufiafm as marks the inhabitants of Great Britain. Chriftmas never vifits us without a train of peculiar rites and ceremonies, to which I fuppofe our Hiftorians have not extended their notice, becaufe they have been unwilling to deal forth their cenfures upon their Countrymen.—How we ought to commemorate this feafon, every one may know; how we do commemorate it, no one is ignorant; and there is perhaps not much diftinction between the omiffions of him who neglects to practife what he knows is right, and of him who is ignorant of what

he

he ought to know. But as it is considera-
bly to my intereſt to bid farewell to my
readers, without leaving them in ill humour, I ſhall lay a reſtraint upon my inclination to moralize, and be very brief
upon a ſubjeƈt which perhaps demands a
more ample diſcuſſion. To the ſerious it
is unneceſſary to ſuggeſt, that the time is
now preſent which they are called upon,
by their Reaſon and their Religion, to welcome with every demonſtration of rational
and ſettled joy. Theſe are refleƈtions to
which they are naturally led without ex-
hortation, and which the gay might indulge without diminution of their happineſs. Yet ſome there are, who without
taſte for the enjoyment of gaiety are never
diſpoſed to ſeriouſneſs ; who, from a trifling
diſpoſition, are devoted to endleſs inſipidity,
and affeƈted mirth ; or, from vicious ten-
dencies, are willing to baniſh refleƈtion, leſt
it ſhould bring with it an interruption to
their ſuppoſed happineſs. But leſt I ſhould
ſeem already to have forgotten my promiſe
of reſtraining my inclination to moralize, I
ſhall

fhall fill up part of my vacant page with
that beautiful Sonnet of Shakſpeare, ſo
well deſcribing the natural appearance of
Winter. If there be any one to whom it
is new, I ſhall be entitled to his thanks ;
and he, to whom it is familiar, cannot read
it again without pleaſure.—Its ſimplicity I
know not how ſufficiently to commend.

When iſicles hang by the wall,
And Dick the Shepherd blows his nail,
And Tom bears logs into the hall,
And milk comes frozen home in pail ;
When blood is nipt, and ways be foul ;
Then nightly ſings the ſtaring owl
Tu-whit, tu-whoo, a merry note,
While greaſy Joan doth keel the pot.

When all around the wind doth blow,
And coughing drowns the Parſon's ſaw,
And birds ſit brooding in the ſnow,
And Marian's noſe looks red and raw ;
When roaſted crabs hiſs in the bowl ;
Then nightly ſings the ſtaring owl
Tu-whit, tu-whoo, a merry note,
While greaſy Joan doth keel the pot.

With

With regard to the tendency of thefe pages which I here offer to the publick, I know my own intentions, and am fatiſfied.—How they are executed, it remains for them to judge.—To the Critics I have nothing to fay.   He who would fhun criticifm, muſt not be a fcribbler; and he who would court it, muſt have great abilities or great folly.

F I N I S.

www.ingramcontent.com/pod-product-compliance
Lightning Source LLC
Chambersburg PA
CBHW020858130726
47900CB00014B/1021